Literature and psychoanalysis

Manchester University Press

Literature and psychoanalysis

Jeremy Tambling

Manchester University Press
Manchester and New York
distributed in the United States exclusively by Palgrave Macmillan

Published by Manchester University Press
Oxford Road, Manchester M13 9NR, UK
and Room 400, 175 Fifth Avenue, New York, NY 10010, USA
www.manchesteruniversitypress.co.uk

Distributed in the United States exclusively by
Palgrave Macmillan, 175 Fifth Avenue, New York,
NY 10010, USA

Distributed in Canada exclusively by
UBC Press, University of British Columbia, 2029 West Mall,
Vancouver, BC, Canada V6T 1Z2

British Library Cataloguing-in-Publication Data
A catalogue record for this book is available from the British Library

Library of Congress Cataloging-in-Publication Data applied for

ISBN 978 0 7190 8673 1 hardback

ISBN 978 0 7190 8674 8 paperback

First published 2012

Typeset in 10/12pt Minion
by Graphicraft Limited, Hong Kong
Printed in Great Britain
by Bell & Bain Ltd, Glasgow

Contents

Acknowledgements and a note on the text

No single book can cover Freud's 7000 pages of writing on psychoanalysis, plus his letters, let alone the bodies of work of those associated with him, or his adversaries. So the book has to be selective. Though Freud is sometimes hard, and Lacan obviously so, reading systematically through the book, rather than just dipping, will make the ideas emerge comparatively straightforwardly. I use the Standard Edition of Freud (called *SE*), translated principally by James Strachey. There are many problems about his translations (see Ornston, 1992, and Laplanche, 1992), but the solid advantage of the *SE* is its footnoting and referencing. I have given plentiful cross-references, to follow ideas through. Given the cramped space, I ask readers to make extensive use of the book's index to check explanations and definitions, and to follow reading suggestions via the Bibliography.

Thanks to all those who have discussed this subject with me over many years: to Bob Pattison for many conversations, especially on Klein, to Howard Booth for comments on the Klein chapter, to Ben Moore and James Smith who both read substantial sections, and to Will Simpson who read the sections on Lacan, and Mark Gardner who read the early sections. Thanks to Jack Sullivan and Jack Wittels for help with the manscript. This book is for Pauline, Kirsten, and Felix, with love.

1

Introduction: Freud's Copernican revolution

Freud's biography

Before discussing psychoanalysis and literature, we must ask the question: who was Freud, creator of psychoanalysis, whose name, as an adjective – 'Freudian' – invokes unconscious thought and motivations, and sexuality?

He was born on 6 May 1856, in Príbor, then called Freiberg, in Moravia, in the now Czech Republic, then part of the Austro-Hungarian empire. He was a mid-Victorian; it was three years before Darwin's *The Origin of Species* appeared; a text fundamental to him. Freud's father, Jakob Freud, was forty-one, and in his third marriage; Amalie, his mother, who died in 1930, was twenty. The family was Jewish but not practising; Jews had been granted emancipation in German countries only since 1802, and the results of this were patchy. In *The Interpretation of Dreams* (1900), Freud writes:

> I may have been ten or twelve years old, when my father began to take me with him on his walks . . . thus it was . . . that he told me a story to show how much better things were now than they had been in his days. 'When I was a young man,' he said, 'I went for a walk one Saturday in the streets of your birthplace; I was well dressed and had a new fur cap on my head. A Christian came up to me and with a single blow knocked off my cap into the mud, and shouted, "Jew! get off the pavement!"' 'And what did you do?' I asked? 'I went into the roadway and picked up my cap', was the quiet reply. (*SE* 4.197)

Freud seems to have found this response insufficiently aggressive. His 'Autobiographical Study' (1925, *SE* 20.7–74) describes the family moving to Vienna when he was four: Vienna had strong, growing antisemitic tendencies, part of the nascent culture of fascism in Europe (fascism, a French term, was first used in Paris in the early 1890s) which would swell towards the Second World War. Freud suffered from antisemitism professionally and personally. How psychoanalysis intermeshes with Judaism – a religion historically marked by exile, and marginal in relation to mainstream European society, and as absolutely based upon interpretation of sacred texts – has been frequently discussed (Robert, 1977, Derrida, 1996).

Freud attended University in Vienna, graduating as a physician in 1881. Interested in nervous diseases, he became a University Lecturer in neuropathology in 1885, the year he studied with Jean-Martin Charcot (1825–1893), Professor of Neuropathology at Paris; Charcot worked at the Salpetrière, the hospital for nervous diseases in Paris, specialising in hysteria; another student was Pierre Janet (1859–1947), who influenced William James (1842–1910). Hysteria (from Greek *husteron*: the womb), which in the nineteenth century was seen as a way to marginalise women, by saying that they were all potentially 'hysterical' on account of their monthly cycle, was not analysed by Freud as having a medical or bodily origin: he recalled later being laughed at for saying that men could be hysterical (*SE* 20.15). Unfortunately for Freud and feminism, *Studies in Hysteria* (1895) discussed only women: despite his theories, he was gendering hysteria as female.

Returning to Vienna in 1886, Freud married Martha Bernays (1861–1951): of their six children, the youngest, Anna (1895–1982), maintained a distinctive tradition of Freudian psychoanalysis in England. One of Freud's earliest writings was on speech disorders, *On Interpretation of the Aphasias: A Critical Study* (1891) (see *SE* 14.209–15). An early collaborator was Josef Breuer (1842–1925), co-author of *Studies on Hysteria*. One patient in that book, analysed by Breuer, and called 'Anna O—', named the new method that was being employed by these two the 'talking cure' (*SE* 2.30). Perhaps the principal difference 'the talking cure' involved was this: Charcot considered hysteria a disease of the nervous system, whose symptoms could be seen generally in different patients. Breuer and Freud, both, initially, using hypnotism, considered the condition as individual, its causes buried in the individual's personal history. These could be disinterred, by hearing the patient speak, and, in Freud's case, by letting patients talk in an unrepressed way, free-associating, with as little intervention from the analyst as possible. Freud's sense of hysteria may be summed up in the phrase 'hysterics suffer mainly from reminiscences' (*SE* 3.7). At the heart of hysteria was a painful memory not sufficiently 'worked through', and therefore repeated incessantly. The German cultural critic Walter Benjamin (1892–1940) quotes from the psychoanalyst Theodor Reik (1888–1969) for the distinction: 'essentially memory is conservative, reminiscence, destructive' (Benjamin, 1999: 402). The way was open for Freud to speak of 'psychoanalysis': a word different from 'psychology', which, as 'the science of mental life', is an objective study of what goes on in the mind, as far as this can be ascertained scientifically (Miller, 1970). Both terms, of course, differ from 'psychiatry', which treats medically those it judges as needing attention for mental disorder.

From 1893 to 1897, Freud held to the 'seduction theory', that the women treated had been victims in childhood of sexual abuse by their fathers. More than Breuer, he felt the memories or reminiscences he was hearing were sexually based (*SE* 20.26). Charcot's influence mattered: Freud recounted, in 1914, hearing Charcot say of a 'hysterical' woman, 'Mais dans ces cas pareils c'est toujours la chose genitale, toujours . . . toujours . . . toujours' (But in these cases, it's always the genital thing – always, always, always), to which Freud thought, 'Well, but if he knows that, why does he never say so?' (*SE* 14.14). The 'talking cure' raised questions of 'la chose genitale', which made Foucault call Freud 'the most famous ears of our time'; listening to people's constructions of themselves as subjects, in terms of various forms of sexual inadequacy, through the confessional means of the psychoanalyst's couch (Foucault, 1981: 112).

At the same time as this work with Brauer, from 1887 to 1902, there was an intense correspondence, and friendship, whose homosexual basis Freud acknowledged, with Wilhelm Fliess (1858–1928), in Berlin. Freud's letters to Fliess show the changes in his thinking. On 24 July 1895, he analysed one of his dreams, on 'Irma', a family friend, treated as a case of hysteria (see *SE* 4.96–121); this affirmed his sense that a dream was 'the fulfilment of a wish' (*SE* 4.121); sleep allows what Freud called 'the primary process' to work unimpeded, combining unconsciously held images in a way which would gratify a wish. For Fliess, Freud wrote the *Project for a Scientific Psychology* (1895), which I discuss in Chapter 3; this set out a course of thinking that Derrida insists he never departed from: its topic was an attempt to examine the 'defences' which are raised against painful memories or feelings ('affects') and to see how these do, or do not, work. 'Defences' include 'repression': the *Project* declares that 'the process of repression remains as the core of the riddle' (*SE* 1.352) that Freud wanted to solve.

At the same time, Freud was going through his own painful crises: in a letter to Fliess of 14 August 1897, he referred to 'my little hysteria' (*SE* 1.259, Masson, 1985: 261, see Anzieu, 1986: 232). On 23 October 1896, Jakob Freud had died, aged eighty, inaugurating Freud's 'self-analysis', reacting to 'the most important event, the most poignant loss, of a man's life' (*SE* 4.xxvi). He began thinking about the centrality of infantile sexuality, and relating sexual fantasies to what came to be called 'the Oedipus complex': the result being *The Interpretation of Dreams*, built up on an analysis of his own dreams (e.g. Irma). Started in summer 1897, it appeared at the end of 1899. It was this sense of sexual fantasy, which he connected with his own, in his 'self-analysis', which made him drop the 'seduction theory' (that does not mean that he ignored sexual abuse towards children). He now had the sense that the unconscious, as he puts it in an all-important letter of 21 September 1897, has no 'indications of reality', 'so that one cannot distinguish between truth and fiction that has been cathected with affect' (*SE* 1.260, Masson, 1985: 264). A technical term has been used here: *cathected with affect* means 'invested, or loaded, with feeling, with emotional force'. An idea has been conveyed, and the psychic system has seized on it, and given it the weight of feeling; it cannot be given up as an idea.

Writing to Fliess (15 October 1897), and saying he is undergoing his own 'self-analysis', Freud calls Hamlet a 'hysteric' suffering from an unconscious sense of guilt; Hamlet cannot kill Claudius because he had contemplated the same murder of his father out of love for his mother. Freud finds Hamlet's sexual alienation from Ophelia hysterical, and thinks he ends in the same 'marvellous' (i.e. uncanny) way as any of Freud's hysterical patients, bringing down punishment on himself 'by suffering the same fate as his father, of being poisoned by the same rival' (*SE* 1.266, Masson, 1985: 272–3). *The Interpretation of Dreams* confirms this interpretation of *Hamlet* (*SE* 4.264–6), and the play remained vivid for him throughout (see *SE* 7.305–10, for instance).

I have emphasised Freud's own neurosis or hysteria, during these years before 1900, when he became 'Freud', the founder of a system of thought, because it must be said that the scientific, empirical data which supports his theories is impressionistic, and thin. Freudian thought is hardly to be considered as scientifically based: Freud is like his own version of Hamlet, producing ideas from his own introspection, which makes them not objective, but resting on a desire to interpret which is in itself literary. Seeing the psyche as a text, he uses textual means to explore it: developing critical theory to read literature. *Beyond the Pleasure Principle* (1920) says that 'physiological or chemical terms' are also 'part of a figurative language' (*SE* 18.60), so he seems to make science a form of poetry, or to think that all language has a poetic basis. As I do not want to annoy scientists reading this, I will simply say that there is no question of contending that Freud was objectively right; the question is what interest there is in his critical theory. And remembering that Paul de Man speaks of texts having a 'resistance to theory', and that Charcot told Freud that, just because a theory exists, 'ça n'empêche pas d'exister' (that doesn't prevent it [i.e. anything] existing) (*SE* 20.13), the question is always how adequate the theory is, and how it needs revision. This book is written in the conviction that the theory has much to say, and is wonderfully suggestive.

After the publication of the 'dream-book', and its companions, *The Psychopathology of Everyday Life* (1901) and *Jokes and Their Relation to the Unconscious* (1905), each the 'royal road to a knowledge of the unconscious activities of the mind' (*SE* 5.608), and with the ending of friendship with Fliess, Freud was established. The rest of his life was bound up with the development of his writings, with complex relationships to fellow-psychoanalysts such as Carl Jung (1875–1961) and Alfred Adler (1870–1937) and Sándor Ferenczi (1873–1933); commentaries on 'case-histories' of patients, theorisings – and constant revisings – of his position, and an attempt to think through the nature of 'drives' (*Trieb*). 'Drive' is a better word to use than the Standard Edition's 'instinct', because 'instinct' implies a force which is biological or natural, whereas 'drive' allows for the power of culture; a 'drive' is a product of the intersection of the body and cultural forces. In 1923, Freud was operated on for cancer of the mouth, and was in pain for the rest of his life; in 1938, with Hitler's occupation of Austria (the *Anschluss*), it was no longer safe to be in Vienna; his books had been burned in Berlin in 1933, and Freud moved to London, where he died, on 23 September 1939, the month the Second World War began.

How can we access Freud's theory? He compared it to Copernicus (1473–1543), who had shown that the Earth was not at the centre of the universe. Freud said that people's self-love had suffered a blow when they learned of this, just as *The Origin of Species* dealt a blow to human narcissism through showing that man was neither different from animals nor superior to them. But Freud saw his work as continuing this decentring, because psychoanalysis, which, if anyone created, he did, he said struck a blow at 'human megalomania', showing 'the ego that it is not master in its own house, but must content itself with scanty information of what is going on unconsciously in its mind' ('The Unconscious', *SE* 16.285, see also *SE* 17.140–1, 19.221).

The 'Copernican revolution' means that psychoanalysis decentres the conscious mind, the ego, showing that it acts not according to rational principles which it has thought out, but because of the unconscious, which in some ways is unknown, but which overrules the conscious mind. The unconscious (*das Unbewusste*), first appeared in *Studies on Hysteria* (*SE* 2.45). It is not the same as the 'subconscious', a term with no psychoanalytic overtones: it is a technical term, inseparable from 'repression', which creates it. It is definitional to say that we do not know what the contents of the unconscious are. I do not know what I have repressed: if I *do* know, that is not unconscious knowledge. Freud was not just practising psychotherapy on his patients, helping them in difficult situations, but helping them by studying the unconscious as the basis of their problems; this was what he considered set him apart from both Breuer and, more importantly, from Janet (*SE* 20.30–1). Freud considered that the unconscious as an idea was one reason for people's dislike of psychoanalysis: it cut at their belief in themselves as centred, rational. Considering Freud's 'Copernican revolution', however, we could supplement Copernicus and Darwin by Marx, who, writing in 1846, declared that thinking was not produced by autonomous individuals: rather, 'the ideas of the ruling class are in every epoch the ruling ideas' (Marx, 1977: 64). Copernicus, Marx, Darwin, and Freud have contributed to a series of shocks which have decentred 'man' from being the centre of his own world. And Lacan thinks that the image of 'decentring' does not go far enough; referring to the astronomer Kepler (1571–1630), he argues for the primacy of the ellipse, which takes away all idea of anything being at the centre, or it being possible to think of a centre at all (Lacan, 1998: 43, Žižek, 2004: 66).

All this gives a first reason for studying Freud, and psychoanalysis, but it needs studying also for the terms it has left as a legacy. 'Narcissism', referred to earlier, was a word virtually invented, in 1899, by the British writer Havelock Ellis (1859–1939), and taken over by Freud, as he used 'ego', or 'megalomania', a term used almost interchangeably with paranoia. Other psychoanalytic terms have slipped into everyday use: Oedipus complex; Freudian slip; *déjà vu*, sexual instinct, death-drive, ambivalence, defence mechanism, superego, sublimation, fixation, to say nothing of sadism, masochism, fetishism, the taboo, and the phallic symbol . . . These terms are part of the texture of expressions about 'modernity', that topic crucial for anyone reading nineteenth-, or twentieth- or twenty-first-century literature; every critic and theorist who has engaged with this has found it necessary to discuss the place of Freud, but not denying his importance: Adorno, Benjamin, Bakhtin, Marcuse, Fanon, Althusser, Foucault, Derrida, Deleuze, Luce Irigaray, or Hannah Arendt, or Žižek. Only Heidegger stood aloof (Derrida, 1987: 357). No approach to theory can fail to engage with Freud's legacy, and his legacy as, substantially, that theory's diversity. A third, crucial, reason is the one I start Chapter 2 with: how Freud illuminates literature, and makes for a very full reading of it. Freud needs attention for what he says about literature, and enables some exciting ways of considering it.

After this – to map the book briefly – Chapter 3 starts with one of Freud's 'case-histories', where he discussed particular examples of analysis: I have chosen the account he gave of someone suffering from *obsessional neurosis*, the 'Rat Man'. I examine what Freud said about this, as distinct from *hysteria*, and then consider Freud on *memory*, in relation to *consciousness*, *repression* and *the unconscious*. Chapter 4 discusses what Freud thought about *guilt*, a central topic of his work, and explores this through several critical texts, 'Criminals from a Sense of Guilt', 'The Ego and the Id', his essays on anxiety, and 'Civilization and Its Discontents'. While Chapter 3 ends with Derrida's critique of Freud and psychoanalysis, Chapter 4 concludes with Freud's auto-critique of psychoanalysis.

Chapters 3 and 4 overlap, while Chapter 5 discusses one of Freud's most exciting followers, Melanie Klein (1882–1960), and *object-relations theory*; here also I make reference to Julia Kristeva; this chapter has most to say about the role of the mother in psychoanalysis. But there is plenty of Freud in this chapter, too, most notably his discussion of the *Fort! Da!* game in *Beyond the Pleasure Principle*.

Chapters 6 and 7 discuss Jacques Lacan (1901–81), first through the main strands of his thought: the categories of *the Imaginary, the Symbolic, and the Real*, then, in Chapter 7, on *paranoia*, and madness, linking both to modernist literature. Chapter 7 also returns to Freud on *hysteria* (the Dora case), and examines him on paranoia in Schreber, and the psychosis of the 'Wolf Man': it raises the question of literature and madness, literature as a form of madness, enabled to be so by psychoanalytic theory about language. This leaves Chapter 8, which goes back to psychoanalytic criticism of literature, through Lacan, and Derrida, on 'The Purloined Letter'.

Lack of space means excluding a lot, especially Freud's contemporaries. From contemporary critical theory, I have only a little on the philosopher Gilles Deleuze (1925–95), whose critique of psychoanalysis, sometimes in collaboration with Félix Guattari (1930–92), develops Foucault's, but I have attempted to discuss Slavoj Žižek (b. 1949), a significant commentator on Lacan. I have said a little about Foucault (1926–84), and quite a lot on Derrida (1930–2003), roughly a third of whose writings are on psychoanalysis. The area where I have said too little, though I have kept alluding to it, is feminism: here another book the same length could be written. Whether psychoanalysis, or literature, is hospitable to feminism – and what kinds of feminist discourse – I consider several times, but don't get much further than thinking how psychoanalysis and literary theory create and respond to Luce Irigaray's statement that 'sexual difference is one of the questions, if not *the* question to be thought in our age' (Irigaray, 1992: 9).

2

Freud and literature

Not only did Freud know literature intimately, and quote liberally from literatures of several languages, he has also inspired twentieth-century writers, as well as artists and philosophers, and created several schools of criticism, in literary and cultural studies. This chapter contains examples of attempts at criticism inspired by Freud. The first uses Freud to consider a poem by William Blake (1757–1827), the second to interpret a familiar Sherlock Holmes short story. These are different, contrasted uses, one requiring reading a lyric poem in all its intensity, the second showing how understanding popular narrative, written as entertainment, requires psychoanalysis, which, in turn makes valuable the close reading of a large-circulation text. Both discussions invoke some Freudian concepts, which I gloss as we go.

Blake

My mother groand! my father wept
Into the dangerous world I leapt:
Helpless, naked, piping loud,
Like a fiend hid in a cloud.

Struggling in my fathers hands:
Striving against my swadling bands:
Bound and weary, I thought best
To sulk upon my mothers breast.
(Blake, 1982: 28)

This is 'Infant Sorrow', one of the *Songs of Experience* (1794), poems which Blake illustrated. The colour picture shows the rich interior of a house, and a mother in red bending over a naked child on the bed. He has the free use of his limbs – he is certainly not in swaddling bands – and is apparently resisting her. The illustration will surprise anyone who deduced from the poem that the 'dangerous world' was so because of poverty, or that the parents were groaning and weeping because being poor they regretted having another mouth to feed. The illustration, which does not show the father, shows a child born into comfort.

Any approach will note that the speaker is the child, and the predominance of first-person pronouns (seven altogether). In the beginning, he presents himself as active ('leapt'), but, by the end, as passive. He seems to be in a completely adversarial relationship to the parents: to the mother, mentioned first, and last, and to the father, mentioned twice, in the first and fifth lines. (The symmetry is noteworthy.) If we assume that the child is male, which seems likely, though not certain, and compare Blake with Freud, it would not be difficult to say that the relationship to the father, fearful and aggressive, has resonances of Oedipus, whom Freud discussed in *The Interpretation of Dreams*; his summary of Sophocles' play *Oedipus the King* (c. 425 BCE) I now quote:

> Oedipus, son of Laius, King of Thebes, and of Jocasta, was exposed as an infant because an oracle had warned Laius that the still unborn child would be his father's murderer. The child was rescued and grew up as a prince in an alien court, until, in doubts as to his origin, he too questioned the oracle, and was warned to avoid his home since he was destined to murder his father and take his mother in marriage. On the road leading away from what he believed was his home, he met King Laius and slew him in a sudden quarrel. He came next to Thebes and solved the riddle set him by the Sphinx who barred his way. Out of gratitude the Thebans made him their king and gave him Jocasta's hand in marriage. He reigned long in peace and honour, and she, who, unknown to him, was his mother bore him two sons and two daughters. Then at last a plague broke out and the Thebans made enquiry once more of the oracle. It is at this point that Sophocles' tragedy opens. The messengers bring back the reply that the plague will cease when the murderer of Laius has been driven from the land . . . The action of the play consists in nothing other than the process of revealing, with cunning delays and ever-mounting excitement – a process that can be likened to the work of a psychoanalysis – that Oedipus himself is the murderer of Laius, but further that he is the son of the murdered man and of Jocasta. Appalled at the abomination which he has unwittingly perpetrated, Oedipus blinds himself and forsakes his home. The oracle has been fulfilled. (*SE* 4.261–2)

Is this poem of Blake's, then, one where, as Freud says, the poets seem to have discovered the unconscious before he did (Trilling, 1970: 47)? Freud compares Oedipus with *Hamlet*, and with Dostoyevsky's *The Brothers Karamazov* (*SE* 21.188–9), for the significance of parricide; but, in Blake, aggression toward the parents seems equalled by a perception of the parents' aggression. This is not the only place in Blake where intense hostility between father and son seems to happen. Full studies of Blake in relation to Freud have been written (George, 1980). But if this poem was 'about' Oedipal struggle, that would be a use of a Freudian model that might be interesting . . . though it would have to be said that this was not the end of the matter, that there was more to be said, and that seeing the poem as Oedipal would be reductive. Can we go further?

Here, we could start by saying that, if this is 'Oedipal', it is consciously so, whereas Freud emphasised the son's *unconscious* hostility – in the legend, as given in Sophocles, Oedipus is travelling away from the man he thinks is his father, because he does *not* want to kill him. The death of Laius is accidental. The child in the poem seems determined to fight his father, indeed, both his parents, as much as they seem aggressive to him. But the statements of the 'I' seem to be fantasies. For instance, how old is the speaker? Is Blake giving the 'thoughts' of an infant, i.e. one who cannot speak, the definition of 'infant'? (The poem even uses the word 'thought'.) Is it the words of someone older, maybe an adult, who is remembering? But how can the first year or so of life be remembered? Can there be thought without language? Unless we assume that the poem is recording the unconscious desires of the child, giving voice to what was unconsciously wished for – which is possible – it would have to be said that the poem was the fantasy of an older person, reading his childhood, creating it, and making a fantasy out of it, so that nothing in the poem is actually reliable: it is a fantasy about the parents, and a fantasy of his own power, which grows in the third and fourth lines. We start with 'helpless', but end with the menace of the fiend in the cloud.

Have we moved away from seeing the poem as the illustration of the Oedipal? No, only changed from seeing it as something that both generations participate in to a fantasy created by someone older, which involves hatred of the father, who is thought of as weeping, as if he knows that his power has gone. Instead of seeing the poem as confirming either Blake's, or our, belief, in the Oedipal, the poem puts such belief into question. But in rightly getting away from a 'reductive' reading – as though we can use this piece of Freud to understand this poem of Blake, an approach this book opposes – we still have not got away from Freud. That is because we are still using profoundly Freudian terms, in speaking of *fantasy*, and *memory*, both concepts Freud was fascinated by, particularly because he was interested in memories of things that had never happened, whereas psychologists are interested 'only' in how we remember what *did* happen.

(Where the concept of fantasy is used in a strictly psychoanalytic, technical sense, I have spelled it *phantasy*: see 'Creative Writers and Day-Dreaming' (1908 *SE* 9, 141–53), which discusses it.) It might be argued that the speaker had just realised the profundity of what he thought had happened to him in infancy. In which case, the poem would be a case of 'deferred reaction', or *Nachträglichkeit* (*SE* 17.45); this means there is a lapse, or delay, between a traumatic event and the time, later on, when the event is felt. A reaction is never punctual with the event it responds to (see below, Chapter 7).

Further, imagine that the illustration was a photograph, and that the poem's speaker could be shown it. It would be obvious either that the fantasies related to a deliberate desire to deceive, because the description in the poem does not match the picture, or that the speaker did not realise how potentially unreal all that he was saying was. This gives another point, at the heart of psychoanalysis: that the subject speaking cannot recognise his or her situation, being a *divided subject*. (For the moment I am deliberately assuming it is a male subject.) The person, or subject, speaking, cannot understand the force of what he is saying; cannot recognise the meaning of the words. Does he know why he fantasises the world as 'dangerous'? Is it a word which expresses his own lost-ness, his own lack of being able to impose a meaning on what is around him? Perhaps this poem is one of protest which shows up the speaker to be an egotist. Perhaps it shows an inadequacy masked as aggression. Certainly what is involved is a strong sense of self-consciousness. The speaker is full of himself, and, in this sense of grievance, Blake has learned from *Hamlet*. That egoism is also why Freud, too, was attracted to *Hamlet*, not just for the idea of the Oedipal, and why this book makes frequent references to it. Psychoanalysis has always been obsessed by *Hamlet*: Lacan, for instance, devoted a seminar to it (Reinhard and Lupton, 2009: 3–90, Rabaté, 2001: 54–68). *Hamlet* marks something new: the modern subject, characterised by interiority, who cannot be analysed because he is beyond knowledge: as he tells Gertrude: 'I have that within which passes show' (1.2.85).

Did Blake write 'suck' or 'sulk' in the last line? Printed versions give 'sulk', but drafts of the poem show Blake wrote 'suck' (Phillips, 1988: 50). These words are opposites. The child who sulks is trying a strategy of resistance; 'sulks' follows on from 'bound and weary'. But sucking might suggest the puckered-up face, which has the expression of a sulk. If the word is 'suck', that returns to the Oedipal fantasy: the child's desire is for the mother's breast, an erotic fantasy. Though the poem has 'sulk', it would be wrong to exclude 'suck', in which case we come into another Freudian concept, derived from *The Interpretation of Dreams*, in which chapter 6 discusses how to interpret a dream image. It argues that each image is '*overdetermined*': meaning that, whenever there is one image in the dream, it comes from several thoughts which have combined together. 'The elements of the dream's content . . . have been represented in the dream-thoughts many times over' (*SE* 4.283). Freud refers to *condensation* and *displacement* (*SE* 4.279–309). An image that is *condensed* fuses two ideas into one, or puts two words – or more – into one. An image that is *displaced* means that, where there are two contiguous ideas which exist in close relationship, term B displaces term A. So 'fire' associates in thinking with 'water', so that to dream of 'water' may suggest that 'fire' has been displaced, perhaps because of repression. So sulk/suck: one term displaces another, but includes the other in it. And, since no one familiar with older print-forms which were current from Shakespeare onwards could forget that s was often written like an f, there even seems a displacement: sulk > suck > fuck. In which case, the word 'sulk' covers over obscene possibilities, as the polite but repressed possibility, but it also suggests that the word is a compromise, and covers over meanings that cannot be reconciled with each other.

If anything of that repressed third word in the associative chain was intended, what of the opening line? 'My mother groaned'? Childbirth? Or is it also a fantasy of the climax of the sexual intercourse which has produced him? If so, that brings us close to Freud, who discusses the idea of the *primal scene* in the analysis of the 'Wolf Man' (see Chapter 7). The fantasy in the primal scene is of forming a mental image of parental intercourse, as Freud thought the Wolf Man had, at the age of eighteen months, and so approaching one's own origins (*SE* 7.29–47). And if other words may be hidden in 'sulk' and have been repressed from the utterance, then it may be interesting to note the word 'hid' in the line that stands equivalent to this one: 'like a fiend hid in a cloud'. The idea of hiding one thing inside another is not foreign to what the poem is speaking of, nor is the idea that meaning is hidden from the speaker.

The speaker fantasises the world as 'dangerous' and of himself as dangerous like it. The child would be swaddled in 'swaddling bands', like Jesus (Luke 2.7), as an act of kindness and of care. But because of the word 'bound' which follows, which suggests imprisonment, do not these swaddling bands seem another form of repression? The illustration shows the child in a state of freedom. But the rhetoric of the poem constructs the friendly gesture of wrapping as an imprisoning gesture. Who could say that there was not a repressed idea in the parents of being aggressive to the child in so swaddling it? This gets to something which fascinates Freud: that a friendly gesture presents itself as something adversarial, and that a way of being someone's enemy is to be friendly towards them. Freud discusses the *ambivalence* of people's feelings about themselves and each other, liking to hate and hating to like, having unconscious emotions ('affects'), and in doing so, follows Blake.

We have moved away from thinking that Freud can tell us about the poem because he writes about Oedipus. That helps neither a reading of the poem nor the cause of psychoanalysis, because it makes it sound as though this was an encyclopaedia of points whose authority could be evoked. There can be no such authority to psychoanalysis: how can we *know* that there is such a thing as the Oedipus complex? Many readers have rejected the idea, and thought that that finally disposed of Freud. My intention is *not* to defend a Freudian idea and say it is right, or has scientific veracity, though the opposite point of view is not defended either: that current psychological or psychiatric theories, or scientific objective accounts of behaviour, are the best way of understanding the human, and people's lives in culture. I do not treat psychoanalysis as a body of ideas which can be explained in the abstract. I take it as a form of literature, while, incidentally, making the point that Freud is a very great creative writer, whose essays question the distinction between writing objectively and writing creatively. Literature's essence, on the basis of what has been said in the analysis of Blake's poem, is that it has no essence. Its precise words turn out to be not quite what is meant to be said, because language condenses and displaces. If so, things are hidden inside other things, and mean something slightly different from what they seem to mean. Psychoanalysis shows that. Literature, when read for that sense of repressed meanings being always a potential in the text, and of statements that mean the opposite of what they say, helps to see psychoanalysis not as a monolithic entity but as drawing together allusive images and concepts that can only ever be provisionally interpreted.

The opposition to psychoanalytic readings of literature – in my experience, people are for it or against it, few are indifferent, or in the middle – is that it detracts from the author's intention and from a commonsense approach to the author's sources. Some then add that psychoanalysis takes away from the enjoyment of literature. But psychoanalysis is a mode of thinking which questions intentions and surface meanings. It does not make literature less interesting, but enriches the importance of close reading. And psychoanalysis engages with what people say they enjoy, and what gives pleasure: one of the points that runs through Freud is the pleasure people take in what hurts them, for example, in the things they repress, or in their determination to enjoy their symptoms. So what of the last two lines of Blake? Being breast-fed should be considered pleasurable; the speaker, however, gives the sense of being determined *not* to enjoy it, but to sulk instead. That, of course, *is* his pleasure.

Is the poem called 'Infant Sorrow' because the speaker thinks all sorrow stems from the way he imagines he has been treated as an infant, before he could speak (and perhaps he describes accurately how he was treated)? But then, how could anyone know from observing from the outside? Was he well, or badly treated? It is assumed that the poem is about a boy, but psychoanalysis insists on the significance of sexual difference. What sort of poem would a girl have spoken?

Sherlock Holmes

'The Adventure of the Empty House', which is easily found, and read, is one of the Sherlock Holmes stories of Arthur Conan Doyle (1859–1930). Doyle started bringing out Sherlock Holmes stories in 1888, with *The Memoirs of Sherlock Holmes* (1894) culminating in Holmes's death, fighting Professor Moriarty, the 'Napoleon of crime', in 'The Final Problem'. Both detective and criminal were supposed to have died at the Reichenbach Falls (Meiringen, Switzerland) in 1891. But Doyle had been too innovatory with detective fiction for the formula to die, and he had to revive Holmes for *The Return of Sherlock Holmes* (1905), in which this story is the first. The coincidence of dates between Holmes and Freud and the similarity of their methods are significant: detective and psychoanalyst both work by looking for clues, traces of the past (Irwin, 1994): if Holmes has become a template for popular fiction, then psychoanalysis has too.

Not the least of the popularity effects of the Holmes stories is readers' readiness to treat Holmes and his companion Watson as real. Holmes's authority is guaranteed by Watson, the narrator, whose honesty, and basic commonsense and lack of imagination, and even the point that he has lost his wife (Doyle, 1981: 488), make him to be identified with in the narrative. *Identification* is a psychoanalytic concept (*SE* 18.115–20), an emotional tie with another person, where the other person is taken into (*introjected*) the ego, made to become part of it; on account of the lack of criticism this involves, Freud sees it as regressive in character.

Dr Watson, narrating 'The Adventure of the Empty House', dates the events as of Spring 1894, ten years earlier. A young gambling aristocrat, the Honourable Ronald Adair, has been found murdered in his Park Lane room. This was locked on the inside, and it seems that the murderer could not have used the window. The names of witnesses at the gambling table include the name of Moran. Watson, in the absence of the Holmes whom he supposes dead, wonders how the murder happened, but is, literally, clueless.

A second part, beginning with the paragraph 'My observations' (1981: 485), is set in Watson's home in Kensington, and shows his unexpected reunion with Holmes, and the revelation, which Holmes tells in five paragraphs, that he has been disguised in London, having escaped from Moriarty, whom he killed, at the Reichenbach Falls. He foiled Moriarty's confederate, who attempted to kill him as he escaped from the Falls. He tells Watson that they are to go out to 'start upon the notable venture of the empty house' (488): the first time that the title of the story is mentioned. (Since Holmes refers to the expedition as (*a*) notable and (*b*) an adventure *before* they have started out, and before they can know whether there will be an adventure at all, it is actually an impossible sentence for Holmes to have said at all; narrative is written from the standpoint of the end, as if Holmes was making them repeat something already done.) Holmes and Watson cross London, to an empty house opposite their old Baker Street quarters, where there is a dummy of Holmes in the window, a bait to catch Holmes's enemies, who are still on his track. The actual potential assailant enters the empty house in the dark, and Holmes and Watson catch him in the act of firing a gun at Holmes's dummy. The police, led by Lestrade, appear to arrest the attacker: Colonel Sebastian Moran, 'once of her Majesty's Indian Army and the best heavy-game shot that our Eastern Empire has ever produced' (492). The air-gun had been made, says Holmes, by 'Von Herder, the blind German mechanic' to the order of Moriarty. Lestrade thinks that the charge to be preferred against Moran is the attempted murder of Holmes, but Holmes says that he has caught the man who shot Adair 'with an expanding bullet from an air-gun through the open window of the second-floor front [flat] of No. 417 Park Lane'.

Back in Baker Street, Holmes's landlady tells Watson that she was involved in setting up the dummy, under Holmes's instructions. Holmes tells Watson about Moran, who was Moriarty's accomplice in various murders, and the other man at the Reichenbach Falls, speculating that Moran shot Adair because the latter had discovered him cheating at cards and was about to expose him. Nothing more is said about Adair; the reader realises that the 'evidence' mentioned ambiguously at the beginning of the story (1981: 484), implying that Moran was just a witness, is actually evidence condemning him for murder.

The main story narrated is not the story expected. We open expecting to hear about Adair's murder (plot 1) but it becomes a story about the return of Holmes from the Reichenbach Falls and the attempts on his life (plot 2). Readers starting plot 1 must have intuited that Holmes would be brought back, which happens at the beginning of plot 2, but only when plot 2 has been concluded do we realise that plot 1 has been solved. A clue connected the two in the name Moran, common to both, but the narrative depends on the reader not noticing this link. The demonstration of how Moran attempts to shoot the Holmes dummy seated behind the closed window of his apartment at Baker Street imitates how Moran kills Adair; it *repeats* it (save that, with Adair, the window was open), but the point, that we are seeing how Adair was shot when watching Moran trying to shoot the dummy, is apparent only on rereading.

The process of writing started from the solution, constructing the mystery to attach to it. When reading, we forget that it was written from the end. So reading has the effect of *repetition* itself: throughout this book, it will become apparent that repetition is a psychoanalytic concept. Watson refers to 'the risk of telling a twice-told tale' (1981: 483), which means that the fiction is that the events and the trial are well known to the reader of 1904/5, but also alludes to the idea that the pleasure of telling the story is that it has no surprises, that it will not disconfirm anything the reader knows. (People reread Sherlock Holmes stories, after knowing the solution, perhaps because of the power of identification, certainly confirming the 'pleasure principle'.) There are two levels of repetition. There is the fiction that reading a story is a process of repetition (the events have happened, now they are being retold), and that the pleasure of reading is to repeat familiar ground, because there is a definite point of clarification to reach. Inside the story is another repetition, which is where plot 2 illuminates how plot 1 happened. And plot 2 contains a repetition. It begins when Watson goes to his home and is followed by Holmes in disguise. Holmes reveals himself, and then narrates his escape from the Reichenbach Falls, and discusses the face of the man above him and trying to kill him. Holmes withholds his name. After the man has been caught, Holmes gives his name, and a narrative about Moran. This gives a pattern:

A. Watson's introduction to Plot 1 (1981: 483–5)
B. Plot 2: Holmes's narrative of himself and his unnamed assailant, in Watson's house (485–8)
C. Plot 2: Watson's account of 'the adventure of the empty house' which begins 'It was indeed like old times' (488), which also conveys the sense that the narrative to follow is no more than a repetition of earlier narratives. (488–93)

D. Plot 2: Holmes's narrative of his now named assailant, in Holmes's apartments. (493–5)
E. Conclusion of Plot 1, starting with Holmes: 'Now my dear Watson, does anything remain for me to explain?' (495–6).

The pattern gives a hierarchy of authorities who can, or cannot be questioned:

1. At the lowest: the police, led by Lestrade, the object of Holmes's sarcasm, (492) and the private detective whom Watson calls absurd (485)
2. Watson, the doctor, doing his professional rounds (483), whom the reader identifies with and trusts
3. Holmes, the highest, whose knowledge of the Falls, wrestling, various parts of the world, and various technologies (488), of both French and German manufacturers (489, 493), and of London (489) makes him the master. His parallel is Moran, whom he admires.

We cannot identify with Holmes, and the police are presented too marginally, but Watson, with his commonsense, sees everything but sees nothing and gives the reader the feeling that s/he might do better and see what Watson cannot. We can see that Watson makes mistakes, though we cannot see what he should be seeing. Realist narrative, like this, flatters the reader into thinking that s/he has a privileged access to the 'truth', but the truth allowed access to is the truth you are intended to see. Holmes flatters Watson into thinking that he knows more than he does. (He does not flatter the police, but Watson is not much brighter.) Flattering the reader suggests that his or her attitudes are basically correct; this confirmation of views already held makes realism basically conservative.

A trope (a literary figure, or metaphor) of hunting and being hunted runs through the text: this is a gun crime, and guns, in Holmes or in Hollywood, connote a hyperactive masculinity, or phallicism. Moran, hunting, does not understand that he is being hunted; as Holmes taunts him when he has trapped him: 'this empty house is my tree, and you are my tiger' (492). The repetitions this produces are:

1. Adair hunted and killed
2. Holmes's narrative of killing, being hunted, and escaping
3. Holmes hunting Moran, Moran hunting Holmes; the reversal when Moran is caught and handed over to the police, the law, which ends the law of the jungle. Holmes springs on to his back 'like a tiger' (491). Arrested, and called a superb shot in hunting tigers, Moran is likened to a tiger (492)
4. Holmes's narrative of Moran as hunter: 'the story is still told in India how he crawled down a drain after a wounded man-eating tiger' (494)
5. The conclusion of the Adair case – 'Colonel Moran will trouble us no more'.

Here is the narrative structure:

A. (Plot 1): the young man Ronald Adair – a figure of innocence? – is shot by someone unknown (Moran)

B. (Plot 2): Holmes narrates how he killed Moriarty, and how someone (Moran) witnessed this, and tried to kill him from above the cliff

C. (Plot 2): In the empty house, Holmes and Watson witness Moran, repeatedly described as elderly or old (a detail to be stressed, though he is only fifty-four), trying to kill Holmes by shooting through the empty window. This leads to the capture of Moran through Watson, and his arrest by the police, but not before Holmes has teased and taunted him. The police are seen as comparatively neutral, unrelated to violence

D. (Plot 2): Holmes narrates the violence of Moran, including murders he has been involved in with Moriarty in London. Holmes has been witnessing Moran's actions

E. (Plot 1): Holmes narrates how the corrupt older man killed the 'youngster', Adair. Is this like the father-figure destroying the son: an Oedipal theme in itself?

Here, A corresponds to E, B to D, and C stands by itself in the middle. The narrative goes into a reverse (a *chiasmus*), pivoting on C. This fits the repetition pattern, where what is important is the reversal of roles between Holmes and Moran. The telling of the story is not the linear A > B > C > D > E, but it shows repetitions, which make the story work, not discernible from the outside.

Roland Barthes emphasises how such structures rest on antitheses, contrasts, emerging within the text, which show the unconscious of the author and his readers (Barthes, 1974: 18–22). They indicate that Freud's 'unconscious' is socially formed, not simply personal. Following the 'Copernican revolution', thought has been decentred, and thinking follows tracks, codes of reference whose authority is laid down as undetectable ideological structures. Living inside those at least partially unconscious structures of thought, we *misrecognise* what we see, under the power of bourgeois ideology in Marxist terms (Althusser, 1984: 170–1). Thinking is not 'master in its own house': we think ideologically, according to a society's ruling ideas; the psychoanalytic study reveals the Marxist point.

Holmes calls Moran 'the best shot in India, and I expect there are few better in London' (1981: 494). The antithesis is India versus London. India symbolises Moran versus tigers in the jungle. London symbolises Holmes versus criminals in the streets. Moran is the best shot in India, but Holmes's unconsciously superior attitude to foreigners appears when he reckons that London has better shots than India has, as though London is more dangerous than being a colonial figure in India.

Linking Freud and Holmes suggests that plots in fiction follow a detective-story pattern, leading to the solution to a mystery. In *Oedipus the King*, Oedipus intends finding out who murdered King Laius. He is told early on in the play, by the blind prophet Tiresias, that the murderer will be found out to be himself. Oedipus rubbishes this explanation, choosing to continue with his investigation. (In Doyle's story: why was the manufacturer of the special air-gun said to be blind? What does blindness connote? Special cleverness? Insight, like Tiresias?) Considering the pressure in international relations between Britain and Germany before the First World War, it is noteworthy that the munitions-creator is German. Oedipus wants to know what has happened. *The Interpretation of Dreams* argued that the 'first sexual impulse' is directed against the mother, and the 'first murderous wish' against the father (*SE* 4.262). Freud makes the male child as aggressive towards his parents, and curious about 'the primal scene', wanting to know what goes on behind the bedroom's locked doors. That curiosity to see (voyeurism), is *scopophilia* (*SE* 7.157); see the 'Wolf Man' case (Chapter 7).

With Oedipus, the investigator is the murderer. That is literally so in some detective stories. But even when it is not so literally, it means that the desire to find out what happened in the past is not innocent. Which side of the law is Holmes on? He is responsible for Moriarty's death (neither Moriarty nor Moran is on police records: they are part of a plot which only Holmes knows, and only he can narrate). Holmes and Moran are on the same wavelength; note Moran's repeated phrase 'You cunning, cunning fiend' (1981: 492), said to Holmes when he has been caught: admiration and hatred together. How Moran watches Holmes, and Holmes watches Moran, and Holmes's account of Moran, indicate a mutuality between the two. If Moran is a criminal, Holmes is not that far off from being one himself. Moran repeatedly tries to kill Holmes; at the end, Holmes has Moran framed: his neck will be 'in the noose' (1981: 495). The attraction of the detective – who is not a policeman – is to be on both sides of the law, maintaining it by subverting it, criminal himself. That compares with what will appear, in Chapter 3 about Freud's ambiguity towards the law, and to criminality, in 'Totem and Taboo' and 'Criminals from a Sense of Guilt' and *Moses and Monotheism*. Obviously, if you kill your father, you are attacking law, as a patriarchal structure . . .

Moran's pleasure is in killing Holmes; the man is 'beside himself with excitement', his two eyes shine like stars, and his features work 'convulsively', with a 'sigh of satisfaction' (1981: 491) when about to shoot. This sounds like sexual pleasure, *jouissance*. It makes this movement to the window – to see and to kill – the absolute centre of the story, and it questions what is meant by pleasure. Only then does the story revert to Plot 1, having brought out something in it. If the detective, like the criminal, is interested in what happened within the locked room, the implicit scopophilia appears when Holmes, Moran, and the readers, through Watson, are led to see what it means in practice when Moran shoots into the provocatively set-up locked room. Watson exhibits less scopophilia than Holmes: Holmes enjoys speculating, but Watson's realism, which wants simple identifications and recognitions, does not; he thinks Holmes is getting fanciful (1981: 494), wanting him to make it 'clear' why Moran murdered Adair (1981: 495), which Holmes cannot do: the issue is unconscious desire.

And Moran? I add numbers and emphases showing the antitheses in his description:

> It was a (1) *tremendously virile* and yet *sinister face* which was turned towards us. With (2) the *brow* of a *philosopher above* and the *jaw* of a *sensualist below*, the man must have started with great capacities for (3) *good* or for *evil*. But one could not look upon his (4) *cruel blue eyes*, with their *drooping, cynical lids*, or upon the (5) *fierce, aggressive nose*, and the *threatening, deep-lined brow*, without reading Nature's plainest danger-signals. (1981: 492)

This is not a description but a collection of antitheses, which could be studied to pick out the significance of the contrasts whose lack of unity (according to Doyle) mark the criminal mind. 'Virile', read psychoanalytically or not, stresses how the whole text revolves around men and their desires against each other, which are, nonetheless, sexually charged: psychoanalysis reveals a dominant *phallocentrism* within culture (and perhaps repeats it: we shall have to consider this later). Blue eyes connote honesty if not attractiveness (in the dark, it is puzzling how Watson could note them), while, on the other side of the antithesis, 'drooping' makes him evasive, even non-masculine, as 'sinister' implies that the virility is qualified by underhandedness, which is unmasculine. Noting these points means seeing how reading is an unconsciously formed process, following through on unconscious, not logical, assumptions. The antitheses, because they point up contradictions, if not perversions in the character, work to ensure the reader recognises Moran as a criminal type. Moran's face had 'great capacities for good or for evil'. Good and evil form a binary opposition, which this story tries to maintain: the detective keeps the streets of London free from danger, which is the triumph of goodness. But Holmes is only 'good' by being 'evil'; it seems that the equivalence between Holmes and the criminal world he understands, and therefore can outsmart, means that goodness disappears as a category, to be replaced by something more interesting and ambiguous – and perhaps it is because of that that narrative remains fascinating. In that way, Freud is at least as ambiguous as Holmes, and psychoanalysis deconstructs the binary opposition between saying something is 'good' or 'evil'.

What mystery must be solved? It is: who shot Ronald Adair, and how? The mystery is compounded by the problem that this is the classic, basic 'locked room' mystery, where the murderer could not have left by the door, because this was locked on the inside. Nor did he escape by the window. The murder has happened before the start, so that the solution to the mystery lies in what comes *before* step A is narrated. So A > B > C > D > E are narrative steps to recreate a point which we can call –A. Half-way through the narrative, the reader is positioned by it in a position where s/he watches the gun fired through the window in order to kill Holmes – Watson: 'But suddenly I was aware of that which [Holmes's] keener senses had already distinguished' (1981: 491). It is essential to note the silence, the darkness, the secrecy, and the pleasure which takes place at that moment. When this narrative is virtually complete, the reader realises that this attempted shooting has acted out the event which was not told: i.e. Moran shooting repeats his shooting of Adair. But, if the original event (–A) can be repeated, it is no longer original, rather, one in a series.

–A and A are Plot 1, B, C and D are Plot 2. E returns to Plot 1, now solved. Getting from A to E means passing through the apparently unrelated B, C and D. They seem to delay the progress, as the story defers from its task of finding the murderer. So we return to the point made earlier in relation to *Nachträglichkeit*: that *deferral*, and *delay* are at the heart of things.

Summarising, a Freudian reading of the Holmes narrative:

(I) shows the basis of narrative in repetition, which is unconscious
(II) shows that the pleasure of the text is identification with what takes place
(III) reveals the Oedipal nature of the detective story. Even if we do not accept the idea of the Oedipal, something odd has happened: the Oedipal still serves as a prop to understand both Freud and the literary text. (Does Conan Doyle support belief in the Oedipal? Is the literary text more knowing, more Freudian, even, than Freud?)
(IV) shows the interest of the 'locked room' mystery, which maps on to the voyeuristic curiosity of the child over the 'primal scene'

(V) suggests that the primal scene is the missing scene which narrative tries to get back to, or fill in for, or replace; narrative pleasure encouraging the reader into searching out that missing scene

(VI) shows that the pleasures of reading narrative fringe on to the transgressive and forbidden or repressed (Moran's pleasure).

Since Freud, it becomes clear that narrative draws on unconscious structures (binary oppositions), which point to repressed – ideological – beliefs inside the culture. Because the beliefs are held unconsciously, the literary text, which they allow, reinforces them at the level of the reader's pleasure: Freud's work makes pleasure not 'natural', beyond investigation, but to be questioned. Pleasure, since it enables an enthusiastic misrecognition of what we see, assenting to what is in reality certainly not the case, can indeed be dangerous. These unconscious layers of ideology are what Lacan calls the *symbolic order*, and their authoritativeness belongs to what Lacan calls 'the Law-of-the-Father'. That is what Holmes establishes, which makes him less than a psychoanalyst, who is more interested in questioning such an order and such a law. But – the point is completely Freudian – law is established by transgressing it. Psychoanalysis, too, looks on both sides of the law.

3

Freud and memory

This chapter strikes out on a pathway of charting how Freud considered memory, as one of the processes working through the subject, and I will do so through a specific 'case-history'. Although Freud thought psychoanalysis was in the pursuit of truth, the speculative nature of his writing, and the different, irreconcilable models of thought, set side by side alongside each other, mean that 'truth' for him could not be single, unitary. The writing is literary: *Studies on Hysteria* says: 'it still strikes me myself as strange that the case histories I write should read like short stories' (*SE* 2.160). In *Notes Upon a Case of Obsessional Neurosis* (*Bemerkungen über einen Fall von Zwangsneurose*) (1909), about the 'Rat Man', Freud writes a modernist novella: the portrait of a young man. What is 'obsessional neurosis'? Here is a working definition: in this condition, people typically worry over what other people think are trivial issues. An anxiety or fear, an 'affectual state', is seen as being too great for whatever seems to be causing it.

The Rat Man's life appears at the end of the account of his treatment (*SE* 10.256–7). He was born in Vienna in 1878, and his father died in 1899, after the son had begun a relationship with a woman called Gisela, who twice (1900, 1903) declined marrying him. After 1902, his obsessional neurosis gave him suicidal impulses. He first visited Freud in 1907, married Gisela in 1910, and died in the First World War. Freud gives notes from his case-history, not in chronological order, but working towards the neurosis, which he describes as comprising:

> an erotic instinct [masturbation, love for women, and Gisela] and a revolt against it; a wish which has not yet become compulsive, and struggling against it, a feat which is already compulsive: a distressing affect and an impulsion towards the performance of defensive acts. (*SE* 10.162)

The Rat Man felt his parents knew his thoughts without him spelling them out: indeed he said of himself, 'I speak my thoughts out loud, without hearing them'; Freud regards this as a manifestation of the unconscious: 'he had thoughts without knowing anything about them' (*SE* 10.164). Compare the later statement: patients 'do not know the wording of their obsessional ideas' (*SE* 10.223). The crucial point is that the Rat Man *is separated from the meaning of his language*; the words he speaks have their own history, and create the unconscious of the thought, of which the patient can only ever be half-aware.

Early on appears the obsessive fear, relating to an army experience, when one army officer, a captain 'obviously fond of cruelty' – note the Rat Man called Freud 'Captain' – described a punishment, when rats were allowed to escape from an inverted pot placed over the buttocks of a prisoner lying face downwards, only by boring their way into his anus. Escape for the rats is only by something worse, and it seems the Rat Man must identify with them, because Freud notes the 'very strange, composite expression' on the Rat Man's face, 'one of horror at pleasure of his own of which he himself was unaware' (10.166–7): a pleasure either in hearing, or in telling the story; which marks him off as a divided subject: sadistic and tortured at once (as *both* prisoner and rats are tortured). The Rat Man felt, when hearing this, that this torture was happening to Gisela, and to his father, but his father was already dead, and he wants to repudiate the meaning the fantasy has for him. One commentary emphasises the patient's identification with the rats' panic, which would replicate his neurosis: they were 'seeking the way out, mistaking the way in as the way out' (Schneiderman, 1973: 48).

Freud brings out, later, the Rat Man's 'wish' (not 'idea', as he euphemistically called it), that his father might die, a wish he had repudiated (*SE* 10.179). What appears is an indestructible hatred (and love) for the father, surviving his death. Examples of obsessional ideas follow, revealing a conflict between hatred and love (*SE* 10.186–95). Freud narrates how the Rat Man's father had married his mother – who was wealthy – rather than the penniless woman he had been in love with (*SE* 10.198), and, in reconstructing the Rat Man's anger against his father, brings out how he was beaten before the age of six and how this, confusedly, linked as a punishment with his having bitten someone: so making him ratlike and suggesting that the rat image *precedes* the Rat Man's specific neurosis, going back a generation (*SE* 10.205–6). The image is literary: it recalls David Copperfield biting his stepfather, Mr Murdstone, and forced, when he goes to school, to wear a board on his back saying he bites. The Rat Man's ambivalence shows in his desire that his father might come back at night between twelve and one (this shows positive love, but recalls the power, and the threat, of Hamlet's father's ghost) to see him masturbating (a fantasy masochistic to the self, and sadistic towards the dead father) (*SE* 10.204).

Rats

When Hamlet impulsively kills Polonius spying on him, by stabbing through the arras, thinking, however irrationally, that it might be his uncle hiding (the man in his father's place), he exclaims 'How now? A rat? Dead for a ducat, dead' (*Hamlet* 3.4.23). Perhaps we can say that this line concentrates in it hatred for all father-figures. As the analysis proceeds, so 'transference' happens: the Rat Man dumps on to Freud the characteristics of his dead father, giving his fears an objective force (*SE* 10.209). He pays Freud in florins, called 'rats', making himself the punisher (giving rats to Freud, the victim), or, alternatively, degrading Freud as a figure of his own father (*SE* 10.213). There is a 'verbal bridge' (*SE* 2.213, 214) joining *ratten* (rats) to *raten* (instalments, paying by instalments) to *Spielratte* (a 'play rat', a gambler), which associated with the Rat Man's father being a gambler (*SE* 10.210), and, because he owed a debt to a comrade, which had not been paid off, imposing a debt on the son. This links, via the thought of money, to anal eroticism, the latter being associated with the Captain's punishment which had such a fascination for him.

Anality, discussed in the *Three Essays on Sexuality* (1905), appears in a parallel essay, 'Character and Anal Eroticism' (1908). This relates interest in cleanliness to a repression centred on dirt and anality:

> wherever archaic modes of thought have predominated or persist – in the ancient civilisations, in myths, fairy tales and superstitions, in unconscious thinking, in dreams and in neuroses – money is brought into the most intimate relationship with dirt. (*SE* 9.174)

Interest in cleanliness accompanies fascination with money, as money, as filth, flaunted or concealed, displaces attraction to filth, meaning faecal matter. Freud then links the rat with other valences: with syphilis; the penis; prostitution (again linking sex and florins), and to children (noticeably, the Rat Man knew Gisela could not bear children) (*SE* 10.215–17). Anger against the father, relating to his perceived interdiction of the erotic, has, as another determinant, his sense that the family wished him to marry a woman who would give him a business connection (*SE* 10.198). Freud also considers the significance of *heiraten*, to marry. The implications of Gisela being infertile and rats being children promotes speculation: was the Rat Man's marriage to Gisela an implicit revenge against the father, since it would discontinue the patriarchal line? Did it involve fear of children as rats? Did it imply that he would have more sexual potency with an infertile woman?

Freud also considers Ibsen's play *Little Eyolf* (1894), which contains the Rat Wife, who comes knocking at the door in the first act, like 'the return of the repressed'. This strange figure goes round the country, taking away all the rats with her, and her dog, Mopsemand. She plays on the pipes, the rats come out and follow the woman and her dog down to the water, she pushes out in a boat and they follow and are drowned: 'And then it's as quiet and nice and dark for them as ever they can want – the pretty little things. They sleep down there, such a long, sweet sleep. All of them, that human beings hate and persecute' (Ibsen, 1958: 225). The Rat Wife has charmed her sweetheart down there, to drown him. By the end of the Act, Little Eyolf, the crippled child, has gone down to the fjord, and been drowned. Freud adds in a footnote to the rat as the child, and thinking of the Pied Piper of Hamelin, that in legends the rat is not so much disgusting as uncanny, a chthonic animal, used to represent the souls of the dead (*SE* 10.215). This ill-treatment of rats Freud says the Rat Man 'had often observed with horror' (*SE* 10.216). The significance of rats, as both destructive *and* vulnerable, appears in the ratcatcher theme which runs through much literature: not just Ibsen, but the brothers Grimm, Goethe, Heine, Browning, and Marina Tsvetaeva (Livingstone, 1999: 12–17, Ellmann, 2010: 14–34). Freud spells it out, even, following Ibsen, identifying by the name the Rat Man the sadistic victim, with the rat embodying doubleness and the uncanny. Further, the associations of the word 'rat' do not just relate to the Rat Man's history; they go back, and include his father's generation, contributing to the sense that the 'rat' as signifier speaks outside, and beyond, the Rat Man's conscious understanding.

Obsessional neurosis

After considering the Rat Man's double response both to his father and to the woman, Gisela, Freud writes a 'Theoretical' section. Its definition of obsessional ideas calls them 'transformed self-reproaches which have re-emerged from repression and which always relate to some sexual act that was performed with pleasure in childhood' (*SE* 10.221). This quotes from 'Further Remarks on the Neuro-Psychoses of Defence' (1896, *SE* 3.169), where Freud first used the term 'psychoanalysis' (*SE* 3.162).

Before that, the essay 'The Neuro-Psychoses of Defence' (1894) compared *hysteria* with *obsessional ideas*, as two forms of *neurosis*. *Hysteria* begins when an idea 'incompatible' with the ego (for example, a sexual desire or prompting which the self finds unacceptable) must be forgotten: 'the subject decided to forget about it because he had no confidence in his power to resolve the contradiction between that incompatible idea and his ego by means of thought-activity' (*SE* 3.47). Freud calls this – for the first time in his writings – a 'defence' (*Abwehr*). Something has been pushed away. But 'both the memory-trace and the affect which is attached to the idea are there once and for all and cannot be eradicated' (*SE* 3.48). The *idea* is the image left by the unacceptable experience or invitation, and the *affect* is the excitement – 'the sum of excitation' – that this stimulation produces. The ego robs the powerful idea of the affect with which it has been loaded (*cathected*), because it wants to preserve 'the pleasure principle'; i.e. it wants stability, restfulness, homeostasis.

The 'sum of excitation' must go somewhere else, if it cannot be 'abreacted' (discharged). It is transformed – converted – into something bodily. The ego has burdened itself with an idea, which acts in consciousness either as 'an unresolvable motor innervation or as a constantly recurring hallucinatory sensation'. So 'the memory-trace of the repressed idea has . . . not been dissolved' (*SE* 3.48–9). Drumming the fingers impatiently on the desk would be a good example of 'innervation': it means, broadly, 'motor activity'. The sum of excitation has become a bodily symptom; and that, for Freud, is *hysteria*.

If that fails to happen, the affect remains in the psychical sphere, and does not work in the body. As with hysteria, the *idea* has been repressed, but 'its affect, which has become free, attaches itself to other ideas which are not in themselves incompatible; and, thanks to this "false connection", those ideas turn into obsessional ideas' (*SE* 3.52, compare *SE* 10.175–6). The 'incompatible' idea, or image, had a sexual basis. Repressed, it re-emerges as an obsessional idea armed (*cathected*) with a huge intensity of affect:

> In mental functions something is to be distinguished – a quota of affect or sum of excitation – which possesses all the characteristics of a quantity (though we have no means of measuring it) – which is capable of increase, diminution, displacement [*Verschiebung*] and discharge, and which is spread over the memory-traces of ideas somewhat as an electric charge is spread over the surface of a body. (*SE* 3.60)

The analyst can 'retranslate' the dislodged or transposed affect into sexual terms (*SE* 3.54). To distinguish again: the quota of affect, or the sum of excitation, returns to the body in the case of the *hysteric*. For the *obsessive*, it is translated into other ideas. 'Abreaction', or discharge, would eliminate such a sum of excitation. The Standard Edition calls this passage Freud's 'theory of cathexis' (*SE* 3.63).

Back to the Rat Man's obsessions: Freud's 'Theoretical' section revises the terms of the earlier definition. 'Obsessional ideas' become 'obsessional thinking', one example being superstitiousness, another the omnipotence ascribed to thoughts, feelings, and wishes, whether good or evil (*SE* 10.229, 233). Freud calls the Rat Man's repression of an infantile hatred of the father 'the event which brought his whole subsequent career under the dominion of the neurosis' (10.238). And Lacan comments about the father that the analysis could succeed only by Freud seeing that the word-chain of associations which held the Rat Man prisoner, discussed above, emanated from the father and his generation. This emphasises, for Lacan, what he calls 'the role of the Other in obsessive neurosis'. As Lacan says, the role of the Other, which seems to be controlling, 'may be served, in obsessive neurosis, by a dead man, and . . . in this case it could not be better served than by the father, insofar as the Rat Man's father had, by his death, acceded to the position Freud recognised as that of the absolute Father' (Lacan, 2006: 499).

The father

This analysis suggests that the Rat Man's father must be understood as more powerful now he is dead. (The argument about dead fathers is pursued in *Totem and Taboo* (1914), which makes the dead father more sacred, in relation to his sons.) It links the Rat Man back to Hamlet as another figure of obsessive neurosis; Lacan emphasises that Hamlet is 'constantly suspended in the time of the Other'. Hamlet can only act, not in his own time but at 'the hour of the Other', and his only freedom is to affect madness (Lacan, 1977b: 17–20).

The Rat Man's neurosis showed in his ambivalence with Gisela. 'His hatred of his lady was inevitably coupled with his attachment to his father, and inversely his hatred of his father with his attachment to his lady' (*SE* 10.238). Each obsessional idea the Rat Man had contains traces of his original repression, so that all his behaviour shows signs of hatred accompanied by forms of 'defence' against this. Hence the doubleness in his thinking. After the Rat Man speaks of the 'ghastly punishment' – the rat-phantasy – Freud says that:

> with the idea there always appeared a 'sanction', that is to say, the defensive measure which he was obliged to adopt in order to prevent the phantasy from

> being fulfilled. When the army-Captain had spoken of the rat-punishment . . . and these ideas had come into his head, by employing his usual formulas (a 'but' accompanied by a gesture of repudiation, and the phrase 'whatever are you thinking of') he had just succeeded in warding off *both* of them. (*SE* 10.167)

The word 'both' tells Freud that the punishment was to be carried out *both* upon Gisela *and* upon his dead father. Freud describes the defensive formula: it was a way of saying '*aber*' (but) which turned into the word *Abwehr*, 'defence'. The Rat Man incorporated into the defence-word the recognition that he was defending himself. That comes out in the next passage:

> Another time he told me about his principal magic word, which was an apotropaic against every evil; he had put it together out of the initial letters of the most powerfully beneficent of his prayers and had clapped on an 'amen' at the end of it. [Later, Freud reveals the word, 'Glejisamen' (*SE* 10.280–1).] . . . I could not help noticing that the word was in fact an anagram of the name of his lady. Her name [Gisela] contained an 's' and this he had put last, that is, immediately before the 'amen' at the end. We may say, therefore, by this process he had brought his *Samen* (semen) into contact with the woman he loved; in imagination, that is to say, he had masturbated with her [with her image]. He himself, however, had never noticed this very obvious connection: his defensive forces had allowed themselves to be fooled by the repressed ones. This is also a good example of the rule that in time the thing which is meant to be warded off invariably finds its way into the very means which is being used for warding it off. (*SE* 10.225)

The feared or hated thing – whatever it is that might happen to the woman; perhaps the rats – and the apotropaic have come together; the first infecting the second. Further, the apotropaic fragments the woman, by making an anagram out of her name. Freud thinks of the Rat Man's obsessions taking the form of 'distortion by omission or ellipsis' (*SE* 10.226), and in doing so draws attention to the point that psychoanalysis works by observation of *language* – that is its interest, and how it connects with literature.

Freud puzzles over the relationship of love and hatred (*SE* 10.239) – the 'ambivalence' which means that both are there – in the Rat Man. He continues with 'the domination of *compulsion* and *doubt*' in the mental life of obsessional neurotics (*SE* 10.241). Doubt (*Zweifel*) means thinking double: it involves the combination of love and hate, producing indecision, failure to act. For the power of this doubt, Freud cites Hamlet's letter to Ophelia, ending 'never doubt I love' (*Hamlet* 2.2.119): but, of course, Hamlet *is* marked by doubt here, and it affects his relationship to 'every lesser thing', including his revenge. Compulsion attempts to compensate for doubt, and

Freud comments on the regression: 'preparatory acts become substituted for the final decision, thinking replaces action, and instead of the substitutive act' – which *must* be carried out – 'some thought preliminary to it asserts itself with all the force of compulsion' (*SE* 10.244).

Obsessional acts conform increasingly 'to infantile sexual acts of a masturbatory character' (*SE* 10.244). A second form of regression follows: 'an early development and premature repression of the sexual instinct of looking [scopophilia] and knowing [the epistophemophilic instinct]' (*SE* 10.245). The latter produces 'brooding', another word associated with Hamlet (*Hamlet* 3.1.165): Hamlet the masturbator. Repression of action means that the intensity that should go into this is displaced into thought, which becomes more obsessive and compulsive, as thoughts require less energy expenditure than actions. For Freud, the Rat Man's passionate and 'evil' impulses have formed his unconscious, while in his preconscious state, 'between which his consciousness could oscillate', he was either kind, cheerful, and sensible, or paying homage to superstition and asceticism, in a reaction-formation against his repressed wishes (*SE* 10.248–9).

The psychoanalytic critic Steven Marcus discusses the Rat Man, and thinks how it might have influenced D.H. Lawrence's short story 'The Prussian Officer' (1914) (Marcus, 1984: 157–63). Another potential link with Lawrence is a story the Rat Man tells of his potential towards criminality. (His father had thought he could become a great man or a great criminal (*SE* 10.205), when he responded to his father's beatings by shouting at him 'You lamp! You towel! You plate', negating the name of the father, reducing him, perhaps, without knowing it repeating his mother's language, as if he had heard the way she talked to him.) The Rat Man says he committed an act of which he was not the author, though he remembered doing it, and he quotes from Nietzsche's *Beyond Good and Evil* (4.68) on the division of the self and how the ego demands that it maintains its orthodoxy and stability at the price of rewriting the past: '"I have done that," says my memory. I cannot have done that – says my pride and remains unshakeable. Finally – memory yields' (Nietzsche, 1998: 58). The story the Rat Man tells is of letting his younger brother look down a gun, which nearly killed him. He cannot think how he can have done it, but for Freud this non-normative triumph of memory over pride indicates that 'you derive pleasure from your self-reproaches as a means of self-punishment' (*SE* 10.81). The passage suggests how criminality is constituted by guilt (see Chapter 4), but, also, it contributes to Lawrence's *Women in Love* (1921) where Gerald Crich has done just that, killing his brother by making him look down the barrel of a loaded gun. Nor does Gerald's friend Birkin think that could have been just ‘accident’: like Freud, Birkin, considers that ‘it all hung together, in the deepest sense’ (Lawrence, 2000: 26, 48–9). Lawrence is fascinated by Gerald’s potential for self-destruction, which indeed produces his death, and which also takes the form of punishing, as in his desire to control animals: the Arab mare and the rabbit. The Rat Man is seen as holding on, as a memory, to his destructiveness. This suggests that his obsessional neurosis is not personal, but typical of an educated and sophisticated generation which was caught up in the war machine (devising punishments, being killed) like Gerald Crich. But the cruelties the Rat Man fantasises are less than the collective destructiveness of the war.

Project for a Scientific Psychology

We have considered two types of neurosis, hysteria and obsessional neurosis, and how they come into existence, from the necessity of warding off an unacceptable idea, or thought. I now want to go further, with Freud’s *Project for a Scientific Psychology* (1895), which influenced all his work, especially *The Interpretation of Dreams* (especially chapter 7), and *Beyond the Pleasure Principle* (Ricoeur, 1970: 69–86). Both Lacan and Derrida commented on the *Project*, and this gives it another acute interest.

The *Project* discusses neurones, chains of communication comprising the nervous system. Freud distinguishes three types. One, the *phi* (Φ), are permeable, so that excitations, stimuli, which are received from the outside and whose impact is sexual, pass through them. The *psi* (Ψ) neurones are impermeable, and are permanently altered by the excitations, called ‘quantities’ (*Q*). Ψ neurones, because they retain the quantity, correspond to memory. (I omit, for simplicity, Freud’s added distinction between *Q* and *Qn*.) The third group, the *omega* neurones, we will come to; they have to do with ‘perceptual consciousness’.

The first type (Φ) corresponds to perception of stimulus from the outside. Here, perception does not reach consciousness. What flow through are ‘quantities’, not consciously registered. As the nervous system desires non-stimulation, homeostasis, ‘the pleasure principle’, *Q* flows between neurones which try to divest themselves of it (*SE* 1.296), by an abreaction, a ‘flight from the stimulus’. Unpleasurable sensations ‘impel towards change, towards discharge, and that is why we interpret unpleasure as implying a heightening, and pleasure a lowering of energic cathexis’ (‘The Ego and the Id’ (1923) *SE* 19.22).

When these excitations, like electrical energy, cannot be abreacted, that build-up is a *cathexis* (Freud’s word *Besetzung* can mean ‘an occupation’, like occupying a building). *Q*s pass through the Ψ neurones via what Freud calls 'contact barriers' (Charles Sherrington called them 'synapses'). These resist discharge, both holding the *Q* and allowing it to pass through. What is retained is memory; which means that to remember is 'unpleasure', painful. *Q*s find permeable pathways, but contact barriers are forms of resistance, which *Q*s overcome; the *Q* passing 'difficultly, or partially' (*SE* 1.299); and of facilitation (*Bahnung*) – so they break, or breach a path. Memory is both the retention of traces of *Q* and the painful process of discharge; these neurones are 'vehicles of memory and probably of psychic processes in general' (*SE* 1.300).

Derrida comments on that: 'memory, thus, is not a psychical property among others, it is the very essence of the psyche: resistance, and precisely, therefore, an opening to the effraction [= breaking open] of the trace' (Derrida, 1978: 201). Some contact-barriers resist more, and some less, so that Derrida can quote Freud, 'memory is represented by the differences in the facilitations between the Ψ neurones' (*SE* 1.300). Memory is installed in the psyche, and *is* it, existing not as a unitary block but as a system of differences, and is in both the retention and the discharge of *Q*.

Derrida's idea that the memory is laid down as a 'trace' comes from *The Interpretation of Dreams* (*SE* 5.538–9). Calling the pathway followed to discharge 'the trace' implies that what is laid down is written. And Lacan, before Derrida, had connected the contact-barriers with language: *Bahnung*, he says, 'suggests the creation of a continuous way, a chain'. Lacan adds: 'it can be related to the signifying chain, insofar as Freud says that the development of the Ψ apparatus replaces simple quantity by quantity plus *Bahnung*, that is to say its articulation' (Lacan, 1992: 39). 'Articulation', implies joining one thing to another, as an articulated truck is joined, and to articulate means to speak. Lacan connects the pathway, which the contact-barriers have become, with whatever it is that allows language, the articulation of one idea connected to another.

Memory as writing: and thus, like writing, a structure of deferral and delay: this idea comes from Freud. Derrida quotes Freud's Letter 52, 6 December 1896, to Fliess, saying that he is working:

> on the assumption that our psychic mechanism has come into being by a process of stratification: the material present to us in the form of memory traces being subjected from time to time by a *rearrangement* in accordance with fresh circumstances – to a *retranscription*. Thus what is essentially new about my theory is the thesis that memory is present not once but several times over, that it is laid down in various kinds of indications. (*SE* 1.233, Masson, 1985: 207)

Memory is laid down by a repetition: that is, the second time creates the first time. The trace only becomes the 'original' the second time round. Memory is necessary to create a 'first time'.

If memory has a linguistic basis, this is not a biological account: for Freud, speech makes memory possible (*SE* 1.365–6). (This develops material from Freud's book on aphasia (Greenberg, 1997: 172–3).) Successive inscriptions of memory traces require a translation from one inscription to another:

> Every later transcript inhibits its predecessor, and drains the excitatory process from it. If a later transcript is lacking, the excitation is dealt with in accordance with the psychological laws in force in the earlier psychic period and along the paths open at that time . . . A failure of translation – this is what is known clinically as 'repression'. (1.235, Masson, 1985: 208)

When a 'translation' has not happened, that is because it would mean disturbance of thought. Translation can be dangerous. When Claudius sees Gertrude weeping after Hamlet has left her, having said so much to her about herself and Claudius, he says 'There's matter in these sights, these profound heaves – You must translate, 'tis fit we understand them' (*Hamlet* 4.1.1–2). But Gertrude does not 'translate' into Claudius's language; she knows it is dangerous. But, leaving that example aside, failure of translation for Freud means that an older memory, expressed in one set of terms, exists side by side with a new one, so that language in the speaker, or the writer, while it seems to relate to a single experience or single set of ideas, really relates to different memories, held, as it were, in different archaeological strata. Listening to one person means hearing what has been inscribed at different, and separate moments of life: it is not a single person who is speaking!

Memory and consciousness

This material must be understood not in terms of physiology but in a psychological sense. Freud cannot identify the 'mental apparatus' with any geographical part of the body. 'Our psychical topography has *for the present* nothing to do with anatomy: it has reference not to anatomical localities but to regions in the mental apparatus, wherever they may be situated in the body' ('The Unconscious' (1914) *SE* 14.175). Biological explanations can think about 'quantities', but go no further. Science deals with quantity, but consciousness with quality, which eludes observation.

The jump from somatic Qs to qualities and to consciousness is not quite explicable, save that Freud has suggested that we are already in language if the memories have a writing, or linguistic character, making them signs, representations, traces of something else. Consciousness itself cannot be directly seen, only through its representations (speech, and behaviour): indeed 'all psychic content is only a representation' (letter to Fliess, 31 August 1898, Masson, 1985: 325). Freud does not know how a quantity of excitation becomes a quality, but he suspects, cryptically, that it may relate to time (*SE* 1.310), and he speaks of another *omega* system of neurones which have to do with sensory perception of the outside world, and links consciousness with that (*SE* 1.309, 311). But – and this is the vital point – I do not start with consciousness, rather, I *become conscious* of something: consciousness is 'a sense-organ for the perception of psychical qualities' (*SE* 5.615), like a computer's ability to read writing that has been encrypted.

Memories are unconscious: Freud emphasises that memory and the quality that characterises consciousness are mutually exclusive (*SE* 5.540; compare Letter 52, *SE* 1.234, Masson, 1985: 208). 'Becoming conscious and leaving behind a memory-trace are processes incompatible with each other within one and the same system' (*Beyond the Pleasure Principle SE* 18.25). This thought is crucial to Walter Benjamin, when discussing Proust, whose theme throughout his great novel, *In Search of Lost Time*, is the impossibility of remembering (Tambling, 2010a: 23–53). Benjamin repeats Freud's point: 'consciousness as such receives no memory traces whatever, but has another important function, protection against stimuli' (Benjamin, 1973: 115).

Memory surfaces in what Proust calls *involuntary memory*, which intrudes itself into consciousness in moments of trauma. Consciousness is shielded from memory. For 'protection against [outside] stimuli is an almost more important function than reception of stimuli' (*SE* 18.27). A protective shield in the psyche forestalls outside stimuli. But there is no shield against excitations from the drives which are within the system, productive of unpleasure [= tension] (compare *SE* 5.616). Excitatory internal material predominates over outside stimuli, save with trauma, a central subject for *Beyond the Pleasure Principle*. In trauma, external excitations 'are powerful enough to break through the protective shield' (*SE* 18.27). This is pain (*Project SE* 1.306–7), or shock (*Beyond the Pleasure Principle* 18.31). Freud calls pain a quality (*SE* 1.320), forcing consciousness.

We can add that shock, for Benjamin, producing a consciousness traumatised by memory, is definitional for city life in modernity (Benjamin, 1973: 117). In Dickens's *A Tale of Two Cities* (1859), a leading motif is the desire *not* to be conscious: as one character imagines saying to Dr Manette, imprisoned, or 'buried alive' – clearly traumatised – for fourteen years in the Bastille, and now to be released: 'I hope you care to be recalled to life?' he imagines the answer: 'I can't say' (Dickens, 2000: 17).

The ego

The *Project* contrasts pain with 'the experience of satisfaction' which a helpless infant receives after undergoing an endogenous [i.e. internal] excitation in the Ψ system. Here the *Project* is clarified by *The Interpretation of Dreams* (*SE* 5.565–6). The excitation – a state of urgency, or wishing, for example, in a state of hunger – can be reduced only by something from outside: supply of nourishment (the breast) which is identified with the proximity of the sexual object (*SE* 1.318). The image of the object which satisfied the need becomes a memory trace. The 'experience of satisfaction' produces 'reproductive remembering' (*SE* 1.319), where the urgency arises again, producing a wish which must be satisfied. There is a 'wishful activation' which produces 'the same thing as a perception – namely a hallucination' (*SE* 1.319). The memory system works whether or not there is an external source of satisfaction, being motivated by phantasy.

This phantasy existence is, however, controlled by a modification from the ego, and this is introduced as a new idea in the *Project*. The ego channels *Q* into another course, diverting it from its normal cathected contact-barriers, into a 'side cathexis' (*SE* 1.323). It inhibits the movement of a *Q* which has been produced from an hallucinatory, or wishful, state, so acting as to indicate reality, not phantasy. Freud calls the ego a 'network' of cathected neurones in the Ψ system, neurones which have had a 'regularly repeated reception' of endogenous quantities (*SE* 1.323). The ego is a solidified bound collection of memories, produced by *repetition*. It separates off the quantities, particularly as regards their power of memory, inhibiting their circulation, so that they do not become 'quality', i.e. consciousness'. But it is not the same as consciousness (*SE* 1.322–6; see Laplanche, 1976: 49–66).

The ego's activity produces a crucial distinction. The system filled with 'reproductive remembering', where *Q*s roam free and mad, is distinguished from one which as a result of the ego accepts reality. The first is the world of *psychical primary processes*, which involve 'wishful cathexis to the point of hallucination and complete generation of unpleasure which involves a complete expenditure of defence'. The *psychical secondary processes* are those which have been moderated by the ego (*SE* 1.326–7). So *Q*s are mobile, free, in a state of process, or else they are bound, rendered quiescent. The distinction between *primary* and *secondary processes*, free and bound, which Freud says he took from Breuer (*SE* 18.31, compare *SE* 2.194), Freud calls 'the deepest insight we have gained up to the present into the nature of nervous energy' ('The Unconscious' (1915) *SE* 14.188).

And this distinction is at the heart of what Freud says about the unconscious, and repression. The ego is a bound network of neurones – 'a complex of neurones which hold fast to their cathexis' (*SE* 1.369). A 'bound', controlled, state, associating with social life, and rational thinking, has little flow from neurone to neurone (*SE* 1.368). In the primary process, psychic activities are associated with wishes and fantasy, calling for release, as in dreams, or creativity: in dreams, apparently utterly real (hallucinatory) unbound neurones are at work. Secondary processes relate to 'the reality principle', ensuring that satisfactions are attained in the real world.

So, pain, and unpleasure, 'the sole means of education' (*SE* 1.370), are at the heart of memory-formation, and at the heart of the ego's formation. Consciousness corresponds to admitting a certain degree of pain. The energies the ego uses to bind energies are themselves the painful *Q*s which were held in the contact-barriers. It seems that, from the start, the ego's existence points to a conflictual existence within the memory system. Putting this another way: Freud tells Fliess (6 December 1896, *SE* 1.234, Masson, 1985: 208), that the ego is the *preconscious* (*Pcs*). It belongs to the secondary, bound processes, whereas the primary process is associated with the unconscious. The preconscious acts as a gatekeeper, to allow images from the unconscious to 'enter consciousness without further impediment' (*SE* 5.541, see Solomon, 1974).

The ego inhibits the primary process's phantasy powers, by remembering and judging what of reality and what of phantasy is inside an image presented to it. Freud gives an instance of how both these are inside the image:

> Let us suppose that the object which furnishes the perception resembles the subject – a fellow human-being (*Nebenmensch*). If so, the theoretical interest taken in it is also explained by the fact that an object *like this* was simultaneously the subject's first satisfying object and further his first hostile object, as well as his sole helping power. [This returns to *SE* 1.318, adding in the infant's ambivalent response to the breast – see Chapter 5 below.] For this reason it is in relation to a fellow-human-being that a human being learns to cognise. Then the perpetual complexes proceeding from this fellow human-being will in part be new and non-comparable . . . The complex of the fellow human falls apart into two components, of which one makes an impression by its constant structure and stays together as a *thing* [*Ding*], while the other can be understood by the activity of memory – that is, can be traced back to information from the subject's own body. (*SE* 1.331)

This suggests how much of phantasy exists in perception. My perception of person A includes my phantasised memory of person B, who was the prime 'satisfying object' (e.g. as the mother). For Freud, 'the aim and end of all thought-processes is thus to bring about a *state of identity*, the conveying of a cathexis *Q* emanating from outside, into a neurone cathected from the ego' (*SE* 1.332). A perception from outside and from the memory-world that the ego organises must be matched up. The *Project*'s sense of how the ego is stabilised, and seeks to stabilise, returns with *The Interpretation of Dreams* which adds a distinction between perceptual and thought identity. The primary process tries to establish a 'perceptual identity': it wants 'a repetition of the perception which was linked with the satisfaction of the need' (*SE* 5.566). It wants to preserve the link between memory and satisfaction, and the phantasmatic, hallucinatory image that seemed to give it satisfaction. The secondary process, however, wants a 'thought identity': it wants to match up memories, concerning itself with 'the connecting paths between ideas, without being led astray by the intensities of those ideas'. It does not want thinking to be interrupted by memories being painful. However:

> condensations of ideas . . . must obstruct the attainment of the identity aimed at. Since they substitute one idea for another, they cause a deviation from the path which would have led on from the first idea . . . It is easy to see, too, that the unpleasure principle . . . puts difficulties in its path toward establishing 'thought identity'. Accordingly, thinking must aim at freeing itself more and more from exclusive regulation by the unpleasure principle and at restricting the development of affect in thought-activity to the minimum required for acting as a signal. (*SE* 5.602)

Ideas, as they exist as memories, are already subject to condensation. That is, all ideas associate other memories with each other, a point fundamental to dream-interpretation (*SE* 4.279–304, and see Chapter 6). No thought is identical with itself, it contains its own 'other' in it, what Derrida calls *differance*. These ideas consistently substitute one for another, in that other dream-process, 'displacement' (*SE* 4.305–9). And the 'unpleasure principle' – which wishes to avoid, or to discharge, unpleasurable tension – makes for difficulties with 'thought identity': thought resists such, which explains why Freud calls thought 'nothing but a substitute for a hallucinatory wish' (*SE* 5.567). Thought is a matter of avoiding unpleasant material, just as dreams, part of the primary process, allow the fulfilment of a wish (*SE* 4.121): dreams and thoughts are not so different.

Melancholia

Let's return to the passage from the *Project* (*SE* 1.331), about recognising a fellow human being. Freud has begun with the other (perhaps the mother), who helps the 'initial helplessness of human beings' (*SE* 1.318). Lacan's Seminar VII, 'The Ethics of Psychoanalysis', quotes the passage, centring on the *Nebenmensch*. He says that that *das Ding* (the thing), cited there, is that element isolated by the subject in his or her experience of the *Nebenmensch* and seen to be 'by its very nature alien, *Fremde* [= strange]' (Lacan, 1992: 52). Everything else in the *Nebenmensch* is perceived through the mnemic traces in the Ψ neurones, but there is always something unrecognisable in the recognisable. Lacan then quotes from Freud's essay, *Verneinung*, 'Negation' (1925):

> The first and immediate aim, therefore, of reality-testing is not to *find* an object in real perception which corresponds to the one presented [i.e. in the memory], but to *refind* such an object, to convince oneself that it is still there. (*SE* 19.237–8: see also 238, footnote 1)

At the heart of psychoanalysis is the 'lost object', which may be thought in relation to the mother's breast, the 'first' source of satisfaction. Everything of looking becomes *repetition*, attempting to refind it. Yet 'something is there while one waits for something better, or worse, but which one wants' (Lacan, 1992: 52). Waiting is always to be satisfied by substitute objects. The absolute Other is only found 'as something missed' (Lacan, 1992: 52). There is always something absent, missing, in all encounters.

The phrase 'lost object' comes from 'Mourning and Melancholia' (1917), one of Freud's most interesting speculative essays. Melancholia is a 'reaction to the loss of a loved object', but the loss is more complex than mourning, because the mourner or melancholic 'cannot see clearly what it is that has been lost', and knows

> *whom* he has lost, but not *what* he has lost in him. This would suggest that melancholia is . . . related to an object-loss which is withdrawn from consciousness, in contradistinction to mourning, in which there is nothing about the loss that is unconscious. (*SE* 14.245)

This leads Freud to his distinction, as he notes that the melancholic suffers – like Hamlet – from a diminution in his self-regard: 'In mourning it is the world which has become poor and empty; in melancholia it is the ego itself' (*SE* 14.246). The melancholic has a sense both of loss and of worthlessness because of his or her ambivalence towards what has been lost. Freud thinks of Hamlet's sense of worthlessness: he is a melancholic in a court which does not mourn the dead adequately (Lacan, 1977b: 39–40).

The melancholic values the lost object, identifies with it, and incorporates it into himself (*SE* 14.249). But 'the loss of a love-object is an excellent opportunity for the ambivalence in love-relationships to make itself effective and come into the open' (*SE* 14.250–1). I identify with what I hate and love. Melancholia means taking the love-object into myself, and so turning onto myself the love and the hatred I felt for the love-object. Even in the passage on the *Nebenmensch*, Freud thinks there was an ambivalence towards the other who sustains the subject in its state of helplessness.

Lacan identifies *das Ding* with Freud's 'impulse to find again' (Lacan, 1992: 58) while noting that what the object or thing is is unstated by Freud. It can only be known as lost. 'The Thing is not nothing but literally is not' says Lacan (1992: 63), adding that the mother occupies the place of the Thing. This makes him say that 'it is *das Ding*, which is the mother, is also the object of incest' which 'is a forbidden good, and there is no other good' (Lacan, 1992: 67, 70). If the lost object relates to the mother, it reappears in strange, yet familiar forms (see Chapter 7, which discusses 'The Uncanny').

Derrida on Freud's *Project*

'In seasons of pestilence, some of us will have a secret attraction to the disease – a terrible passing inclination to die of it. And all of us have like wonders in our breasts, only needing circumstances to evoke them' (Dickens, 2000: 292). What Dickens evokes in *A Tale of Two Cities* is a death-drive. I will come to that concept in these closing sections, by returning to Derrida's essay 'Freud and the Scene of Writing' (Derrida, 1978: 196–231, see Johnson, 1993: 65–108), already quoted in this chapter. Derrida starts with the *Project for a Scientific Psychology*, underlining points already made: how the contact-barriers produce a system of differences between them, places where memory slips through, places where it does not, in the one system, and that everything is laid down as memory-traces, as images, or signs, of what has been. 'Quantity becomes *psyche* and *mneme* through differences rather than through plenitudes' (Derrida, 1978: 201). A memory is the marker of something that has been; it is not plenitude, but marked by absence. Resistance is primary: Q cannot go straight through an impermeable Ψ system. Memory is the result of resistance, so it arises in a system marked by deferral:

> in accordance with a motif which will continue to dominate Freud's thinking, this movement is described as the effort of life to protect itself by *deferring* a dangerous cathexis, that is, by constituting a reserve (*Vorrat*). The threatening expenditure or presence are deferred with the help of breaching or repetition. Is not this already the detour (*Aufschub*, lit. delay) which institutes the relation of pleasure to reality? (*Beyond the Pleasure Principle*). Is it not already death at the origin of a life which can defend itself against death only through an *economy* of death, through deferment, repetition, reserve? For repetition does not *happen to* an initial impression; its possibility is already there, in the resistance offered *the first time* by the psychical neurones. (Derrida, 1978: 202)

Derrida makes many points here, suggesting how the *Project* impacts on *all* of Freud, especially *Beyond the Pleasure Principle*, that key text which proposes that there is a death-drive. There Freud even says that 'the aim of all life is death', adding that 'inanimate things existed before living ones' and that the primary drive is 'to return to the inanimate state'. But not directly, rather, by 'making ever more complicated *détours*, before reaching its aim of death' (*SE* 18.28–39). Not coincidentally, in the extract given above, Derrida uses the same word.

Psychoanalysis as a system of thought recognises detours; it does not deliver immediate truths, but works by delay and deferral, and difference, key terms for deconstruction; as if psychoanalysis was deconstructive thinking. Detours are forms of repetition. Breaching happens by repetition, which enforces the role of pain in constituting a psyche, links repetition to a system of delay and connects repetition to death. Since the ego, conferring identity, is formed by repetition, as we have seen, its role seems to be to bind the memories in the primary process. That constricting is a step on the way to death, so that Freud speaks of the 'ego-instincts' as exercising pressure towards death (*SE* 18.44). Identity, it seems, conferred by the ego, is death.

Derrida begins with the trace as 'difference', *not identity, or presence.* He says that *The Interpretation of Dreams* thinks of primary processes as a 'theoretical fiction', and of the secondary processes as subject to delay (*Verspätung*), so: 'it is the delay which is in the beginning' (*SE* 5.603, Derrida, 1978: 203). Everything in the psychic structure is anachronistic, out of time, producing delayed reaction (*Nachträglichkeit*) and *Verspätung*, 'concepts which govern the whole of Freud's thought and determine all his other concepts' (Derrida, 1978: 203). If the primary process is a matter of displacement and condensation, as has already been quoted (*SE* 5.202), there is nothing originary in it; no pure starting concept of identity or presence.

Derrida's fascination with delay, with *Nachträglichkeit*, appears in the *Project*, in a passage which serves as a revision for much of what has been said in this chapter. Freud cites a case of hysteria in a woman called Emma, unable to go into a shop by herself (Freud compares this with agoraphobia). Aged eight, she had twice gone into a shop, and the shopkeeper had attempted to grope her, sexually. But this carried no traumatic significance. At the age of thirteen, she had felt the shop-assistants were laughing at her clothes, and that one of them pleased her sexually, and she ran away in 'an affect of fright'. That triggered a memory of the earlier incident, and produced in her a sexual release which is dated to the first occasion, remembered through the idea that one of the assistants pleased her. Freud writes:

> Here we have the case of a memory arousing an affect which it did not arouse as an experience [i.e. when she was eight], because in the meantime the change brought about in puberty had made possible a different understanding of what was remembered [. . .] We invariably find that a memory is repressed which has only become a trauma by *deferred action*. (*SE* 1.356)

This example illustrates much of what this chapter has discussed. Hysteria results from an 'unacceptable idea' (the sexual proposition) which translates into bodily behaviour (Emma cannot go into shops by herself). But the memory is not from the first time round: it is created by a second occasion, which has the effect of creating the first time: this has striking parallels with the Sherlock Holmes story, where the solution to the second problem was the solution to the first. Repetition establishes the first time, gives it, indeed, an ontological reality. The first time, there was a repression, shown in the point that Emma went back to the shop, repeating her behaviour, even as if, unconsciously, seducing the shopkeeper. Only the delay brings out the trauma, and produces the affects which are retrospectively dated to the first time. The failure of repression means the dominance of the primary process.

For Derrida, the *Project* accounts for the psyche 'in terms of spacing, a topography of traces, a map of breaches' (Derrida, 1978: 205). The unconscious does not contain a truth which may be accessed, as through dreams, since 'the unconscious text is already a weave of pure traces, differences in which meaning and force are united – a text nowhere present, consisting of archives which are *always already* transcriptions' (Derrida, 1978: 211). Obviously, Derrida is going back to Letter 52 (see p. 32 above). The implications are crucial: there is no truth to be got from the unconscious. Psychoanalysis, for Derrida, is *not* in the business of telling you what is wrong with you, or that you have got an Oedipus complex etc. It is *not* a system for delivering truth. Derrida claims that Freud is antagonistic to what deconstruction criticises as 'the metaphysics of presence', i.e. to the sense that the self is punctually accessible, in 'the purity of the living present' (Derrida, 1978: 212). Rather, 'meaning' is reconstituted after deferral. 'Writing' has as its property *spacing*: that is, it exists temporally, spread out in a way which brings out deferral, delay, and difference, the latter being 'the articulation of space and time' (Derrida, 1978: 217, 219).

'The Mystic Writing-Pad'

Freud, since the *Project*, distinguishes between a Perception Consciousness, which receives perceptions from the outside, but does not retain them, and a system of memory which, of course, does, as 'a potential for indefinite preservation and an unlimited capacity for reception' (Derrida, 1978: 222). Freud's essay 'A Note Upon the "Mystic Writing-Pad"' (1925, *SE* 19.225–32), illustrates the distinction. It describes a child's toy: a commercial product, a wax slab, overlaid with a liftable transparent sheet, comprising two layers: a transparent piece of celluloid under which is thin translucent waxed paper. You write on the celluloid, and the waxed paper presses onto the waxed pad, and the incisions or traces created by the writing show up as the waxed paper adheres to it. They appear as writing on the celluloid. To erase the writing, you pull the paper up. The loss of contact between the paper which receives the stimulus and the wax pad means the loss of perception of the incisions, but they remain, as traces, on the wax slab.

The celluloid acts only as a layer of protection to the waxed paper: Freud compares it to the 'protective shield against stimuli' discussed in *Beyond the Pleasure Principle* (*SE* 18.27). The waxed paper compares with Perception Consciousness, which receives no permanent trace. 'The appearance and disappearance of the writing' is like 'the flickering-up and passing away of consciousness in the process of perception' (*SE* 19.231). The writing vanishes when the contact is broken. The wax slab is like the unconscious.

The point that contact is made and broken between the two systems, 'as though the unconscious stretches out feelers, through the medium of the system Perception Consciousness towards the external world and hastily withdraws them as soon as they have sampled the excitations coming from it' (*SE* 19.231), makes Freud think that the intersection of these systems may be connected to how a sense of time is created. He concludes with a sense of the two systems at work, imagining 'one hand writing upon the surface of the Mystic Writing-Pad while another periodically raises its covering-sheet from the wax slab'. That gives a representation of 'the functioning of the perceptual apparatus of our mind' (*SE* 19.232). The 'mystic writing-pad' gives an image of this, indicating that writing takes place all the time in 'the scene of writing'. (There is no pregiven permanent inscription in the soul, as Plato thinks, no 'metaphysics of presence' in Derrida's terms.)

Derrida discusses Freud's essay, but says that this apparatus does not run by itself: it needs two hands, one to write, one to lift the paper. Freud, by making the writing-pad stand alone, idealises, while writing without ink on to a surface desexualises the apparatus: Derrida quotes from *The Interpretation of Dreams* (*SE* 5.356) to argues that the apparatus is phallic, and from *Inhibitions, Symptoms and Anxiety* (*SE* 20.90) to make writing a sexual act, both of these being forgotten in the image of the 'mystic writing-pad'. Derrida rethinks what it means to separate the subject from the apparatus which gives memory; the writing-pad is a process of writing which is not simply a question of the autonomy of technology, showing that technology just goes on, nor is it a matter of permanence, for 'an unerasable trace is not a trace' (Derrida, 1978: 230). And it always undergoes repression, writing being unthinkable without repression, including, in western philosophy, the repression of writing itself.

> Pure perception does not exist: we are written only as we write, by the agency within us which always already keeps watch over perception, be it internal or external. The 'subject' of writing does not exist if we mean by that some sovereign solitude of the author. The subject of writing is a *system* of relations between strata: the Mystic Pad, the psyche, society, the world. Within that scene, on that stage, the punctual simplicity of the classical subject is not to be found. In order to describe the structure, it is not enough to recall that one always writes for someone; and the oppositions sender-receiver, code-message etc. remain extremely coarse instruments. We would search the 'public' in vain for the first reader: i.e. the first author of a work. (Derrida, 1978: 226–7)

Related to this is the question, what is consciousness? Freud makes it 'a surface exposed to the external world' (Derrida, 1978: 212), appearing as such by the stimulations which run through the system, and the excitations which come from the outside. But 'neither outside nor inside' (Derrida, 1978: 204) can be supported; Freud's image, and the suggestions of writing which Derrida draws on, show that there is no question of a consciousness simply on the inside. Freud's image of the paper over the wax slab gives an image of consciousness, but this consciousness, which does not bear a permanent memory, but which is also marked by what is behind, what is unconscious, is not that of a unique, ideal, self-present 'punctual' subject.

Derrida shows that this is implicit in Freud – as part of his Copernican revolution – but not quite stated, because Freud retains a sense of the ideality of the self.

Realising that consciousness is not that of a single subject changes everything; it means that psychoanalysis, as the study of what has influenced a single psyche, is too narrow; the subject is the effect of inscriptions which are at work throughout. Freud thinks of what is written, Derrida thinks of what writes, and how the power of technologisation creates the memory, and the subject (Derrida, 1996: 13–20). Such powers of inscribing include what Foucault calls 'the constitution of the subject' (Foucault, 1981: 60), where structures of power, working through the active force of discourse, label and construct the individual subject, in a whole field of constructed subjects. Kafka's short story 'In the Penal Colony' exactly describes that process of inscription. Homing in on the single subject looks as though the individual was sovereign, not constructed by discourse. That is a weakness of psychoanalysis, which, in its American versions ('ego psychology'), makes it seem that the subject is being elevated as supreme.

Summary

For clarification, let us summarise what this chapter has shown. First, the Rat Man is internally split, between love and an unconscious hatred for what the father represents, producing compulsive behaviour where unacceptable ideas have been displaced on to other ideas, apparently endlessly. Second, the unconscious is material which exists as freely mobile, unbound, material in the 'primary process'. Third, the ego is formed by painful repetition, creating the secondary process, which is rational, and ordered, pursuing 'thought identity'. Fourth the secondary process is aligned with the preconscious, which binds the energies of the primary process, and acts as a censor to admit, or refuse mental impulses or instinctual wishes or incompatible ideas into it, since, once they have passed into its space, they can become conscious (*SE* 16.295–6). Fifth, repression is 'turning something away, and keeping it at a distance, from the consciousness' (*SE* 14.147). Repression is not always successful, and must be repeated. Unconscious material always struggles to become articulate, as in dreams, jokes, and those strange forms of behaviour called 'the psychopathology of everyday life'. Sixth, the ego, acting by repetition, binds the energies of the primary system, which is a step towards the death-drive. At the same time, in the 'Rat Man', it encounters the compulsive repetitions of obsessional neurosis.

4

Freud and guilt

'Criminals from a sense of guilt'

Macbeth

Is guilt – like the 'Rat Man's' – the primary theme of literature? In 'Some Characters Met With in Psychoanalytic Work' (1916), Freud discusses some 'surprising traits of character' (*SE* 14.311) which he has detected in his patients: forms of resistance to treatment, ways in which the character refuses forms of help. He illustrates these through literature. So the first essay evokes Shakespeare's Richard III, who considers himself an 'exception' on account of his deformity: that permits his criminality, makes him resistant. Freud then turns to women embittered against their mothers, because they have come into the world as women, not men (*SE* 14.315), so also licensed by their exceptional circumstances. Then we get 'Those Wrecked by Success', people who apparently cannot tolerate their happiness. So Lady Macbeth 'collapses on reaching success, after striving for it with single-minded energy' (*SE* 14.318).

Freud asks why, noting that the play, which fascinated him (Jekels, 1943, Lukacher, 1994: 152–79), was written for James I. James's accession to the throne of England, as well as Scotland, demonstrated 'the curse of unfruitfulness [in Elizabeth] and the blessings of continuous generation' (*SE* 14.320; compare 15.96, and 4.266, saying the tragedy's subject is childlessness). Freud recalls the witches' prophecy to Banquo: when Macbeth reminds Banquo of that – 'your children shall be king' – Banquo replies: 'You shall be king'. That second comment actually veils a threat to Macbeth's future, cancelling it, and Macbeth knows it; though he may strike against Duncan as king and father, he does not become a father (see also *SE* 17.187). The witches ambiguously call Banquo 'lesser than Macbeth and greater', 'not so happy yet much happier' (*Macbeth* 1.3.65–86). Perhaps the point is that Macbeth is marked by personal ambition, whereas Banquo, already a father, has a more erotic drive, so 'happier'. When Macbeth becomes king, and Lady Macbeth queen, frustration – a key word in this section – enters the woman's childlessness, convinces her 'of her impotence against the decrees of nature' (*SE* 14.322).

Freud finds it strange that the play's speed of events, by which the Macbeths collapse quickly, is different from Shakespeare's source, Holinshed, where Macbeth rules well for ten years before attacking Banquo, as if then taking revenge against his childlessness which makes him 'lesser' than Banquo. Freud speculates that the two Macbeths comprise a single character, both obsessed by childlessness. What Macbeth fears 'in his pangs of conscience is fulfilled in her; she becomes all remorse and he all defiance. Together they exhaust the possibilities of reaction to the crime' (*SE* 14.324). Her collapse is his: the woman's frustration acts out the man's sense of what it is to have no children. It may be speculated that Macbeth's desire to be a man, and that his wife should 'bring forth men-children only' (1.7.46, 73), masks a fear of being feminine, which even his wife intuits, when she thinks he has too much 'milk of human kindness' (1.5.17). Lady Macbeth tries to masculinise herself, but even she feels that she cannot murder Duncan, because, asleep, he resembles her own father (*Macbeth* 1.5.40–54, 2.2.12–13).

Rosmersholm

Freud's speculation on one woman's childlessness evokes the third character, Rebecca West, the free-thinking woman in Ibsen's play *Rosmersholm* (1886), partly complicit in the suicide of Beata, Johannes Rosmer's first wife. Beata felt guilt – which Rebecca has intensified – because she is childless. When Rosmer proposes marriage, Rebecca refuses – at the point when she has in her grasp what she apparently wants – and she retreats, revealing herself, as Freud says, as 'a criminal in a voluntary confession to Rosmer and Rector Kroll, the brother of the woman she has got rid of' (*SE* 14.326). Rosmer ignores this revelation of how she ill-treated Beata, but Rebecca cannot and tells him she has 'a past' – i.e. she has had sexual relations with another man. The secret of that comes from Kroll, the pastor of the village of Rosmersholm, who, in Act 3, accuses her of having committed incest with her father, Dr West, being both West's adopted daughter (if not his real daughter) and his mistress. One guilt-feeling, her treatment of Beata, to which she confesses masks another.

Freud suggests that Rebecca's behaviour in Rosmersholm has repeated earlier behaviour; (1) she displaced her mother (Dr West's mistress) to be with West; (2) she eliminated Beata to be with Rosmer. For Freud, psychoanalytic practice shows how frequently 'a girl who enters a household as servant, companion or governess will consciously or unconsciously weave a day-dream, which derives from the Oedipus complex, of the mistress of the house disappearing and the master taking the newcomer as his wife in her place' (14.331). There are elements of the *Pamela* (1740) or *Jane Eyre* (1847) narratives here, and of Henry James's *The Turn of the Screw* (1898), and of the case-history of Miss Lucy R, which Freud had written about in *Studies in Hysteria* (*SE* 2.116ff) – a text which possibly influenced James (Cargill, 1963: 238–49). Comment on Freud discussing the governess's typical relation to her employer could point out, first, that he ignores questions of class here, that make the idea of marriage to an employer more than a matter of sexual desire; second, that he ignores the manipulativeness of the male employer: the opening page of *Anna Karenina* indicates many a male employer's attitudes to a young governess.

Analysis of Lady Macbeth and Rebecca West circles back to the problem of having been born female, deprived both in relation to the mother, whose object of desire she can never be, unlike the boy, and in relation to the father, whom she cannot equal. Having no child accentuates the loss, or even sense of guilt. Freud writes a third section, 'Criminals from a Sense of Guilt', whose argument, while short, is fascinating: criminal deeds attempt to mitigate a sense of guilt. The sense of guilt is related to the Oedipal desire of killing the father – who holds back both Lady Macbeth and Rebecca – and having sexual relations with the mother, but the larger question is, does this obscure feeling of guilt as a form of causation work to produce crime? While excepting adult criminals who commit crimes without guilt-feelings – who either have no moral inhibitions or, in their conflict with society, consider themselves justified in their action – Freud argues that, with others, a feeling of guilt leads to crime, in a desire for punishment. Freud concludes:

> A friend [perhaps Lou Andreas-Salome, to whom Nietzsche proposed marriage, and who trained as a psychoanalyst with Freud] has since called my attention to the fact that the 'criminal from a sense of guilt' was known to Nietzsche too. The pre-existence of the feeling of guilt, and the utilization of a deed in order to rationalize this feeling, glimmer before us in Zarathustra's sayings 'On the Pale Criminal'. Let us leave it to further research to decide how many criminals are to be reckoned among these 'pale' ones.

Freud's words imply the relevance of Dostoyevsky's *Crime and Punishment*: Nietzsche saying of Dostoyevsky, in an aphorism devoted to 'the criminal', that he was the only psychologist from whom he had anything to learn (Nietzsche, 2004: 65). It is not that crime leads to punishment, punishment produces the need for crime. 'On the Pale Criminal' appears in *Thus Spoke Zarathustra* (section 1.6), commenting on the violence of a man whose bodily instincts are wild, not at peace with one another; his soul interprets that conflictual state as 'murderous pleasure and greed for the joy of the knife', but after he has, therefore, murdered, his reason persuades him to find a motive: '"What is the point of blood? Do you not at least want to steal something too? Or to take revenge?"' So he listened to his reason, because 'he did not want to be ashamed of his madness'. The man becomes a victim of his own self-interpretation, which makes him construct himself as – or narrow himself into being – a single subject: 'he now saw himself as doer of a single deed'. So 'the exception now became for him the essence'. This 'pale man' is now sentenced by the 'scarlet judge', who is ignorant of this inner conflict; his interpretation, in sentencing the man, confirms what he has thought of himself, confirming him as that reified type, 'the criminal' (Nietzsche, 2005: 33–5).

It is part of Freud's interpretative brilliance to see what Nietzsche describes as related to his thesis, just as his interpretation of Ibsen reveals that below the confidence of Rebecca West, which makes her so able to judge the guilt-ridden atmosphere of Rosmersholm, is a past guilt which traps her. Perhaps Rosmer and Rebecca form two parts of a single identity, hence they commit suicide together. With Macbeth, it is significant that conscience frustrates him the moment he hears about the possibility of becoming king (*Macbeth* 1.3.147–2). And it seems that this has been a phantasy for him (Tambling, 2004). Banquo, the 'lesser' great and 'happier', is not tempted to criminality: needing to do nothing, he is Macbeth's conscience. Macbeth must free himself from a prior guilt, whose concomitant – he must murder Banquo and eliminate his son – is childlessness.

'The Ego and the Id'

Freud continues to work with guilt in essays published in the 1920s. I will discuss two, 'The Ego and the Id' (*Das Ich und das Es*, 1923) and 'Inhibitions, Symptoms and Anxiety' (*Hemmung, Symptom und Angst*, 1926). The first makes distinctions to supplement the conscious/unconscious division. Here 'consciousness' (*Bewusstheit*) is a passive, as is hinted at in the expression 'I became conscious of something'. As suggested in Chapter 3, we do not start with consciousness, but come into it through the 'preconscious', which is 'a state of latency', while, in the primary process, there is also the 'unconscious', which includes the preconscious but gets its 'dynamic' quality because it is made up of 'the repressed' (*SE* 19.15). Freud calls the ego that 'coherent organisation of mental processes' in each individual (*SE* 19.17), but it will be remembered from the *Project* that the ego also has something in it which is unconscious, and which represses material from it.

Considering the unconscious as both repressed and unrepressed leads Freud towards thinking of another 'structural' model (the superego, the ego, and the id), to replace the earlier 'topographical' model, which had worked on the principle that the two systems, consciousness and unconscious, were separate ('The Unconscious' (1915) *SE* 14.173). Consciousness is a surface, and a perceiving surface (*SE* 19.20), i.e. it interconnects with the world. With this '*Pcpt*' system, as Freud calls it: where a perception takes place, consciousness, not a memory trace, is formed (*SE* 5.539–40). The *Pcpt* 'provides our consciousness with the whole multiplicity of sensory qualities' but 'our memories are in themselves unconscious'.

Beneath consciousness is the unconscious, and preconscious. Unconscious thought-processes comprise 'thing presentations', visual images contained as memory-traces, and words treated as things, while, in the preconscious, the memory image becomes associated with a verbal image (a 'word presentation'). 'The Unconscious' says: 'the conscious presentation comprises the presentation of the thing plus the presentation of the word belonging to it, while the unconscious presentation is the presentation of the thing alone' (*SE* 14.201). A presentation which is not seen as 'only' words remains in the unconscious, in a state of repression (*SE* 14.202), and takes a more visual form. Freud says that 'thinking in pictures . . . is only a very incomplete form of becoming conscious . . . It stands nearer to unconscious processes than does thinking in words' (*SE* 19.21). Visual symbolism, for Freud, represents an older way of thinking than thinking in words: the point is relevant for art criticism, and surrealism responds directly to it, as the art of the primary process. Only by word-presentations do internal thought-processes become conscious perceptions (*SE* 19.23).

Now Freud returns to the ego, engaing here with Georg Groddeck (1866–1934), a radically minded medic based in Baden-Baden, who corresponded with Freud after 1917. His correspondence shows his disagreement with Freud's reading of *Rosmersholm*. He denies the argument that Rebecca West has guilt for her past – 'it is an ironical tragedy that a splendid woman like Rebecca should perish because of the milieu of Rosmersholm and a "noble human being"'. He regards Rosmer, as apparently Freud did too, as sexually impotent (Groddeck, 1977: 44, 45). He also, incidentally sent Freud a copy of Dürer's print of 'Melencolia', which he regards as 'an illustration of the consequences which ensue when the erotic principle of life is denied' (Groddeck, 1977: 103). Groddeck is cited as saying that 'what we call our ego behaves essentially passively in life', and that we are 'lived' 'by unknown and uncontrollable forces' (*SE* 19.23). Freud thinks that Groddeck has taken the idea from Nietzsche (Groddeck, 1977: 76), presumably from Nietzsche's sense of Dionysus. But Groddeck and Freud mean different things: Groddeck's view of the force, the 'id', as Freud calls it, *das Es*, the 'it', may be unconscious, but it is a more essentialist concept, not quite Freud's 'id', formed out of the repressed consciousness. Using Groddeck, Freud discusses the individual as a 'psychical id, unknown and unconscious, upon whose surface rests the ego, developed from its nucleus, the perceptual system' (*SE* 19.24). 'The ego is that part of the id which has been modified by the direct influence of the external world' and tries to bring the influence of the external world to bear on the id; hence it is 'reason', 'common sense' as opposed to the id which contains the 'passions' (*SE* 19.25). More: 'the ego is first and foremost a bodily ego; it is not merely a surface entity but is itself the projection of a surface' (*SE* 19.26).

This statement puts the ego at the surface, where the body and the outside world interact; it makes the ego what rises to the surface from bodily sensations, which is how awareness of it rises. And, as a surface, it touches other surfaces, as the hand is used to touch the self. That would suggest self-consciousness, and Freud visualises the ego as seeing itself, as though it was like an image projected on to a flat screen. It then becomes, on the screen, a surface imitation of a surface, an image the ego looks at. The ego comes into full consciousness by looking: the point is taken up in Lacan discussing the mirror stage (see Chapter 6). This doubling, by which the ego is looked at, is not just potentially narcissistic, it also opens it up to critical inspection. Freud to conclude the chapter speaks of 'the faculties of self-criticism and conscience', and says that these may be unconscious, including giving 'an unconscious sense of guilt' (*SE* 19.27). For 'the ego . . . is under the influence of perception' (*SE* 19.40).

Narcissism

Freud now introduces another distinction, in referring to a differentiation within the ego by which it narcissistically looks at itself. He had considered narcissism when discussing the artist and creativity, in 'Leonardo da Vinci and a Memory of His Childhood' (1910), and further in 'On Narcissism, an Introduction' (1914, see Sandler, Person, and Fonagy, 1991). We can take the essay on Leonardo first. For Freud, Leonardo's homosexual drives, never activated, were sublimated (= diverted) into art and science. In this speculative essay, Freud used a faulty translation, which used the word 'vulture' instead of 'kite' in recording a childhood memory of Leonardo's. Freud wanted to connect the Egyptian hieroglyph of a vulture (supposedly standing for the mother) with the Egyptian goddess Mut, who combined maternal and masculine characteristics, and to link her with the German 'Mut' (mother) (*SE* 11.93–4). For this reason, some of the detail of the analysis may not stand, but much of it, nonetheless, retains its fascination (Halpern, 2002: 59–85).

Freud says the phantasy recorded in the memory indicates 'the existence of a causal relation between Leonardo's [unbroken] relations with his mother in the childhood, and his later manifest, if ideal homosexuality' (*SE* 11.98). The absence of a father as an object to turn the boy towards heterosexual choices means that the boy identifies with the mother and her object-choices. He has returned to autoeroticism, 'for the boys whom he now loves as he grows up are after all only substitutive figures and revivals of himself in childhood – boys whom he loves in the way in which his mother loved *him* when he was a child. He finds the objects of his love along the path of *narcissism*, as we say, for Narcissus, according to the Greek legend, was a youth who preferred his own reflection to everything else' (*SE* 11.100). The fascination of the Mona Lisa portrait contains the 'riddle' of her smile, which implies that the picture is, as it were, Egyptian itself, in containing hieroglyphic, riddling significances resisting definition. It suggests the 'erotic life of women; the contrast between reserve and seduction, and between the most devoted tenderness and a sensuality that is ruthlessly demanding – consuming men as if they were alien beings' (*SE* 11.108). The enigmatic, then, has to do with women's sexuality. When Leonardo was encoded into the values of the father, as happened later, his attention became divided: his scientific speculations required that he set aside authority in favour of the study of nature. But, 'if we translate scientific abstraction back into concrete individual experience, we see that the "ancients" and authority simply correspond to the father, and nature once more becomes the tender and kindly mother who had first nourished him' (*SE* 11.122). The creative drive rests with the mother, and a narcissism related to being with her.

Freud notes the then newness of the word 'narcissism'. The mythical Narcissus of Ovid (43 BCE – 17 CE, *Metamorphoses* Book 3 lines 339–510), the youth who pines away for desire of his reflected image in the pool, and dies, is not wholly a narcissist since he does not know he is in love with himself; his pride makes him disdain the advances of others. He is loved by Echo, the very principle of sound, but 'Echo, that "acoustic personification of a reflection of the self" [the phrase of Otto Rank] is herself disqualified, as entailing a first element of symbolisation or difference' (Laplanche, 1976: 68). Narcissus desires a youth, so his wish is homosexual, even though it is actually a desire for himself. Is it that narcissistic desire leads to homosexuality, or does Ovid make homosexuality the basis of narcissism? At the birth of Narcissus – who was, not incidentally, born from the rape of the mother, Liriope by the river god Cephisus – the old blind prophet Tiresias says he will live till he is old 'if he never knows himself' (3.348) (Ovid: 1.148–9). Narcissus is proud, which means that he does not know or judge himself – he sees himself in the pool, but does not know it is him; he does not know that his desire is same-sexual. Not knowing the self, it may be noted, links Narcissus to Oedipus, who is also untroubled and transgressive and in a way narcissistic until he knows himself; Tiresias – who else? – tells Oedipus he knows nothing of himself, and Oedipus at his most ignorant prides himself on his knowledge that enabled him to solve the Sphinx's riddle (*Oedipus*, lines 300–462 and 397; Sophocles, 1994: 353–71).

Narcissism, as a love of the self, belongs with the constructions of deviant sexuality in the nineteenth century that Foucault's *History of Sexuality* discusses. Freud's essay makes such narcissism not deviant but 'the libidinal complement to the egoism of the instinct of self-preservation' (*SE* 14.73–4). He speculates on 'primary narcissism' (*SE* 14.88) which is associated with 'the first autoerotic sexual satisfactions' which derive from the organism's desire for self-preservation. The child loves himself or herself, and the woman who nurses him, and therefore preserves him, as virtually the same thing. Then Freud adds – and here Sarah Kofman finds Freud at his most affirmative about women (Kofman, 1985: 36–97) – that males lose this primary narcissism, but women, 'especially if they grow up with good looks', keep a certain narcissistic self-contentment, which is essential for 'the erotic life of mankind' since:

> Another person's narcissism has a great attraction for those who have renounced part of their own narcissism, and are in search of object-love. The charm of a child lies to a great extent in his narcissism, his self-contentment and inaccessibility, just as does the charm of certain animals, which seem not to concern themselves about us, such as cats and the large beasts of prey. Indeed, even great criminals and humorists, as they are represented in literature, compel our interest by the narcissistic consistency with which they manage to keep away from their ego anything that would diminish it. It is as if we envied them for maintaining a blissful state of mind – an unassailable libidinal position which we ourselves have long abandoned. (*SE* 14.88–9)

Such narcissism of women is just what cinema has encouraged for the benefit of men who have surrendered their narcissism: the cult of Marilyn Monroe may be considered here. Women are brought into relation with the charm of children and big cats, which may include tigers, and panthers, associated with Dionysus, whose appearance in Euripides' play *Bacchae* makes him a narcissist. Milton's Satan from *Paradise Lost* may exemplify great criminality. Perhaps Molière's Tartuffe (*Tartuffe*), or Dickens's Mr Pecksniff (*Martin Chuzzlewit*) attract because, as humorists, they are beyond the self-criticism – or guilt – others have. All are criminals, but not from a sense of guilt. Is Oedipus, that unconscious criminal, narcissistic? The chapter ends with Freud seeing parents finding their own narcissism again in the way they regard their offspring; this suggests that object-love – whoever the object – is not separable from narcissism.

However, the ego institutes repression. Primary narcissism gives way to setting up of an ideal ego within the self by which the actual ego is measured: the formation of an ideal is the conditioning factor of repression, and the ideal ego is the target of the self-love that the actual ego enjoyed in childhood. 'The subject's narcissism makes its appearance displaced onto this new ideal ego, which, like the infantile ego, finds itself possessed of every perfection that is of value' (*SE* 14.94). The image of the ego as the projection of a surface, already discussed, gives the same idea: the ego as 'the projection of a surface' has features in it of an ego-ideal.

But this self-confirmation is not everything; Freud speculates that 'a special psychical agency' sees to it that the ideal ego can be a source of narcissistic satisfaction. Hence 'conscience', which internally polices this ideal ego, making sure it is behaving itself. So armed with a conscience, the ideal ego becomes the superego, though Freud's essay does not actually use that term. Freud speaks of delusions of being watched – this is the negative aspect of the narcissism, where the ego regards itself admiringly – of patients feeling that all their thoughts are known (this happened with the 'Rat Man'), and that voices are speaking to them in the third person: 'now she's thinking that again', or 'now she's going out'. This constitutes the split subject, divided not only in that one part is observing the other but because the acting self is spoken of as though it was an object, and, almost, not there. And:

> The complaints made by paranoiacs also show that at bottom the self-criticism of conscience coincides with the self-observation on which it is based. Thus the activity of the mind which has taken over the function of conscience has also placed itself at the service of internal research, which furnishes philosophy with the material for its intellectual operations. This may have

> some bearing on the characteristic tendency of paranoiacs to construct speculative systems. (*SE* 14.96)

So the critically observing agency not only watches but speculates, producing 'philosophic introspection', as with Hamlet. The self finds ample reasons to justify itself, or to create a complete fantasy world, for example by believing in a complete religious system, into which it fits. This material in Freud may be compared with what he says of Schreber (see Chapter 6), an instance of paranoia, a state less narcissistic than megalomaniac (like Shakespeare's great criminals: Richard III, Iago). This critical agency not only observes the ideal ego, but *is* it, and in 'The Ego and the Id', is called the 'superego'.

Freud connects this part of the ego with consciousness, as much as the id is unconscious. He says that the ego identifies with what it attaches itself to, so that, especially in melancholia, which mourns the 'lost object', 'the character of the ego is a precipitate of abandoned object-choices' and 'contains the history of those object-choices' (*SE* 19.29). My ego is the sum of all those people I have identified with, and introjected into myself. Leo Bersani calls it 'an affective dump' (Bersani, 2002: 93). There can be no question of 'I'm goin' to wash that man right out of my hair' (*South Pacific*)! Such a process of internalising the figure with whom I have identified in love-terms desexualises the relationship. The chief figure to be introjected is the father, as a prime object-choice, towards whom, in the case of the male especially, feelings are ambivalent, (1) since the child's feelings towards both parents are complicated by the child's own bisexuality, (2) because of a sense of rivalry towards the parents (both are to be preserved and destroyed). Both parents (Freud argues that both are installed in the ego) are inside, as an 'ego ideal or superego' (*SE* 19.34). The superego is a reminder of earliest object-choices, but also an 'energetic reaction' to those choices, saying both that 'you ought to be like this' (like the father) and that 'you may not be like this' (*SE* 19.34), meaning, in the latter case, that the child cannot have the same freedoms that the father has. This superego is the 'moral' aspect of the self: Freud decentres any morality founded on religious arguments, invoking here the argument of 'Totem and Taboo'. Essentially, it *cannot be obeyed*, because as a law it says two opposite things at once; obeying it in one respect would mean not obeying it in another.

Freud recalls the two classes of drive working in the ego and the id. These are the sexual drive plus the self-preservative drive, and the death-drive of *Beyond the Pleasure Principle*. No resolution between these is possible; Freud thinks 'dualistically' (*SE* 19.41). These drives are fused together; not separable. 'Defusion', a coming together of the alternative drives in a detectable form, takes place in sadism, which destroys the sexual object, and therefore shows something of the death-drive, and in epilepsy, discussed in 'Dostoevsky and Parricide' (1928). That speculative essay begins calling *The Brothers Karamazov* (1880) 'the most magnificent novel ever written', outstripping psychoanalysis – 'before [which] the problem of the creative artist analysis must, alas, lay down its arms' (*SE* 21.177). The murder of the father is central to it, and Freud sees behind the novel Dostoyevsky as criminal-like, as in 'his choice of material, which singles out from all others violent, murderous and egoistic characters . . . and also . . . his passion for gambling and his possible confession to a sexual assault upon a young girl' (*SE* 21.178). At the same time, Freud makes Dostoyevsky masochistic, calling his epileptic attacks hysterical, 'self-punishment for a death-wish against a hated father' (*SE* 21.183). Freud pairs Dostoyevsky's gambling with his epilepsy, the first as a challenge to the father, as the superego, as Fate (the gambler wants to lose), and the epilepsy as self-punishment, deriving from the father. Dostoyevksy's gambling, as addictive, replaces masturbation, 'the primal addiction' (letter to Fliess (22 December 1897, Masson, 1985: 287), which, as autoeroticism, makes the subject both active and passive (*SE* 14.132).

Discussion of drives in 'The Ego and the Id' and their non-separability, which makes them *ambivalent* (active and passive together), and the sense that love and hate may be in each of the separate classes of drives, yields to an argument that they themselves contain a displaceable force. That means that the object of the erotic drive becomes a matter of indifference. 'Neurotic acts of revenge can be taken against the wrong people . . . punishment must be exacted, even if it does not fall upon the guilty' (*SE* 19.45), because punishment serves traits in the ego and the id, not in the more objective world of justice. In contrast, 'the death instincts are by their nature mute' (*SE* 19.46), unobservable. Having commented on the drives, the last chapter returns to the superego, which behaves as the 'categorical imperative' (from Kant's *Critique of Practical Reason*), demanding moral duty (*SE* 19.48). It produces guilt, though perhaps unconsciously: the patient 'does not feel guilty, he feels ill' (*SE* 19.50). 'A great part of the sense of guilt must normally remain unconscious' because the Oedipal struggle is unconscious. Hence the paradox: 'the normal man is not only far more immoral than he believes, but also far more moral than he knows' (*SE* 19.52). Hence, too, the argument we have sketched out, that criminals are so out of a sense of guilt.

'Unconscious sense of guilt' is a remarkable phrase; it makes anxiety a normative state, and implies that the condition of being socialised is an increase in guilty feelings. Freud stresses the superego's violence:

> the excessively strong superego which has obtained a hold upon consciousness rages against the ego with merciless violence, as if it had taken possession of the whole of the sadism available in the person concerned. Following our view of sadism, we should say that the destructive component had entrenched itself in the superego and turned against the ego. What is now holding sway in the superego is, as it were, a pure culture of the death instinct, and in fact it often enough succeeds in driving the ego into death, if the latter does not fend off its tyrant in time by the change round into mania [from melancholia]. (*SE* 19.53)

Further, if the id is non-moral, the superego can be 'supermoral and then become as cruel as only the id can be' (*SE* 19.53). That is, of course, because the superego relates to the id, as shown before: it relates to the father, or to both parents, as desired, and inside the ego as abandoned object-choices, as much as feared. The least aggressive person may have the most aggressive superego, and the more someone checks their aggression, the more intense becomes the ego ideal's aggressive tendency. 'It is like a displacement, a turning round upon his own ego' (*SE* 19.53). 'The Economic Problem of Masochism' (1924) calls the 'unconscious sense of guilt' a 'need for punishment' (*SE* 19.168). So a desire to punish, and a desire to be punished, both construct the self, but, in terms of cause and effect, have little to do with each other. The superego is sadistic, and the ego masochistic (*SE* 19.169), but not in relation to each other.

At this point, it is worth considering one of the revisions of Freud which are made by Slavoj Žižek, discussing Lacan. Žižek brings out the sadism of the superego, when he says that it gives 'the obscene injunction to enjoy' (Žižek, 2006: 98: the point is in Lacan (Lacan, 1998: 7). The imperialism of the command accords with what Foucault suggests about the 'constitution of the subject' in *The History of Sexuality*. The Panoptical controls that Foucault discusses, the compulsion to confess that power operates, are a form of the superego, but the control is not by repressing people, but rather by telling them to act out what they are, which is, of course, what they are constructed to be. That acting out makes for a deep conformity to prevalent standards of the discourse which has the power of control, but it seems to promise enjoyment.

And before we leave 'The Ego and the Id', its two contradictions should be underlined. The id and the superego are conflictual in relation to the ego and each other, and yet also ambivalent themselves, for the father who is feared is also the father who is or was desired. It is not a question of the 'Law-of-the-Father' being something that has a cold, legalistic impact merely, though Freud has emphasised that in his reference to its cruelty, and as part of 'a pure culture of the death instinct'; it is also desired. That contradiction should be compared with what is said about bisexuality, where Freud has already said, introducing the superego, that 'the relative strength of the masculine and feminine sexual dispositions is what determines whether the outcome of the Oedipus situation shall be an identification with the father or with the mother'. He calls the Oedipus complex 'twofold, positive and negative', and due to the child's bisexuality:

> a boy has not merely an ambivalent attitude towards his father and an affectionate object-choice towards his mother, but at the same time he also behaves like a girl and displays an affectionate feminine attitude towards his father and a corresponding jealousy and hostility towards his mother. (*SE* 19.33)

So the child ends up with two identifications, (a) and (b), installed in, or precipitated into, the ego (*SE* 19.34). (a), identification with the mother, includes her object-choice. (b), identification with the father, includes his object-choice. While both identifications are made, (a), with a boy, instantiates homosexuality, in terms of both the boy's femininity and his desire for the male. (a), for a girl, instantiates bisexuality. (b), for a boy or girl, inscribes bisexuality. There seems no escaping from the at least bisexual nature of the superego, so that the system of law which the superego involves already contains its own guilt, in terms of the ideology which makes heterosexuality, not homosexual, lesbian or bisexual positions, the only one unfailingly tolerated and enforced. The Oedipal is more complex than it commonly seems to be, because it necessitates a homosexual taboo as much as an incest taboo in prohibiting the sexual relation with either parent (Butler, 1990: 64). To consider the contradictions in the self, between id and superego, and to map these on to a basic bisexuality, another contradiction, is to feel that Freud's models of the mind can never be settled, clear-cut; they are modes of attempting to accommodate ambivalence. While the superego seems split, its task seems to be to maintain the ego as heterosexual, and as a single subject.

Anxiety

Guilt, and fear of punishment, articulates with anxiety, considered most fully in *Inhibitions, Symptoms and Anxiety*, which reverses more commonsense assumptions held in earlier writings, such as that anxiety came from unspent sexual libido (*SE* 3.81), or resulted from the repression of energies which were then transformed into it (see *SE* 9.60f, 14.155).

Similarly, Freud had argued that anxiety responded to a trauma. 'The Ego and the Id' considered birth as the cause of anxiety, if not trauma, following Otto Rank's *The Anxiety of Birth*. But the present essay rejects that (*SE* 20.161), on the view that this assumes an ego to start with, rather than an ego which emerges. Now he argues that anxiety constitutes the ego. (See Kearney, 1970: 127–9, Weber, 1982: 48–60.) The significance of anxiety was stated in 'The Ego and the Id' – 'the ego is the seat of anxiety' (*SE* 19.57) – and that is restated now (*SE* 20.140). So, rather than repression producing anxiety, anxiety induces repression.

Anxiety has the effect of a signal, warning of the danger of castration, and it creates a phobia, a fear of something, which displaces the fear of castration from the father (*SE* 20.125–7). It relates to a feeling of helplessness in relation to separation, or loss of a loved object, or fear of death, which Freud considers as fear of being abandoned by the superego (*SE* 20.136, 138, 140 (compare 130, and 143), and it generates symptoms, which are called any 'inhibition which the ego imposes on itself' (*SE* 20.144). With Lacan, who devoted Seminar X to anxiety, the ego is to be identified with a state of desire. Desire and anxiety are two sides of the same coin: what I desire I am anxious about, which means that what I am anxious about I also desire. Anxiety prevents something happening, which means it goes before it (Latin: *prevenio*); in other words, anxiety gets there first, breaking all chronologies. 'Anxiety has an unmistakable relation to *expectation*: it is anxiety *about* [*vor* – "before"] something' (*SE* 20.165). So it goes right round whatever it is that is feared, which is itself indefinite, not an object. Dickens's *Great Expectations* could with much justice be called *Great Anxiety*.

Freud connects anxiety and femininity with hysteria (there is a problematic sexual politics here) and anxiety and masculinity with obsessional neurosis (*SE* 20.143). *Hamlet* considers 'anxiety', first in the speech of the Player Queen, stating an issue: that love and fear are the same (desire and anxiety together) and then, echoing that, the real Queen, who feels guilt, which she must repress:

> For women's love and fear hold quantity,
> In neither aught, or in extremity.
> (*Hamlet* 3.2.162–3)

> To my sick soul, as sin's true nature is,
> Each toy seems prelude to some great amiss,
> So full of artless jealousy is guilt,
> It spills itself in fearing to be spilt.
> (4.5.17–20)

Every minor thing, to both Queens, seems to herald some disaster. When the soul is repressed, guilty, it gives itself away the whole time. The more anxious, the more repressed.

Yet comedy, of course, plays with anxiety: it has been said that, if we want to know what people laugh at, we should know what makes them anxious. In the early modern period, for instance, it was hanging, and cuckoldry. Hanging is laughed at in such plays as Thomas Kyd's *The Spanish Tragedy* (Act 3 scenes 5 and 6), while fear of cuckoldry, producing laughter, runs through numerous *fabliau* tales, such as Chaucer's 'The Miller's Tale', or 'The Reeve's Tale', and innumerable city comedies, such as Middleton's *A Chaste Maid in Cheapside*. Yet, of course, cuckoldry can be a theme of tragedy, as with *Othello*, or *The Winter's Tale*. We come back to the double nature of anxiety. As the other side of desire, anxiety is fascinated by what it fears.

'Civilization and Its Discontents'

Guilt, and its origins, dominates 'Civilization and Its Discontents' (*Das Unbehagen in der Kultur*, 1930): 'Unbehagen' may be translated 'unease', or 'anxiety', or 'malaise': it was originally *das Ungluck* ('unhappiness'). Uneasiness is the symptomatic form unconscious guilt takes (*SE* 21.135–6). The essay intends 'to represent the sense of guilt as the most important problem in the development of civilization, and to show that *the price we pay for our advance in civilization is a loss of happiness through the heightening of the sense of guilt*' (*SE* 21.134, my emphasis). A footnote quotes *Hamlet* (3.1.82): 'Thus conscience doth make cowards of us all.' This becomes more significant when we remember that, for Shakespeare, 'conscience' also means 'consciousness': consciousness is the problem.

The essay opens responding to the writer Romain Rolland (1866–1944), to whom Freud had given a copy of 'The Future of an Illusion' (1927, *SE* 21.1–56). Its subject is religion as an illusion which Freud would like to see disbanded. One of religion's faults is that it has never diminished the sense of guilt: indeed it works to increase it. Rolland replied by speaking of the 'oceanic feeling', where people have a sense of feeling unbounded, complete (another religious state). Freud considers this as a state where the ego has a sense of a complete bond between it and the external world, one that pre-existed in infancy, and he considers it as the 'restoration of limitless narcissism' from a state of feeling the need, in childhood, for a father's protection. If the oceanic feeling is a sense of being consoled, then desire for happiness becomes the theme of the essay (compare *SE* 21.76, 86), happiness which can only come from the sense of being loved. In view of what appears later, about the instituting of conscience to create guilt, such a sense of 'oneness with the universe' can only be a trick wherein religion maintains its hold on the subject.

Freud contends in chapter 3 'that what we call our civilization is largely responsible for our misery' (*SE* 21.86) and confronts the question of this hostility to that which 'protects men against nature and . . . adjusts their mutual relations' (*SE* 21.89). He says that the first act of civilisation was control over fire, and links this – via Gulliver micturating to put out the fire in Lilliput – with homosexual eroticism. The footnote says that the 'natural force of fire' was tamed, rather than extinguished, 'by damping down the fire of his own sexual excitation'; thus: 'this great cultural conquest was the reward for [man's] renunciation of instinct' (*SE* 21.90). Hence, women become guardians of the fire (as with the Vestal virgins). We can enlarge the point: civilisation is argued to result from the renunciation of an ambition expressed in homosexual competition, a dephallicising of man's relation to the world. Fire, whose flames are suggestively phallic, must be rendered 'natural', not a phallic menace. Civilisation itself involves the learning of order, which Freud calls a 'compulsion to repeat' (*SE* 21.93) working in educative training processes which are endemic to becoming civilised. The third chapter concludes with how much civilisation is dependent on a renunciation of instinct, for instance the child's fascination with anal eroticism, producing what he calls a 'cultural frustration' (*SE* 21.97).

This generates more speculation on the origins of civilisation, as in chapter 4, where the extensive footnotes make Leo Bersani consider sexuality as the repressed which is found in the marginal notes, and the dominant showing by its existence text the establishment of civilisation (Bersani, 2002: xiii–xvii). Civilisation seems unsatisfactory in its repression: imposing genital heterosexual love as the means to happiness; hostile to women, whom Freud sees as opposed to its patriarchy; insisting on sexual relationships 'on the basis of a solitary, indissoluble bond between one man and one woman'; and disliking sexuality 'as a source of pleasure in its own right' (*SE* 21.105). Yet, as Bersani implies, sexuality, in the text's margins, is also problematic. The first extended footnote, separated from the text, draws out how man's upright position – different from animals – divides the sense of smell from the rest of the body, indexing a distaste for sexual functions, including anal eroticism. The last massive footnote glosses a statement in the main text that 'something in the nature of the [sexual] function itself . . . denies us full satisfaction' (*SE* 21.105).

The gloss picks out three forms of dissatisfaction, beginning with the repression of bisexuality, and the linking of active/male and passive/female.

The second is the presence of aggression, if not sadism, within the sexual. Freud recognises this, thinking it dysfunctional. The third is the repugnance which is felt for the sexual function itself, which has come about from the ideology associated with the upright posture, and which brings Freud back to the earlier footnote of the same chapter. (The sense of the body as having the head (reason) on top and its sexuality below suggests a hierarchy which Bakhtin contests with the sense of carnival as 'the world turned upside down', placing reason below and the sexual above (Bakhtin, 1984: 18–24).) The chapter, then, picks on civilisation as problematic, and the sexuality it permits, and on sexuality as that which man in civilisation also regards as problematic.

The fifth chapter continues the argument about aggression by locating it in the heart of civilisation, an argument that makes Freud say that everything so far is but 'common knowledge' (*SE* 21.117). He rehearses the distinctions he has made between the ego-instincts and the object-instincts (to which he gives the name 'libido') and indicates how both are complicated by a drive towards destruction, spoken of in *Beyond the Pleasure Principle*, and said to be working silently (*SE* 21.119), not detectable by itself, but only when it is inside the erotic instincts. Its sadism Freud connects with narcissistic enjoyment, and to a wish for omnipotence, which returns, therefore, to the 'oceanic feeling'. The struggle between Eros and Death, which implies aggression, produces chapter 7, where aggressiveness is 'introjected, internalised', directed not outwards, towards the world, but towards the ego:

> There it is taken over by a portion of the ego which sets itself over against the rest of the ego, and which now, in the form of 'conscience' is ready to put into action against the ego the same harsh aggressiveness that the ego would have liked to satisfy upon other, extraneous individuals. The tension between the harsh super-ego and the ego that is subjected to it, is called by us the sense of guilt; it expresses itself as a need for punishment. (*SE* 21.123)

Civilisation insists upon a renunciation of instinctual satisfactions, as discussed in Freud's chapter 4; this is presented as a threat of a loss of love from the external authority (*SE* 21.124), and it presses for punishment, 'since the continuance of the forbidden wishes cannot be concealed from the super-ego' (*SE* 21.127). To repression is added a sadistic and masochistic destructiveness which constitutes the split subject. Freud points out how misfortune comes to the aid of reinforcing renunciation, and the temptation towards morality, drawing attention to the severity of conscience in the best, most tractable people. His explanation of these points he takes to be entirely the province of psychoanalysis, which, we may say, proceeds by putting common ideas into reverse (as with criminality being caused by a sense of guilt):

> Conscience (or more correctly, the anxiety which later becomes conscience) is indeed the cause of instinctual renunciation to begin with, but . . . later the relationship is reversed. Every renunciation of instinct now becomes a dynamic source of conscience and every fresh renunciation increases the latter's severity and intolerance. If we could only bring it better into harmony with what we already know about the history of the origin of conscience, we should be tempted to defend the paradoxical idea that conscience is the result of instinctual renunciation or that instinctual renunciation (imposed on us from without) creates conscience, which then demands further instinctual renunciation. (*SE* 21.128–9)

Every renunciation, for example of aggression, intensifies the power of conscience, making it *more* exacting, *more* aggressive, hence increasing the sense of guilt. Aggression has not been reduced, only turned back.

Aggression against the father, the agent of authority, which must be renounced, is compensated for by 'identification' with the 'unattackable authority' – i.e. the father: this force turns into his superego, so that 'the child's ego [that which is punished] has to content itself with the unhappy role of . . . the father who has thus been degraded'. In a reversal of the situation, the child becomes the vengeful superego punishing the father as child with all the aggression that the child feels towards the father. Hence the idea, which Freud reverts to, from 'Totem and Taboo', of the sons killing the father. Identification with the father comes from a sense of guilt; the child can do nothing about it, and the severity of the superego accords exactly with the amount of aggression addressed to the father (just as much as it accords with the actual violence of the father: Freud holds the two views together). Conscience, in the form of the internalised father, arises through the suppression of an aggressive impulse, and is reinforced by fresh suppressions of the same kind (*SE* 21.130). It is an aggression felt against civilisation, symbolised in the father, whose reward is that the values of civilisation now reign as the superego.

The chapter ends distinguishing guilt, and conscience – feeling guilty – from remorse. Freud here distinguishes himself from such a phrase as 'the remorse of conscience', the Latinising form of the medieval English phrase 'the agenbite of inwit'. Remorse, for Freud, is not to do with feelings of guilt; it results from ambivalence. The actual killing of the father – or whatever symbolises civilisation – causes remorse because the father is loved as much as hated. So, then, remorse for whatever has been done

(*SE* 21.131–2, 137) is always a memory of the ambivalent reaction to the father.

The last chapter, after summarising, comments on the Christian injunction to 'love thy neighbour as thyself', Freud saying 'what a potent obstacle to civilisation aggressiveness must be if the defence against it [i.e. the command to love] can cause as much unhappiness as aggressiveness itself' (21.143).

'Analysis Terminable and Interminable'

There are signs in the Freud of the 1930s of pessimism about his life's work, but none of giving up. A near-last essay is 'Analysis Terminable and Interminable' – *Die Endliche* [properly, 'finite'] *und die Unendliche* [Infinite] *Analyse* (1937). It states a problem central to Freud's psychoanalytic work, and one relevant to all cultural studies which engage with issues of gender, especially 'queer theory' if that term means taking a position that there is nothing 'natural', pre-, or God-given, about any sexual choice. As Freud says in *Three Essays on Sexuality*, 'it seems probable that the sexual instinct is in the first instance independent of its object; nor is its origin likely to be due to its object's attractions' (*SE* 7.148). The sexual drive has no predetermined object, or aim (Dean, 2003: 245).

Half-way through, Freud asks whether analysis can achieve a permanent cure (*SE* 23.234), and turns his attention to the 'normal ego' as a fiction, and to the 'mechanisms of defence' that it uses to avoid danger, anxiety, and unpleasure. Repression, the ego's resource in these matters, results in distortion, or alteration, of the ego. In section 6, Freud turns to different types of ego, and reflects on the resistance so often encountered to recovery; a spirit wanting to hold on to illness and suffering, and to the need for punishment. He reflects afresh on the conclusion that mental events are not exclusively governed by the need for pleasure, rather by the need for suffering: Eros and the death-drive in antithesis (*SE* 23.243). That leads into consideration of destructiveness. Freud thinks of bisexuality, and argues, as so often, that there is nothing but bisexuality. But 'a man's heterosexuality will not put up with any homosexuality, and *vice versa*' (*SE* 23.244). Here we fringe on to homophobia and compulsory 'heteronormativity'. That heterosexuality and homosexuality should be at war with each other puzzles Freud. That homosexuality should repudiate heterosexuality may be understandable, in terms of the marginalisation made by the former – a point he ignores – and, of course, the work of Foucault would suggest that 'the constitution of the subject' which constructs homosexuality is also alienating, a mode not of liberation but of imprisonment within a discourse which makes homosexuality directly opposite to heterosexuality. Yet that is not Freud's point; he is more interested in choices expressing themselves as antagonisms to an other position. After a meditation on Empedocles who considered that love and strife were always at war with each other, he turns to the distinctions between the sexes. He argues that there is, in women, and in men, a 'repudiation of femininity' (*SE* 23.250); in women, the 'desire for a penis', and the masculinity associated with that, and in males, 'the struggle against passivity'. Are there shades of Macbeth here again?

He reflects on the impossibility of convincing a man 'that a passive attitude to men does not always signify castration, and that it is indispensable in many relationships in life'. Yet, a footnote adds, such men often display 'a masochistic attitude' towards women: they reject 'not passivity in general, but passivity towards a male', and he attributes this 'masculine protest' (a term he takes from Adler) to 'castration anxiety'. So he concludes that what is repressed in both sexes is a passive attitude, and what is repudiated in both is femininity. If masculine identity, and its triumphal assertion, are left as the problem, the implications here should be developed in relationship to Lacan (Chapters 6 and 7).

Feminists will contest the proposition that women repudiate femininity, on the basis that that is a social, and male, construct, to say nothing of being a male observation about the 'other'. They will add that it assumes that femininity has an equal status with masculinity, as opposed to a marginal one. Here the arguments about heterosexuality and homosexuality map on to the arguments about the feminine; the rejection of passivity is an argument about homosexuality, because what is in question is how men react to men (answer: aggressively).

While much of the argument is unacceptable as it stands, it nonetheless has the force of Freud's self-criticism behind it. He is contesting any form of reactive behaviour, and placing the issue of what seems 'normal' – i.e. masculine heroism, and masculine assertiveness – into question.

5

Klein and 'object-relations': the mother and creativity

William Wordsworth (1770–1850) was writing his autobiographical poem *The Prelude: The Growth of a Poet's Mind* for much of his life. Though there was a completed version by 1805, the work appeared only posthumously, after long revisions. The 1805 version of lines 2.233–54, quoted below, says that it attempts to trace 'the progress of our being'. A philosophical poem, interested in how the mind is formed inside, and from the outside, it speculates on the infant as an active agent, from the time of being at the mother's breast:

> Blest the infant Babe
> (For with my best conjecture I would trace
> Our Being's earthly progress), blest the Babe
> Nursed in his Mother's arms, who sinks to sleep
> Nursed on his Mother's breast, who with his soul
> Drinks in the feelings of his Mother's eye!
> For him, in one dear Presence, there exists
> A virtue which irradiates and exalts
> Objects through widest intercourse of sense.
> No outcast he, bewildered and depressed:
> Along his infant veins are interfused
> The gravitation and the filial bond
> Of nature that connect him with the world.
> Is there a flower, to which he points with hand
> Too weak to gather it, already love
> Drawn from love's purest earthly fount for him
> Hath beautified that flower; already shades
> Of pity cast from inward tenderness
> Do fall around him upon aught that bears
> Unsightly marks of violence or harm.
> Emphatically such a Being loves,

> Frail creature as he is, helpless as frail,
> An inmate of this active universe.
> *The Prelude* (1850), 2.232–54
> (Wordsworth, 1979: 79)

Wordsworth's baby, suckled and sleeping on the mother's breast, is different from Blake's infant: 'I thought best / To sulk upon my mother's breast.' Nonetheless, comparing these two Romantic poets hints at the overwhelming significance of the mother in literature; and psychoanalysis, especially that deriving from Melanie Klein (1882–1960), has responded to that. Her work provides the substance of this chapter.

Wordsworth writes in an almost incantatory style. He repeats 'blest' and 'nursed' and 'mother' from line to line, speaking of the mother's arms, breast, and eye, while rhyming 'sinks' and 'drinks', later repeating 'love' from line to line, while similar constructions, such as 'already . . .' keep appearing. Paul de Man notes how the word 'eye' comes in as a displacement of the word 'breast', and so introduces the *face* of the mother, which is never referred to but which nonetheless haunts the passage (de Man, 1984: 83–92). The absence of the face, in a literal sense, yet its unconscious presence, is a perfect instance of how Wordsworth's writing, in its indirectness, which cannot be paraphrased, anticipates psychoanalysis.

The sense is that the mother gives much more than milk, that contact with her, as the embodiment of 'one dear Presence', means that every other object is now invested with life, as having traces of the mother, so that there is an active life in which the child participates in an unalienated way, as linked with nature. The example of the flower, and of anything that bears marks of violence or harm, suggests that the value of these things has been supplemented since the child sees them in the light of an 'inward tenderness' received from its mother. The child, even sleeping, is not passive, and though it is 'frail' (repeated), is part of an 'active' universe, making it in turn active. So, a few lines later, Wordsworth speaks of the 'the first / Poetic spirit of our human life' (2.260–1): creativity, poetry (*poeisis* means 'what is made'), making and shaping come out of this contact with the mother, whose milk-giving is a form of creativity.

Klein, who discussed this last point in *Envy and Gratitude* (see below), accepted the view that the child is active, from what Wordsworth calls the very 'dawn of life', the time of 'the hiding places' of his own poetic power (*The Prelude* 12.278–9). Kleinian and post-Kleinian psychoanalysis stresses the child's feelings towards the mother, though, unlike Wordsworth, Klein stressed how these were ambivalent, emerging from the child's sense of vulnerability, which made it see the mother ambivalently. Other analysts influenced by Klein, especially D.W. Winnicott (1896–1971), put equal emphasis on the relation that the mother has to the child, and their work became more fully concerned with 'object-relations', with the to and fro of states of feeling between the child and the mother.

Klein and object-relations theorists took from Freud, who took from Ferenczi, the term 'introjection': that for the ego, 'in so far as the objects which are presented to it are sources of pleasure, it takes them into itself, "introjects" them . . . and . . . it expels whatever within itself becomes a cause of unpleasure' which is 'the mechanism of projection' ('Instincts and Their Vicissitudes', *SE* 14.136). Klein, unlike other psychoanalysts, makes no distinction between introjection and incorporation. The infant incorporates, introjects, what it perceives as the mother's qualities, which become therefore inner objects, good and bad, within the self, as it projects bad and good objects on to the mother.

It has often been argued that Freud's work neglects the mother, concentrating on the father's centrality to the Oedipal, but the mother, the child, and the psychoanalysis of very small children was basic to Klein, when she began writing in the mid-1920s, in London, where she had come to live, from Berlin, following a divorce, and the death of her analyst, Karl Abraham. She was surrounded by argument, both personal and professional, and some of it involving bad faith: there was a clear antagonism in relation to Anna Freud, which produced the 'controversial discussions'. These were held in London between October 1942 and February 1944 and they defined what were emerging as separate schools: Anna Freud versus Klein; Klein was backed by other women psychoanalysts such as the Manchester University-educated Susan Isaacs (1885–1948), the Russian Paula Heinemann (1899–1982), and Joan Riviere (1883–1962), author, amongst much else, of an essay that was to be taken by feminists as definitive for how women's femininity had to be simulated in patriarchal culture: 'Womanliness as a Masquerade' (1929) (Riviere, 1986). Klein held that object-relations with the mother begin soon after birth; Anna Freud held that these developed later after a period of autoeroticism and primal narcissism. At stake here is how primary the mother and the breast are in relation to the child's development (Grosskurth, 1986: 313–33, Hinshelwood, 1989: 251–3). One difference that emerges is that Klein, and the 'object-relations' school generally, which influenced her as much as she influenced it, held more than Anna Freud to the existence of an early ego, an ego present virtually from birth, however 'unintegrated' it might be: this term being taken by Klein from Winnicott (Likierman, 2001: 141–2, 163–6, Klein, 1975c: 4). This sense of an unintegrated, or integrated, ego, especially one from near birth, associates the 'school' with an essentialism about identity and gender different from Freud, or Lacan.

Klein

What follows presents an account of what Klein's work means, and its significance for producing thought about creativity, about writing, and about art. Klein's essay 'Infantile Anxiety Situations Reflected in a Work of Art and the Creative Impulse' (1929) begins with a one-act opera *L'Enfant et les sortilèges* ('The Child and the Queer Goings-On') which had premiered four years earlier. The music was by Maurice Ravel (1875–1937), the words by the French author Colette (1873–1954); she had originally planned the work for a ballet. In this 'fantasie lyrique', a child sits in a room doing his homework; his mother ('maman') comes in to see how he is getting on: she exists on stage only as a huge skirt and a voice, because everything has been scaled up in size to suggest the child's view. He sulks and is rude to her. Shut in the room as a punishment, he becomes wildly destructive with the furniture and the pets in the room, declaring that he is free. The furniture comes alive, mocking him in a foxtrot – which Ravel took from then contemporary American popular music – complaining how it has been desecrated. After a love-duet for two cats, from which the child is excluded, and which the feminist psychonanalyst and literary critic Julia Kristeva (b. 1941), in her book on Colette, calls 'a displaced image of the parents' desired and feared coitus' (Kristeva, 2004: 129), the scene changes to the garden. Here, too, everything complains about his (and other humans') misuse. The garden fills with sound, and with animals and insects and the child calls out in a lonely way, 'Maman'. Significantly, he speaks this, as if he is outside the music, as if the music was the other that he had excluded himself from. This produces a destructive reaction. The animals suddenly become angry against him, but also turn on themselves, and a squirrel is injured. The child spontaneously binds the wound with a ribbon, and the animals, amazed, lead the child back towards the house, whose windows have again been lit up, and the opera ends with the child again singing, now confidently, 'Maman'. That is the last word in the opera, giving it its German title, *Die Zauberwort* ('The Magic Word'), which is how Klein knew it (Klein, 1975a: 214).

Klein's plot-summary is a clue to her work, and we can follow it with terms emerging later in her writing. The child in fantasy destroys everything of the mother (what Klein will call 'the paranoid-schizoid position'), and his destructiveness equally tears to pieces his inner world. She describes the events seen on stage when the room is damaged:

> The shreds of the torn wallpaper begin to sway and stand up, showing shepherdesses and sheep. The shepherd's pipe sounds a heart-breaking lament; the rent in the paper, which separates Corydon [pastoral name for a male shepherd] from his Amaryllis [female], has become a rent in the fabric of the world! (Klein, 1975a: 211)

A pictorial image – a symbol – a tear in the wallpaper – has become something real but indescribable – 'a rent in the fabric of the world'. We will come back, via Lacan, to this lack of distinction between something which is symbolised (shepherds and shepherdesses separated in the state the wallpaper is in) and what is real but unsymbolisable: the idea of a tear in the child's world. The child must repair the damage he has done, to the whole garden, which is symbolically the mother's body, by binding up the wound on the female squirrel's paw. This looks towards the restoration of the mother, being what Klein calls 'the depressive position'. This essay hints at this state, describing the melancholia of a painter, here named Ruth Kjär (perhaps a Danish artist, Ruth Weber), whom Klein had read about through the feminist writer Karin Michaëlis (1872–1950). Kjär would say 'there is an empty space in me, which I can never fill' (Klein, 1975a: 215). Painting the empty space on the wall related to this empty space, and had to do with the desire to make reparation for a mother destroyed in fantasy (Olsen, 2004: 34–42). In just the same way, the critic and educationist David Holbrook, in an early appropriation of Klein and Winnicott, read Shakespeare's *The Winter's Tale* as describing an overwhelming desire to make reparation for Hermione, the wife and mother who has been insulted, and as if destroyed (Holbrook, 1964: 85–6).

This material can be unpacked further. Klein was alive to the idea of the child's 'primary sadism' (Klein, 1975a: 212). What she wrote about schizophrenia in children was based upon her clinical observation of them (the radical move in her psychoanalytic practice), as with the four-year-old Dick, whom she discusses in 'The Importance of Symbol-Formation in the Development of the Ego' (1930, Klein, 1975a: 219–32). Klein draws on Freud's concept, from the *Three Essays on the Theory of Sexuality* (1905), of different phases in the child, who is activated by desire from the very start.

These first two phases, in Freud, are pre-genital: the zone for sexual satisfaction is first the oral, or cannibalistic; the focus is on the mouth, and the child's desire is to incorporate the object (typically, for Klein, the mother's breast), and, by incorporating it, to identify with it (*SE* 7.198). The second stage is sadistic and anal: here the child now aims for mastery (to hold back) by gaining control of the sphincter muscles, but it also desires to give; sexual life has become both active and passive (*SE* 7.198). And giving, in the anal stage, is associated with the faeces, as themselves a gift, which the child has the power to give or to withhold. In these first stages, the child's disposition is 'polymorphously perverse' (*SE* 7.191); i.e. sexuality is not related to normative sexual choices (neither mouth nor anus is gendered). With the move to the third stage, which for Freud is under the compulsion of the Oedipal, sexuality becomes associated with specific parts of the body, and is associated now with what will become heterosexual or homosexual sexual choice.

Klein begins 'The Importance of Symbol-Formation' with sadism in the one-year-old child, specified as 'an oral-sadistic desire to devour the mother's breast' (Klein, 1975a: 219). She identifies a situation where the child's reaction to the breast is profoundly ambivalent, in that the breast is seen as both good (giving goodness) and bad (withholding). The reaction to the bad breast is negative: the child wants to destroy it. In this reaction, the Oedipal is already involved, for Klein dates the Oedipal concept much earlier than does Freud. These phantasies also involve the father, for the penis is like the breast, an object standing for the whole, so that 'the child's sadistic attacks have for their object both father and mother, who are in phantasy bitten, torn, cut, or stamped to bits'. Klein amplifies that: in phantasy, 'the excreta are transformed into dangerous weapons: wetting is regarded as cutting, stabbing, burning, drowning, while the faecal mass is equated with weapons and missiles' (Klein, 1975a: 219–20). Klein adds to this phantasy of sadistic destruction that 'the attacks give rise to anxiety lest the subject should be punished by the united parents [this is clearly an Oedipal anxiety, and recalls Blake's 'Infant Sorrow'] and this anxiety becomes internalised' – which means the development of the superego. So excess of sadism leads to anxiety, which the child must master: Klein adds later, after discussing Dick, that the phantasised objects (faeces, urine, penis) may not only be objects to attack the mother's body, but are 'a source of injury to himself as well' (Klein, 1975a: 226): 'the child's reality is wholly phantastic; he is surrounded with objects of anxiety, and in this respect, excrement, organs, objects, things animate and inanimate are, to begin with, equivalent to one another' (Klein, 1975a: 221). This system of equivalences sets in motion a way of thinking about symbolism. Objects symbolise each other, and anxiety is the motor-force making the child move from the world of phantasy, where everything is immediate, to the ability to symbolise objects of hate and of love. The failure of the ego, as it reacts to sadism, to move to a 'symbolic relation to the things and objects representing the contents of the mother's body, and hence, of the relation to the subject's environment and to reality' (Klein, 1975a: 232), is the basis of lack of affect, and anxiety, which Klein makes the basis of schizophrenia. Its characteristics, Klein writes in a later essay, are a 'withdrawn, unemotional attitude', narcissism and 'detached hostility', a feeling of being 'estranged and far away', saying to the psychoanalyist: 'I hear what you are saying. You may be right, but it has no meaning for me'. Or else, says Klein, '[schizophrenics] say they feel they are not there' (Klein, 1975c: 18–19).

'Symbol-formation' in Freud implies a movement from 'thing presentation' to 'word presentation': it is a prevalent topic also in Lacan, where it means the movement to the symbolic order (see Chapter 6). Not to consider phantasies as real events, but to be able to see them in symbolic forms, means salvation from schizophrenia: we recall how, in *L'Enfant et les sortilèges* the rending of the wallpaper was seen as a rent in the world: the symbolic and the real have not been separated. Lacan, in the essay 'The Function and Field of Speech and Language in Psychoanalysis' (the 'Rome discourse' of 1953), discusses how 'subjectivity gives birth to the symbol' when he focuses on the *Fort! Da!* game (Lacan, 2006: 262). That is, of course, a reference to the second chapter of *Beyond the Pleasure Principle*, which I will now discuss, through Freud and Lacan, as well as through Klein.

Fort! Da!

Freud discusses the death-drive, and trauma, and how trauma surfaces in repetition, and repetitive behaviour. He then turns to the analysis of a child of one and a half. (What Freud does *not* say is that the child, Ernst, was his grandson, and the mother written about, Sophie, his daughter (1893–1920), who had died just before his writing the text. Sophie died when the child was five, he says, in a footnote.) The child played 'gone' with his toys, saying as he threw them what Freud decided was the word '*fort*' (gone).

> The child had a wooden reel with a piece of string tied round it . . . What he did was to hold the reel by the string and very skilfully throw it over the edge of his curtained cot, so that it disappeared into it, at the same time uttering [*fort*!]. He then pulled the reel out of the cot again by the string and hailed its reappearance with a joyful '*da*' ('there'). This, then, was the complete game, disappearance and return. (*SE* 18.15)

This repeated game Freud reads as the child's overcoming loss of the mother: allowing the mother to disappear without protesting. A passive situation, by being turned into a game, allows the child to become active. Freud also speculates that throwing away the object was an impulse, suppressed in actual life, to revenge himself on the mother for going away: in which case, the revenge includes a measure of self-suffering, since the child loses the mother by sending her away: the attempt to achieve mastery is inseparable from self-punishment. Indeed, as Freud suggests, desire for 'mastery' is inseparable from the impulse to revenge: by sending the mother away, she is made to feel the pain that he has felt. This 'revenge' is taken on as a substitute.

'Revenge' becomes therefore part of Freud's chapter about the child learning to create a symbol, which is actually a symbol of the mother. Revenge involves *repetition*. For the child continued playing the game, and *reversal*. The cotton reel is sent away, as under the domination of the child; it does not disappear of its own accord: revenge wants to *reverse* the course of events, in which the mother has gone away without the child's permission. So, if Freud's subject in *Beyond the Pleasure Principle* is the compulsion to repeat, we can say that revenge – that subject of Greek and Renaissance tragedy and inseparable from guilt-feelings which often motivate it – is part of that compulsion. But the compulsion to repeat is also to work over an unpleasant experience, to associate it with the 'pleasure principle', the desire for non-stimulus, homeostasis.

Freud emphasises the play, and the substitute object, which is, of course, a symbol. Lacan's sense of the *Fort! Da!* game is that it means the entry into language, and into the symbolic order: into language as a system of symbols. The work of the structural linguist Roman Jakobson (1896–1982) suggested that all possible linguistic sounds are divisible into a system of binary opposites comprising twelve sets altogether, and Lacan adopted that idea when speaking of the *Fort! Da!* sounds as the child's entering on to the 'dichotomy of phonemes, whose synchronic structure the existing language offers up for him to assimilate' (Lacan, 2006: 262). The child becomes a structuralist in learning how to play, because play obeys the laws that everything fits into a binary structure.

Language and objects are both symbolic modes of engaging with reality: Lacan implies that language-acquisition is premised on death, awareness of the death of the mother as the imagined complete 'other', and presaged in the mother's occasional in-life disappearances. As Lacan says, 'the symbol first manifests itself as the killing of the thing [we can connect this idea of killing with the revenge that Freud has spoken of], and this death results in the endless perpetuation of the subject's desire' (Lacan, 2006: 262). For Lacan, the birth of symbolism, the entry into language as a symbolic structure, is absolutely connected to the birth of desire: in other words, language *is* desire. Being in language reminds me always that I do not have what I desire, I am always using language because I have not come to the end of the desire which its being awakens in me.

The *Fort! Da!* game is essential material for Klein. In 'The Significance of Early Anxiety-Situations in the Development of the Ego', an essay in *The Psychoanalysis of Children* (1932), she sees in it the child's desire to overcome unpleasurable experiences, including controlling stimuli by developing apprehension: the object thrown away is a threat, 'a source of danger to the child' – because of the absence it symbolises – and yet a support against anxiety (Klein, 1975b: 176–8). So there is an ambivalent response to the symbol, too. A later essay, 'On Observing the Behaviour of Young Infants' (1952), returns to the topic of losing the mother, and so to the melancholia associated with 'the lost object', and sees the activity of the child as the need to overcome not only a sense of loss but the 'depressive position' (Klein, 1975c: 111). But speaking about 'the depressive position' is to anticipate: we must return to the earlier stages of Klein's thinking.

We may also note Luce Irigaray's further, feminist point, noting the curtained, or veiled cot for Ernst, where the veil suggests the feminine, and so the presence of the mother, central, but not discussed in Freud's account (Irigaray, 1993: 28–32, discussing Derrida, 1987: 307–20). It is as though throwing the reel into the cot unconsciously mimes incest with the mother.

The paranoid-schizoid and depressive positions

In 1935, five years after 'The Importance of Symbol-Formation', Klein expanded the material in 'A Contribution to the Psychogenesis of Manic-Depressive States' (Klein, 1975a: 262–89). This summarised what had already been said: 'the development of the infant is governed by the mechanisms of introjection and projection' (Klein, 1975a: 262). Introjection means taking into myself, and seeing as part of myself, outside qualities. The child introjects the breast, splitting it into both the good and the bad object 'for which the mother's breast is the prototype'. This is also a process of projection, whereby the child 'projects its own aggression on to those objects that it feels them to be "bad" and not only in that they frustrate its desires: the child conceives them as actually dangerous' (Klein, 1975a: 262). An intricate process is at work whereby the child installs – introjects, incorporates – inside itself what it phantasises as from the outside. This is also aggressive, since the child must deal with the phantasised evil breast;

it means that the child installs in itself the aggression of the parents, as a superego.

At the same time the child expels from itself all that aggression it feels to the parents, especially the mother. It makes the outside, then, a projection of its internal aggression. This is part of a complex process of splitting which the anxious ego of the child carries out to protect itself: splitting the breast of the mother into two, the good and the bad, but internalising both, and splitting its aggression off towards the outside world. There is an identification with the good breast and an attempt to destroy the bad breast, out of a paranoid state of persecutory anxiety: persecutory towards the mother, out of a paranoid fear of being persecuted and destroyed.

This phantasy of destruction is followed by a melancholia called 'the depressive position', emanating from a sense of a loss of the loved object. Here, Klein references Freud's 'Mourning and Melancholia', which she discusses in an all-important paper 'A Contribution to the Psychogenesis of Manic-Depressive States' (1935), and its virtual sequel, 'Mourning and Its Relation to Manic-Depressive States' (1940). The ego has introjected everything of the mother into itself, good and bad, and, as it becomes aware of the mother as a separate being, feels despair since it realises that it has effectively torn her into pieces. The task is to restore the loved object in a state of perfection:

> If we compare the feelings of the paranoiac with those of the depressive in regard to disintegration, we can see that characteristically the depressive is filled with sorrow and anxiety for the object, which he would strive to unite again into a whole, while to the paranoiac the disintegrated object is mainly a multitude of persecutors, since each piece is growing again into a persecutor. This conception of the dangerous fragments to which the object is reduced seems to me in keeping with the introjection of part-objects which are equated with faeces (Abraham), and with the anxiety of a multitude of internal persecutors to which, in my view, the introjection of many part-objects and the multitude of dangerous faeces gives rise. (Klein, 1975a: 272)

Klein takes from Karl Abraham the idea that faeces are the prototype of the 'internal object', the outer world inside the ego (Hinshelwood, 1989: 299). The phantasies of faeces within imply both a threat from and a degradation of the other, the mother, as well as being what can be expelled from the ego. The plurality of faecal elements corresponds to the sense that what is introjected is split up, cut up, reduced as much as possible to fragments. 'Part-objects' (Klein, 1975a: 285) are fragments of the object-world outside, like the mother's breast, and they are all that the infant can think of in relation to the other. In the depressive position, there is the desire to reunite what has been destroyed, or fragmented.

The successor essay, 'Mourning and Its Relation to Manic-Depressive States' (1940), considers the melancholia which is implicit in the depressive position, which is now called 'the central position in the child's development' (Klein, 1975a: 347). But the melancholia spoken of means mourning:

> the object which is being mourned is the mother's breast and all that the breast and the milk have come to stand for in the infant's mind: namely love, goodness and security. All these are felt by the baby to be lost . . . as a result of his own uncontrollable greedy and destructive phantasies and impulses against his mother's breast. (Klein, 1975a: 345)

Klein's 1940 essay concentrates on the child's inner world, as this comes about from having 'incorporated' the parents. It may well be a world of peace. It is constantly compared with the outer, with the objective mother, which may be a source of correction to the destructive phantasies in the inner world, and a way of establishing 'good' inner objects, as opposed to those 'bad' ones which have also been introjected. The 'bad' objects require manic defences to control or master them, and protect the 'good' objects from them: actions repeated obsessionally, being an example of such effort to control. Fear that such defences fail only means that the objects which were to be restored become persecutors, reviving paranoid fears. What is desired is a kind of 'triumph' over the parents, but such triumph can only produce guilt in its turn:

> The triumph over his internal objects which the young child's ego controls, humiliates and tortures is part of the destructive aspect of the manic position which disturbs the reparation and re-creating of his inner world, and of internal peace and harmony; and thus triumph impedes the work of early mourning. (Klein, 1975a: 352)

One feature of this hypomania is making exaggerated evaluations, either of admiration and idealisation, or of contempt and devaluation: features of a megalomania which is a defence against 'fear of losing the one irreplaceable object', the mother, who is still mourned at bottom. And all this is based on denial: the excessive reparation is denied because the cause for reparation is also denied, 'namely, the injury to the object' and the consequent sorrow.

Impossible mourning

Klein joins this desire for reparation to mourning, as this appears in 'Mourning and Melancholia', saying that mourning includes an awareness of having lost the internal good object, which must be reinstated, rebuilt as the inner world. She comments on the 'triumph' that the manic position feels in relation to the parents, and so problematises mourning, in that 'infantile death wishes against parents, brothers and sisters are actually fulfilled whenever a loved person dies, because he is . . . a representative [i.e. a substitute] of the earliest important figures' (Klein, 1975a: 354). In mourning, too, the external world is felt to be 'artificial and unreal' because 'trust in inner goodness' is gone (Klein, 1975a: 361). Mourning must restore that. The manic depressive, and the person who fails in the work of mourning, has been unable, in early life, 'to establish their internal "good" objects and to feel secure in their inner world' (Klein, 1975a: 369).

Before going further with Klein, we should note that the significance of being able to mourn is attended by its impossibility. If Klein speaks of its necessity, as does all psychonalysis, its impossibility is what deconstruction has discussed in relation to literature. Jacques Derrida, commemorating the literary critic Paul de Man (1919–84), founder of 'American deconstruction', says that he finds de Man's work 'traversed by an insistent reflection on mourning, a meditation in which bereaved memory [memory which itself feels inadequate, and which has lost the subject which it is trying to remember] is deeply engraved'. If this memory is 'engraved', it exists as the 'trace, which is always the trace of the other, the finitude of memory, and thus the approach, or memory of the future'. Before death has taken place, memory of the other contains in it the thought of the future, which includes death within it. Hence Derrida says 'there can be no *true mourning*' which would mourn and then complete itself (Derrida, 1986a: 22, 29) with a sense that the loss was known and definable. Memory is always allegorical in the sense that all memory, because of its finitude (because I cannot remember everything), brings in the death of the other.

Derrida compares the work of mourning with narcissism, and with Narcissus, who pines away in death because he sees his friend reflected in the water, and is separated from him. Derrida suggests this as an allegory of 'impossible mourning': mourning is threatened by narcissism, because it is not the other who is mourned but the self, who feels its own loss, and we may add that there is even a triumphalism associated with mourning: I am the survivor, over the one who has died. The process links to 'introjection', which, as Derrida says, going back to its use in Ferenczi, 'expands the self' (Derrida, 1986b: xvi). Introjection may be distinguished, as by the two psychoanalysts Nicolas Abraham and Maria Torok, from incorporation, which they read as a way of refusing to mourn a loss, rather, 'I pretend to keep the dead alive, intact, *safe inside me*' (Derrida, 1986b: xvi). Introjection gives something to the ego, while incorporation implies a failure to mourn, as with Norman Bates's mother in Alfred Hitchcock's 1960 film *Psycho*. Instead, the dead person is preserved within the living, the real loss is rejected and the person is encrypted within the self. Incorporation presents its own difficulties, in that it implies the power of the living dead inside the self; introjection includes in mourning something narcissistic in its assimilation of the other.

Projective identification

Having noted the complexity of what it means to mourn, we can return to Klein. By 1946, in 'Notes on Some Schizoid Mechanisms' (1946), she was borrowing from the work of the Edinburgh-based psychoanalyst W.R.D. Fairbairn (1889–1964). The result is that she now calls the sadistic state, where the child has introjected the bad breast into itself and in phantasy destroyed it, and so, in effect, destroyed the mother, not just a paranoid, but rather a '*paranoid schizoid*' position (Klein, 1975c: 2). Klein refers to such essays by Fairbairn as 'A Revised Psychopathology of the Psychoses and Psychoneuroses' (1941), 'Endopsychic Structure Considered in Terms of Object Relationships' (1944), and 'Object-Relationships and Dynamic Structure' (1946). Fairbairn assumed the primacy of object-relationships, as when he asks the question why the baby sucks its thumb. Freud had answered that in terms of the oral stage of sexuality, the mouth being an erotic zone (*SE* 7.179–83, 198). Fairbairn supplies another answer: 'because there is no breast to suck. Even the infant must have a libidinal object, and if he is deprived of his natural object (the breast), he is driven to provide an object for himself' (Fairbairn, 1952: 33). Schizoid characteristics, for Fairbairn, occur from the failure to establish object-relations, or from a sense of loss of the object. The word 'endopsychic' suggests that the ego is not, as in Freud, constructed from the unconscious id and the power of the superego, but is already a primary and dynamic structure in the self (Fairbairn, 1952: 106): in that sense, Fairbairn's psychoanalysis is based upon – as Freud's is not – a sense of personality in the infant. The child in Klein alternates between the paranoid-schizoid and the depressive positions. Using the word 'position', as opposed to, say, 'stage', implies that these are never grown out of. The alternation of the two positions creates a 'manic-depressive state' since these two are not separate from each other, though the depressive position rises out of the paranoid-schizoid.

Klein's essay of 1946 evokes another term which has been implicit before, to express a child's phantasy of – to put it over-simply – getting into the mother's body:

> The phantasised onslaughts on the mother follow two main lines: one is the predominantly oral impulse to suck dry, bite up, scoop out and rob the mother's body of its good contents . . . The other line of attack derives from the anal and urethral impulses and implies expelling dangerous substances (excrements) out of the self and into the mother. Together with these harmful excrements, expelled in hatred, split-off parts of the ego are also projected on to the mother, or . . . into the mother. These excrements and bad parts of the self are meant, not only to injure but also to control and take possession of the object. In so far as the mother comes to contain the bad parts of the self, she is not felt to be a separate individual but is felt to be the bad self.
>
> Much of the hatred against parts of the self is now directed towards the mother. This leads to a particular form of identification which establishes the prototype of an aggressive object-relation. I suggest for those processes the term 'projective identification'. (Klein, 1975c: 8)

The mother is identified with the aggressive and bad parts of the self. She has become the bad self of the child, which is not repressed – as would be the case for Freud – but projected outwards. But equally, she is identified with the good parts, for 'projective identification' works there too. 'Identification' Freud calls 'the earliest expression of an emotional tie with another person', but he stresses that it is 'ambivalent from the very first', that is, it can be with someone hated. 'It behaves like a derivative of the first *oral* phase of the organisation of the libido, in which the object that we long for and prize is assimilated by eating, and is in that way annihilated as such' ('Group Psychology and the Analysis of the Ego' (1921) *SE* 18.105). What is projected on to the mother is the self with which the child identifies, while it is also introjected so that the child both preserves and destroys what it both repudiates and identifies with.

Klein's point about 'projection' is that it involves the child splitting itself, so that the good, or the bad parts are separated from the self, and go into the other: it is a schizoid position. Splitting off parts of the self and projecting them on to others is crucial for 'object-relations' whether these are good or bad: the object is invested with qualities of the self, and symbolises these. The ego feels impoverished, dependent on what it identifies with, while, at the same time, there is also anxiety, that what is projected outwards and into the mother may be trapped there, and persecuted, as much as there is fear of what has been sent back from the outside into the inner world (what is introjected). In the section called 'Schizoid object relations' of Klein's essay, she sees the conditions of this schizoid projective identification to be narcissistic, controlling, and paranoid, and then emphasises its relation to manic depression, finding it difficult to distinguish between melancholia and the schizophrenia defined earlier (Klein, 1975c: 18), and calling this schizoid state, despite its appearance of apathy, a state of anxiety (Klein, 1975c: 21).

Further implications of projective identification are explored by Wilfred Bion (1897–1979) (see Jacobus, 2005: 173–253). Bion analysed Samuel Beckett in the years 1934–35, but, in the 1940s, Bion became associated with Klein's work. Bion's essay 'Attacks on Linking' (1959) explains projective identification with regard to the transference made by someone on to him as psychoanalyst:

> when the patient strove to rid himself of fears of death which were felt to be too powerful for his personality to contain he split off his fears and put them into me [so making the psychoanalyst, or else the mother the container], the idea apparently being that if they were allowed to repose there long enough they would undergo modification by my psyche and could then be safely reintrojected. (Bion, 1967: 103)

Speaking of the process as it happens to the mother, Bion adds that 'an understanding mother is able to experience the feeling of dread, that this baby was striving to deal with by projective introjection, and yet retain a balanced outlook' (Bion, 1967: 104). For Bion, the basis of the child being able to think is premised on its ability to contain its nameless dread within the mother. The case of the mother who cannot so act as a container, but pushes the fear back towards the child

> leads to a destruction of the link between infant and breast and consequently to a severe disorder of the impulse to be curious on which all learning depends. The way is thus prepared for a severe arrest of development. Furthermore, thanks to a denial of the main method open to the infant for dealing with his too powerful emotions, the conduct of emotional life, in any case a severe problem, becomes intolerable. Feelings of hatred are therefore directed against all emotions including hate itself, and against external reality which stimulates them. It is a short step from hatred of the emotions to hatred of life itself. (Bion, 1967: 107)

This idea of the mother as a container for the child's dread compares with Winnicott's sense of psychoanalysis providing for the analysand a 'holding environment' (Adam Phillips, 1988: 11, 30, 66, 98, 100). It recalls Wordsworth's 'babe' held 'nursed in its mother's arms'. Bion's 'A Theory of Thinking' (1962) speaks of an 'alpha function' which comes about from successful projection and introjection. No alpha function is possible when the child has reintrojected 'not a fear of dying made tolerable, but a nameless dread' (Bion, 1967: 116). There is now a failure to symbolise, which, as the basis of thinking, comes from the mother. 'Beta-elements' are those sense impressions and emotional experiences which have not been transformed.

Klein and creativity

One art-critic psychoanalysed by Klein between 1929 and 1936, with follow-up sessions in 1938 and 1948 (Read, 2007: 89–103), was Adrian Stokes (1902–72). In his turn he was an influence upon Richard Wollheim (1923–2003), the philosopher of art with a strong interest in Freudian psychoanalysis. Stokes's first books, *The Quattro Cento* (1932) and *Stones of Rimini* (1935), develop his interest in stone, and in two forms of expression: carving – a cutting away – and modelling – a building up. Stokes makes this distinction basic to art. He gives the difference between carving and modelling in sculptural art:

> Whatever its plastic value, a figure carved in stone is fine carving when one feels that not the figure but the stone through the medium of the figure, has come to life. Plastic conception, on the other hand, is uppermost when the material with which, or from which, a figure has been made appears no more than as so much suitable stuff for this creation. (Stokes, 1978a: 230)

A figure carved in stone brings out, for Stokes, the depressive position; it is the desire to create a 'self-sufficient object, fully corporeal in essence' (1978c: 12). The moulded, or modelled, work corresponds to the paranoid-schizoid position, in the ways that it subordinates the material which has been worked on, for the figure. It implies more manipulation, more treatment of the material as an object, without seeing it as other, so that the artwork is not free of the spectator, but is dependent on him/her. This dependency accounts for what Stokes calls, in a late essay, 'The Invitation in Art', the '*compelling* invitation to identify – the incantatory process' (Stokes, 1978c: 271). The spectator is pulled towards the work, which means that the reparative process which creates art comes in response to the work of art, which is seen as the breast, which, of course, the child internalises, and tears to pieces, and so is absolutely not separate from it.

Stokes's work has been carried into film analysis, making distinctions between montage and realist cinema. We can quote Rosellini, the Italian neo-realist filmmaker, that 'montage is no longer necessary. Things are there . . . why manipulate them?' This would be a position which sees film as an art analogous to carving (O'Pray, 2004: 109). In this argument, Italian cinema, even when black-and-white, shows more allegiance to colour, which for Stokes, represented 'the carving conception' (Stokes, 1978b: 24). O'Pray allies black-and-white films as with *film noir*, and Hitchcock with 'modelling', and so with the paranoid-schizoid. It is more related to narrative (less to mood, as in colour films), more promoting of thought, and more enigmatic in the power of shadow. Black-and-white cinema has the ability to generate, and to allow for, anxiety (O'Pray, 2004: 185–212).

This interest in different forms of creativity associates with the relationship between Klein and 'object relations' psychoanalysts: Fairbairn, already mentioned, whose work was particularly taken up by Harry Guntrip (1901–75), and Donald Winnicott, whose work was adopted by Masud Khan (1924–89). Winnicott, a paediatrician, was associated with Klein in the 1940s, but there was a break with her in 1951, on account of his paper 'Transitional Objects and Transitional Phenomena', which became the basis of *Playing and Reality* (1971). 'Transitional phenomena' refer to objects held on to by the child (soft toys, a blanket) which are a 'not-me' possession. For Klein, the breast was the 'not-me', but, for Winnicott, it is the symbol (this place given to the symbol suggests the importance of art) which represents the not-me, and is how the child moves on towards independence. The difference between Klein and Winnicott is over mothering: while Klein says little about the specific mother/child relationship, Winnicott is interested in how the child moves away from the literal breast to what symbolises it. This implies an interest in something other than psychoanalysis, i.e. in child development; however, Winnicott associates the process with the depressive position, which gives the creative impulse.

Winnicott is interested in what blocks creativity. He begins with a basic 'predisposition to bisexuality' which enables him to speak of a 'pure female element' in males and females, and a male element. The first relates to the breast and to the mother: Winnicott holds that 'the pure female element establishes what is perhaps the simplest of experiences, the experience of *being*'. In contrast, 'the object-relating of the male element to the object presupposes separateness' (Winnicott, 1971: 80). 'The male element *does* while the female element (in males and females) *is*. Here would come in those males in Greek myth who tried to be at one with the supreme goddess. Here also is a way of stating a male person's very deep-seated envy of women whose female element men take for granted, sometimes in error' (Winnicott, 1971: 81). We can read literary texts, on this basis, for their contrast between false 'male doing', which shows itself in action, versus female 'being', which is more contented to be than to do, and triumphs over the male: Will Brangwen versus Anna in D.H. Lawrence's *The Rainbow* (1915), followed by Anton Skrebensky versus Ursula; or Gerald Crich in *Women in Love*.

Winnicott's position, however, takes no account of the elements in Klein which consider the child's hatred of the breast, and violence towards it, which fragments both what is introjected and the psyche which contains introjected material. These things assume the aggression within the death drive: Klein takes from Ferenczi's essay 'Notes and Fragments' the concept that:

> most likely every living organism reacts to unpleasant stimuli by fragmentation, which might be an expression of the death instinct. Possibly, complicated mechanisms (living organisms) are only kept as an entity through the impact of external conditions. When these conditions become unfavourable the organism falls to pieces. (Klein, 1975c: 5)

But Winnicott, in contrast, 'simply cannot find value in Freud's idea of a death instinct' (quoted in Adam Phillips, 1988: 163). That seems a limitation: Žižek has emphasised that psychoanalysis' sense of the death-drive responds to Hegel, who says that 'the life of Spirit is not the life that shrinks from death and keeps itself untouched from devastation', and challenges the philosopher into 'looking the negative in the face, and tarry with it' (Hegel, 1977: 19). This 'tarrying with the negative', which Žižek uses as a book-title, means accepting that philosophy, as a system of thought, is built around death, which as an absolute absence, because nothing can be said about it, allows us to think of knowledge as split, and always containing something unknown, absent, inside it. In a contrasted way, Žižek criticises Deleuze for a similar non-tarrying, referring to his adherence to Spinoza, whose sense is that everything is immanent, that there is no gap or loss, or silence, within knowledge, no negativity (Žižek, 2004: 35). Winnicott's refusal of the death-drive, which is quite outside any response to Continental philosophy, nonetheless pushes his thinking towards an essential knowledge where failure is because of empirical circumstances, not because knowledge and being are incomplete. Here any thought of such fragmentation must point to the failure of the 'holding environment', that is, everything that is meant by the mother (Adam Phillips, 1988: 123). As with John Bowlby (1907–90), whose *Childcare and the Growth of Love* (1965) puts emphasis on the mother as the primary carer, there is an implicit departure from psychoanalysis to considerations of child development, which are premised on secure conceptions of gender and femininity, and of normalcy.

The question which arises – and which is for our next section – is how much this sense of the maternal, as a recognition of difference from the patriarchal structure, works for and against feminism.

Klein, Kristeva and the mother

Klein's late, short book, *Envy and Gratitude* (1957), sums up and crystallises some of her ideas, and reviews much of her earlier work. Taking envy as one of the seven deadly sins, she quotes from Chaucer, and cites Shakespeare's Othello, who destroys the object he says he loves, and Spenser, and Satan in Milton's *Paradise Lost* for examples of envy. Klein says that the primal good object for the infant is the mother's breast, prototype of patience, generosity, and creativeness. Envy involves the feeling of being deprived of what would gives gratification, by the breast withholding it. So 'envy is the angry feeling that another person possesses and enjoys something desirable – the envious impulse being to take it away or to spoil it' by filling it with badness (bad excrements and bad parts of the self) (Klein, 1975c: 181). It is not so much the weaned child's envy of younger siblings at the breast which characterises envy as a reaction to the breast itself, and so to the mother. 'The breast attacked in this way has lost its value, it has become bad by being bitten and poisoned by urine and faeces' (Klein, 1975c: 186). The thought dries up the possibility of ever feeling gratitude or generosity, for 'the more often gratification at the breast is experienced and fully accepted, the more often enjoyment and gratitude, and accordingly the wish to return pleasure, are felt' (Klein, 1975c: 189, Tambling, 2010b: 105–9).

Since literature is a prime form of creativity, it is important to see Klein's interest in literary texts, as with her essay, 'Some Reflections on *The Oresteia*', which was published posthumously. It considered the meaning of this trilogy by Aeschylus (525–456 BCE), which, centring on Orestes murdering his mother, Clytemnestra, because of her murder of her husband and his father, Agamemnon, contrasts with Sophocles' *Oedipus the King*. After Orestes has killed her, he immediately feels guilt, symbolised by the Furies who rise up and attack him. 'The fact that nobody but Orestes can see the Furies shows that this persecutory situation is an internal one' (Klein, 1975c: 284). For 'the cruel and destructive impulses of the infant create the primitive and terrifying superego' (Klein, 1975c: 290) in the form of revenging female figures. This is, of course, a much simpler view of the superego than Freud's, in 'The Ego and the Id'. Orestes's torment can be resolved only by the trial he undergoes at Athens, where Apollo, with his 'contempt for women's fertility' (Klein, 1975c: 285), speaks for him, by disparaging the role of the woman in childbirth. Athena also speaks for Orestes, as the goddess who never knew a mother. Drawing support from Gilbert Murray, the translator of the version of *The Oresteia* Klein used, she calls Orestes 'manic depressive', but when in Athens, on trial, moving towards the depressive position (Klein, 1975c: 286). She also invokes Murray for the idea of the splitting of the Earth into the figure giving life and fruitfulness and polluted by blood and calling for revenge, and, from there, to the perception of the mother as split into a good and bad one. That split in the perception of the mother is also present in the duality of the two women, Clytemnestra and Athena, the latter 'the mature superego' (Klein, 1975c: 297).

For Klein, the gods' various symbolic roles correspond to the 'diverse, often conflicting impulses and phantasies which exist in the unconscious'. Thinking of the power of phantasies to pervade mental life from the beginning, and of the drive to attach them to various objects, 'real and phantasied', she draws on Winnicott:

> These symbols first represent part-objects and within a few months whole objects (that is to say, people). The child puts his love and hate, his conflicts, his satisfactions and his longing into the creation of these symbols, internal and external, which become part of his world. The drive to create symbols is so strong because even the most loving mother cannot satisfy the infant's powerful emotional needs. In fact no reality situation can fulfil the often contradictory urges and wishes of the child's phantasy life. It is only if in childhood, symbol formation is able to develop in full strength and variety and is not impeded by inhibitions, that the artist can make use of the emotional forces which underlie symbolism. (Klein, 1975c: 299)

Ability to symbolise is at the heart of all later creativity. Julia Kristeva, in her biography of Klein, and throughout her work, as in *Powers of Horror* (1980) and *Black Sun* (1987), has focused on the third and fourth sentences in the quotation above, and virtually focused on the need for 'matricide' as 'our vital necessity' (Kristeva, 1989: 27). Killing the mother is to be able to symbolise (Kristeva, 2001: 133), but it is a source of depression, or melancholia, especially for the woman, whose identification is with the mother (Kristeva, 1989: 28–9). Kristeva's argument is a radical rereading of what Lacan had said about language coming into being in relation to the death of the mother. Klein's sentence that symbolism is necessary because the mother cannot satisfy the child's emotional needs is explained by the following: the child's desires are conflictual, ambivalent, and the physical mother cannot symbolise them, either in her literality or because thinking depends on ambivalence.

In Julia Kristeva's psychoanalysis, the first, pre-Oedipal attachment of the child is to the maternal body, which is the *chora*, the space of the semiotic, where the mother and child coexist in a world of mutual bodily signs (laughing – pre-eminent for Kristeva – crying, touching, communicating through breast-feeding), in a non-differentiated space which precedes its division and articulation in the symbolic order institutionalised by the father (Kristeva, 1980: 283, 1984: 25–30). The *chora* is the 'receptacle', a term taken from Plato, to designate 'an invisible and formless being which receives all things and . . . partakes of the intelligible and is most incomprehensible' (quoted in Kristeva, 1980: 6). Kristeva takes the terms *semiotic* and *symbolic* from Lacan, and looks for, in poetic language, semiotic rhythms in language, underneath structured language. These evoke the body, and do not conform to the gender expectations within language as patriarchally given. Such a language is punning, playing at the level of the signifier, not the signified; it responds to language as excess, as *jouissance*, non-signifiable enjoyment, not language as meaning, hence her interest in the poetry of Stéphane Mallarmé. Clearly such a sense of language can only be pointed to, not demonstrated; Kristeva evokes a Utopian possibility in poetic language, which is, for her, like music. The way it can be transposed allows her to speak of 'intertextuality', of text flowing into text. Intertextuality does not mean the study of sources, or of influences on a given text, which is how it is often misused; it is the sense that one text keeps being transposed into another, as Freud, in discussing dreams, thinks of these as comprising processes of condensation and displacement (Kristeva, 1984: 59–60).

This poetic language sides with the mother, but the mother must be given back to culure to be retrieved as 'sign, image, word' (Kristeva, 1989: 63). Kristeva's arguments about the mother involve her questioning the symbolic role of the maternal in Western culture (Oliver, 1993: 48–68). In her essay 'Stabat Mater', whose title is taken from the hymn of the Franciscan Jacapone da Todi (1230–1306), praising Mary, the mother of Jesus, for standing at the foot of the cross of Christ (a hymn several times set to music), Kristeva considers how maternity, and especially virginal maternity, has been the preferential lens for people to consider and to idealise women (Kristeva, 1987: 234–63). Does maternity as a concept challenge feminism, by suggesting that the only way for a woman to be fulfilled is by being a mother? Yet even maternity in western culture is 'mystified' (= disguised by ideology), since the preferred, ideal mother in this culture is the Virgin Mary, a woman without *jouissance*. The topic of *Powers of Horror: An Essay on Abjection* considers abjection, which is the male's violent repudiation of the 'other' in order to establish borders round himself, to be centred on the mother's body as the embodiment of the feminine; this, for Kristeva is 'the "other" without a name' (Kristeva, 1982: 58). It is 'nameless' in escaping, exceeding, the capacity of patriarchy to represent it, and confine it. 'Abjection' is the direct opposite of intertextuality, being the desire to protect borders and systems from contamination from what is outside, from other bodies, specifically the mother's. The feminine, in patriarchy, must be coded as the mother, and the mother as the Virgin.

Kristeva's work like Klein's, is fascinated by the mother, and the sense of the access to the semiotic that it gives makes her argue for the maternal. She argues that, in childbirth, women identify with their mothers; in that sense at least, she privileges the role of the woman as mother over other forms of feminism which have wanted to challenge that codification.

6

Introducing Lacan

This chapter engages with Jacques Lacan's influential 'return to Freud', and that requires engaging with some Freud texts examined only partially so far: *The Interpretation of Dreams, Jokes and Their Relation to the Unconscious*, 'Instincts and Their Vicissitudes' and *Beyond the Pleasure Principle*. I discuss four of Lacan's essays in the *Écrits*, and Seminar XI – *The Four Fundamental Concepts of Psychoanalysis*.

Lacan's biography is easily available (Roudinesco, 1994, Schneiderman, 1986, Clément, 1983), but reading Lacan necessitates taking in several intellectual histories, for he intersects with names and movements associated with French structuralist and post-structuralist (i.e. deconstructive) thought beginning in the 1960s going through to at least the end of the twentieth century. This 'turn to theory' in literature and cultural studies was also a 'linguistic turn': a new attention to language. Part of that turn to theory included recognition of the centrality of psychoanalysis to literary criticism. If literature has no other basis with which to work except language, we can begin considering Lacan with the point that he always argued that language was Freud's concern, and that 'psychoanalysis has but one medium: the patient's speech' (Lacan, 2006: 206). Psychoanalysis, Lacan felt, had ignored the signifier; ignored not just the point that the 'talking cure' works on speech, but that psychoanalysts were oblivious to what speech is.

Contexts for Lacan

The term 'the signifier' comes from the structuralist linguistics of Ferdinand de Saussure (1857–1913), which was applied by Roman Jakobson (1896–1982), and by the anthropologist Claude Lévi-Strauss (1908–2009), in 'Structural Analysis in Linguistics and Anthropology' (1945), followed up by *The Elementary Structures of Kinship* (1949). Saussure had made three pairs of distinctions. The first was between the *signifier* and the *signified*. The signifier is the terms in any language system, A-B-C-D-E, and the signified is the meaning: a sign comprises the signified (S) over the signifier (*s*) (Saussure, 1974: 67). While holding on to the idea that there are signifieds, i.e. things which have meaning, Saussure held that the signifier cannot guarantee meaning by itself. There is no magic connection between any signifier and its signified, rather, meaning emerges from difference: B has meaning because it is not A or C. An alteration within the chain of signifiers moves all meaning along, changes everything. Nor is there any signifier which has a certain meaning outside this chain: instead, 'in language, there are only differences, without positive terms' (Saussure, 1974: 120).

The second pair of terms, the *langue* and the *parole*, develops this. The langue is that structure of language, of terms whose differential relationship to each other establishes a meaning of which the speaker is unaware. The individual speaks the 'parole'; this is language deriving, not from the infinite possibilities of one language, but from language as it appears at the moment. Althusserian Marxism calls that 'langue' ideology; Foucault calls it discourse. In Lacan, it is the symbolic order, and it is unconscious; the speaker cannot grasp the way that one signifier inflects the other with meaning, and how, if B means because it is not A or C, then A and C become the unconscious of B, terms which give it its meaning.

The third pair is the *diachronic* and the *synchronic*. Linguists, and philology before Saussure, looked at the individual, separate, diachronic history of words and their meanings in the language. Saussure turned attention to the synchronic: to words as they are used in one particular moment; asked, then, for attention to be given to the langue.

Structuralist thought, following Saussure, argued that the signs which constitute language can be considered in terms of binary opposites. Post-structuralist thought owes much to Foucault, and Derrida, and to the post-Nietzschean philosophers Bataille, Blanchot, Levinas, and Deleuze. There was also the Marxism of Louis Althusser, and the feminism of Julia Kristeva, who had studied with Barthes, Hélène Cixous, and Luce Irigaray. Discussing Lacan means navigating a pathway past these and other names.

Paris-born, Jesuit-trained, Lacan (1901–81) – for a short time a young member of the royalist Action française – studied as a medic, taking a doctorate in psychiatry on 'Paranoid Psychosis and Its Relation to Personality' in 1932. He began psychoanalysis with Rudolph Loewenstein; in 1933, he began attending lectures on Hegel's *Phenomenology of Spirit* (1807) given by Alexandre Kojève (1902–68), which continued until 1939 and drew enormous interest from intellectuals in Paris (Macey, 1988: 95–9). Kojève's impact, as an early commentator on Hegel in France, is crucial for understanding the significance of 'the other' in Lacan, though Kojève is not mentioned in the *Écrits*. Kojève concentrated on the sections where Hegel discusses lordship and bondage (Hegel, 1977: 111–19). The lord can require the service of the bondsman, but he cannot control his desire for freedom. Self-consciousness is only such when it exists for another, by being recognised. The servant demands recognition; and the future is with him; the lord must, then, desire the desire of the other; that is, he desires that the slave will look at him and serve him appreciatively. Desire, then, becomes the key: desire goes beyond the limits of the biological. In Lacan, 'desire is desire of the other', a statement we shall discuss later in this chapter, and desire is born out of a sense of lack, which the other must – impossibly – fill. It is that 'lack', or absence, incidentally, which for Žižek marks Lacan's relationship to Hegelian thought, which puts death at the centre; in contrast, Deleuze has no such thought of anything missing in the subject; all is present, or immanent.

In 1934, Lacan joined the SPP, the Société psychanalytique de Paris, which was part of the IPA, the International Psychoanalytic Association. In 1936, at Marienbad, at a meeting of the IPA, he presented a paper on the 'mirror stage' (see below). His relationship with Sylvia Bataille, who had been married to Georges Bataille, the radical thinker and dissident surrealist, began in 1939: they married in 1953 (his second mariage), and Lacan's daughter from that relationship married Jacques Alain-Miller, the philosopher and psychoanalyst, and guardian of Lacan's papers, in 1966. A revised version of the essay on 'The Mirror Stage as Formative of the Function of the I' (1949), preceded by 'Aggressivity in Psychoanalysis' (1948), did much to establish Lacan, and we will begin, below, with these texts.

In 1953, Lacan and his followers split from the SPP and formed the Société française de psychanalyse (SFP). That was inaugurated with the all-important 'Rome Discourse' – Rome being where the lecture 'The Function and Field of Speech and Language in Psychoanalysis' was given. It introduces Lacan's terms 'the Imaginary' (*l'imaginaire*), 'the Symbolic' (*le symbolique*), and 'the Real' (*le réel*) (Lacan, 2006: 255), which govern much of his thinking, and it received an early pioneer translation and analysis (Wilden, 1968). Lacan was not admitted to the IPA, and, as a result, separated from the SFP at the end of 1963. Invited by the historian Fernand Braudel, he resumed the seminars he had been conducting since 1951, at the École pratiques des hautes études, and, helped by Louis Althusser, began his public teaching again at the École normale supérieure. This produced a new society, the École freudienne de Paris (EFP). Lacan's *Écrits* appeared in 1966, and the first of his seminars, no. XI, *The Four Fundamental Concepts of Psychoanalysis*, the lectures of 1963–64, in 1973. Further seminars were to appear, others, of the 24, have not yet been published. In 1980, Lacan dissolved the EFP in favour of the new École de la cause freudienne.

Lacan's work divides followers of Freud, being regarded either as absolutely heretical or as still caught in too many Freudian concepts to go far enough (very loosely, Foucault, Derrida, and Deleuze and Guattari), or as anti-feminist, though perhaps allowing a space for feminism (Mitchell and Rose, 1982: 1–57, Grosz, 1988: 147–87), or as profoundly exciting and to be put into the context of Marxism (as with Žižek). No account of Lacan, especially one committed to putting him into the context of his significance for literature, can hope to be other than partial, selective, and of course, too brief, and any account is bound to contain error, since Lacan's difficulty is not in doubt. Further, unlike Freud, who was always systematising his work, and revising concepts, as if trying to keep a consistent narrative, Lacan was much less systematic or consistent, and accounts of his work often risk making his work more of a narrative than it is. As he says himself, 'obscurity is characteristic of our field' (Lacan, 1979: 187). The statement is not just a comment on how much his theory has to do with vision, with seeing, with the gaze! We will look at his work, and at the challenges to it from deconstruction and from feminism, both psychoanalytic and not.

The imaginary

I start with the writings centred on the mirror stage. It is apparent that Lacan is opposed to any philosophy based on the cogito: i.e. the system of René Descartes (1596–1650), which starts with the subject who says 'I think, therefore I am' (*cogito ergo sum*). In that way, he follows Freud's Copernican revolution. The opposition which Lacan has to Jean-Paul Sartre (1905–80) is apparent: Lacanian psychoanalysis does not presume the presence of an early ego, a founding subject, hence his hostility to American 'ego psychology', which presumes an ego which may need therapy, or massaging, but which is fundamentally capable of doing what it wants to do. The infant begins, for Lacan, at around eighteen months, with an act of *identification* – identity, for Lacan, is premised on who, or what, I identify with. The child identifies with the image seen in the mirror, which becomes the 'ideal I', which Freud spoke of in writing on narcissism, and in 'The Ego and the Id'. What I see in the mirror is me and not me (half my size, and, of course, my face in reverse), and it produces an ongoing drama where the identification with what is seen creates the I. But at the same time, I realise that I am not that: there is a space between me and what I see, and that opens up desire, the need to close the gap, which, however, cannot happen: in Lacan, there cannot be the satisfaction of desire, which would end it:

> the mirror stage is a drama whose internal pressure pushes precipitously from insufficiency [because the child does not have, as yet, full control] to anticipation [of such control] – and, for the subject caught up in the lure of spatial identification, turns out fantasies that proceed from a fragmented image of the body [the *corps morcelé* – the body in pieces] to what I will call an 'orthopaedic' form of its totality – and to the finally donned armour of an alienating identity that will mark his entire mental development with its rigid structure. Thus, the shattering of the *Innenwelt* [inner world] to *Umwelt* [environment] circle gives rise to an inexhaustible squaring of the ego's audits. (Lacan, 2006: 78) [Ainsi la rupture du cercle de l'*Innenwelt* à l'*Umwelt* engendre-t-elle la quadrature inépuisable des récolements du *moi*. (Lacan 1996: 1.96)]

The 'I' constituted by the act of identification with what is seen in the mirror is caught by a 'lure', which is the attraction of the idea of being able to appropriate (i.e. to own) a body and a space. On the one side, it produces (literally, 'machines') a fantasy of being the body in pieces, torn to fragments. The body in pieces is later glossed as meaning that the ego is here 'an inchoate collection of desires' (Lacan, 1993: 39). On the other, it produces the fantasy of totality, of completeness, which Lacan calls 'orthopaedic' – i.e. which has learned to walk straight, which has been trained. (Lacan is remembering the machines devised by Schreber's father: see Chapter 7.) 'Orthopaedic' reappears later, when Lacan speaks of 'the orthopaedics of group relations' (Lacan, 2006: 233): being in a group keeps the person 'straight', upright. The climax is the assumption of the armour of an alienating identity, which implies (1) that identity is an alienating idea, because it separates a fantasised 'I' from everything 'other' in the self, (2) that this identity is worn as self-protective and combative armour, aggressive and paranoid, even Fascist (Foster, 1991: 64–97) and (3) the alienation makes identity other to what I am, in other words, the 'ideal I' that I identify with and desire to be is not me. The word 'alienation', since it contains the Greek *allos*, other, means then that the identity assumed is indeed other to me: identity is truly an alienated identity. The armour Lacan also calls a rigid structure. The last sentence of the quotation may be translated as 'the breaking of the circle from the inner to the outer world engenders the inexhaustible itemising survey of the properties of the self'. The subject who emerges in the mirror stage, the *moi* (= me, whereas *je* is the subject, *moi* is the object: the subject who looked in the mirror has been objectified by the process) now must spend all its time verifying itself, trying to 'square' – i.e. to equalise on all sides – what it has been said to be. It must attempt to square the circle, in a process of trying to rationalise everything of itself, an impossible task, just as the circle cannot be squared. The French *récolements* applies to (1) an official reading back to a witness what they have just said, to verify it, and (2) to a bailiff's inventory of the goods they have seized. The first sense implies repetition: my identity comes from a constant repeating to myself of what I am, not letting anything escape. The second sense suggests that I have to examine every part of what constitutes me, to make sure that it all coheres, and there is nothing wrong in the sum of the things.

The relevance of this material for literature is clear, in so far as this is fascinated by the question of what is meant by a history of subjectivity. How do I learn to say 'I', for example, in a confessional statement, or in autobiography, a term associated with the beginning of the nineteenth century? (Wordsworth's *The Prelude* is one of the first autobiographies in English.) It is clear that to say 'I' is to be objectifying the self, recognising that what is said misses the point, because, as the French poet Rimbaud wrote, 'I is an other' (Rimbaud, 1962: 6).

Lacan draws on Klein, for the phantasies of the child fragmenting its inner world. Lacan's sense is similar, but there is a difference; the inner self which is constructed by the act of identification fears its own fragmentation, and appears in dreams in the form of disjointed limbs, or organs seen in 'exoscopy'; i.e. seen from the outside. He compares the body, as the subject sees it, to the fantastic pictures created by Hieronymus Bosch (c.1450–1516), for example in *The Garden of Earthly Delights*, painted c.1500: bodies with wings, or else ready to carry out internal persecutions on themselves. An example is the monstrous figure in Hell (the right panel of Bosch's triptych) with a body which is an egg-shell, the back part cut away. Inside it, there is a tavern-scene; where the rump should be, figures climb up ladders into it, as if carrying out such 'internal persecutions'. Hell is the sphere of paranoia, and Lacan's choice of Bosch suggests a new moment in western consciousness (the same moment that Dürer painted the first self-portrait (1500), using a mirror), when the self becomes aware of itself as a body, complete, ideal, or, possibly, shattered, nothing, depressed, as in Dürer's *Melencolia* (1513).

The 'I' (*je*) is symbolised in dreams as a fortress, or as a stadium (*stade*), rather like the *Tower of Babel* of Breugel (1525–69), which shows the King,

Nimrod, at the site of the unfinished tower which he has commanded into being. Remembering the original date of the essay, we can say that the 'I' as a stadium may recall the 1936 Olympics in Berlin; certainly the 'mirror stage' (*le stade du miroir*) does not mean a stage as when we speak of 'a stage we all go through', but the I as a fortified state, performing as on a scaffold – another meaning of 'stade' – or walling itself around. At the end of the sixteenth century, Hamlet affirms his own unique identity, and that 'I have that within which passes show' (*Hamlet*, 1.2.85), so that he asserts that he cannot be understood by anyone standing outside his own life. Lacan thinks of the I being surrounded by gravel-pits and marshes; things repudiated and waste and undefined, while inside the stadium's outer wall is a 'proud, remote inner castle' (Lacan, 2006: 78) which is the id. More than anything, the 'I' must protect the id from becoming exposed to an enemy: the id is that which the I, the superego, tortures the ego (the *moi*) over, because the id's activities are threatening to identity, in that they introduce 'other' elements into the self. This image of the castle may be compared with what Abraham and Torok think of as the crypt. (The language by which the subject has to say 'it's me' (c'est moi) is discussed as involving a historical, seventeenth-century change, in Lacan's 'Function and Field', 1953: 233–4).

What appears is a 'paranoiac alienation' which dates from when the 'specular *I*' – the I seen in the mirror (Latin, *speculum*) – 'turns into the social *I*' (Lacan, 2006: 79). This happens at the end of the mirror stage. Lacan refers to the developmental psychologist Charlotte Bühler (1893–1974) and to her work on *transitivism*. *OED* dates this word from 1924 onwards; in transitivism, a patient attributes to others his or her own experiences and sensations, which indicates how fragile the hold is upon identity as secure inside the body of the self. Paranoiac identification implies that the subject has misidentified with the image it has seen in the mirror. As the following essay, 'Aggressivity in Psychoanalysis', says, the subject has identified with the visual *Gestalt* (pattern, form) of his own body, which is 'an ideal unity, a salutary imago' (Latin: image: an 'imago' is a stereotypical version of the other). This *Gestalt*, this corporeal unity, is also invested with the distress and vulnerability that the child of this age has (physically, the child at the time of the mirror stage is far less independent and in control than any other animal). Hence the anxieties apparent in transitivism where 'a child who beats another child says that he himself was beaten; a child who sees another child fall, cries' (Lacan, 2006: 92).

Identification with the other means that the child has not yet worked out what is of itself, and what of another. In an erotic relation 'the human individual fixates on an image that alienates him from himself'; here, 'we find the energy and the form from which the organisation of the passions that he will call his ego originates'. This conflictual state where what is of the other appears in me produces 'awakening of the desire for the object of the other's desire'. So 'man's ego is never reducible to his lived identity', and the ego is capable of saying both: 'What happens to me has nothing to do with what I am' (negating himself), and 'there's nothing about you that is worthwhile' (accusing the other). These statements are interchangeable, indeed, indistinguishable (Lacan, 2006: 93). Put together, they constitute the paranoid structure of the ego, which shows itself in three delusions: jealousy, where I fear that what I have will be taken by someone else; erotomania, where I am convinced that the other loves me, without having reason for saying so; and interpretation: the need constantly to interrogate and overinterpret the motives of other people. Interestingly, Lacan evokes Klein, on the child's paranoid aggressiveness towards the mother, for these arguments.

The 'Aggressivity' essay returns to Bosch's paintings for 'an atlas of all the aggressive images that torment mankind', saying that what psychoanalysis discovers is pictured in Bosch:

> images based on a primitive autoscopy of the oral organs and organs derived from the cloaca is what gives rise to the shapes of the demons in Bosch's work. Even the ogee of the *angustiae* of birth can be found in the gates to the abyss through which they thrust the damned, and even narcissistic structure may be glimpsed in the glass spheres in which the exhausted partners of 'The Garden of Earthly Delights' are held captive. (Lacan, 2006: 85–6)

An autoscopy is where the individual sees his body from a position outside his body. In Bosch's work, demons fly in and out of bodies, like birds, showing the porosity of the body's openings, which are invisible to itself (mouth, anus, vagina), but capable of penetration and so making impossible any single, discrete identity. Lacan sees the double-S shape – which evokes the narrowness of the vagina through which the child has come into the world – with the attendant trauma of birth Freud speaks of, imaged in the Hell-gates through which the demons thrust the damned. He notes how many of the lovers seem to have glass bodies, as though possessed of a fragile narcissism. The fear of having a body made of glass comes out in a short story by Cervantes, *The Glass Graduate*, one of his *Exemplary Stories* (1604). Bosch's art represents a new moment when the body is perceived as individual, and as vulnerable, inducing 'paranoiac knowledge' (Lacan, 2006: 91).

That phrase links to the fourth 'thesis' Lacan is arguing: 'aggressiveness is the tendency correlated with a mode of identification I call narcissistic, which determines the formal structure of man's ego and of the register of entities characteristic of his world'. The ego is an aggressive structure; this comes about from the identification the subject makes with the reflected, alienating image of itself, which it must protect, while aware of the disparity between itself and the image. The moment of identification Lacan thinks of as a stagnation, saying that it is akin to the most general structure of human knowledge, which constitutes the ego and objects as having the attributes of 'permanence, identity, and substance'. The identification made fixes objects with the sense that they are unified, and unchanging. Paranoid knowledge, which makes for 'objective identification', is the fear that they are not (Lacan, 2006: 91). Objects must remain static for the ego to be so too. Narcissism comes in because the ego must be defended at all costs; it can be so only by maintaining other things to it in a constant relation.

'Paranoiac knowledge' is illustrated in D.H. Lawrence's *Women in Love* (1921), in 'Breadalby', a chapter describing an aristocratic weekend party to which Rupert Birkin has been invited: he is surrounded by Hermione, whose desire for certain knowledge is called a 'will', and by Sir Joshua Malleson (who has elements of Bertrand Russell). 'Knowledge is, of course, liberty', says Malleson, and Birkin replies that it is, 'in compressed tabloids' (tabloids are pills; tabloid newspapers = papers where the information has been predigested, narrowed into thinking which has already been sorted out, so that the reader need not think). Hermione asks what Birkin means:

> 'You can only have knowledge, strictly', he replied, 'of things concluded, in the past. It's like bottling the liberty of last summer in bottled gooseberries.'
>
> 'Can one have knowledge only of the past?' asked the baronet pointedly. 'Could we call our knowledge of the laws of gravitation, for instance, knowledge of the past?'
>
> 'Yes', said Birkin. (Lawrence, 2000: 86)

Birkin contends that there cannot be a present knowledge; all knowledge is what I used to have; in the present, I meet the other afresh, and cannot use my past knowledge to cover the present. Many people will know the experience of starting to say something that they thought they knew and now realising that it no longer seems true. Sir Joshua thinks of knowledge as permanent and objective, and the use of the word 'laws' is significant; once knowledge has been made into formulable laws, there is no question of it defying the subject, by becoming different. But of course, we have no present, direct knowledge of gravity, and to speak about it as a 'law' is tabloid thinking.

Lacan's essay is fascinated by how the self formed in the mirror stage relates to the other. So he evokes 'the aggressive motives behind all so-called philanthropic activity' (Lacan, 2006: 87). Lawrence does the same with the industrialist Thomas Crich, in *Women in Love*, who 'liked hearing appeals to his charity' (Lawrence, 2000: 216). He gets a meaning for his life by exercising charity to his workmen. In philanthropy, the self gains a sense of itself; its narcissism is increased.

What has been described is 'the imaginary' (Lacan, 2006: 202). The child has identified with an image: the imaginary is a narcissistic state. The identification is a lure which draws the infant in, and, in 'The Mirror Stage', Lacan, who rejects Sartre's sense of the 'self-sufficiency of consciousness' (Lacan, 2006: 80), specifically distances himself from Freud's sense that the ego is centred on the 'perception-consciousness' system, or organised by the reality principle, which would limit the fantasies of the primary processes, and be a way of accepting reality. Rather, the ego comes from *méconnaissance*, a misrecognition; Lacan speaks of 'the function of *méconnaissance* that characterises the ego' (Lacan, 2006: 80). *Connaissance* means 'knowledge'; *reconnaissance* 'recognition'; Lacan's punning word, which can mean 'failure to recognise' (Wilden, 1968: xv), makes knowledge mis-knowledge, while also adhering to Freud's sense that to know something is to know it again, as in the essay 'Negation' (see Chapter 3, above). Knowledge which does not know is at the heart of Lacan's work, and the instability implied from this accounts for the paranoid and aggressive manner in which the sense of the ego is preserved. The lure that draws in and creates the ego is attractive because it is an image, yet it is a two-dimensional image that gives the subject an illusion of having a spatial, that is, three-dimensional, sense of itself. Animals, when they know that the image in a mirror is an image, lose interest (Lacan, 2006: 75). But, for humans, the point of interest is that what is seen is 'only' an image.

The symbolic

The 'symbolic order', a phrase from Lévi-Strauss, means language taken as a system, or structure of signs which the subject is brought into, under the authority of the father. Lacan discusses it in 'The Function and Field of Speech and Language'. The father severs the dyadic relationship between the child and the mother which is, in any case, broken by the mirror stage, when the infant gains a sense of a unique self, which is not related to the mother. The father's authority compels the child to route its demands of the mother through speech, so enframing the child within language. The first lesson the symbolic order teaches is sexual difference; the child assumes a position as male, or female, and we should note, as Lacan-inspired feminism shows, that the symbolic order is thus patriarchally imposed; it is 'the name of the father' (Lacan, 2006: 230) which establishes this: 'le *nom du père*' (Lacan, 1996: 276), where 'nom' puns on 'non': the father's 'no'. Entering this order means learning that we are inside a system which stretches on either side far beyond individual utterance. The *langue*, it will be remembered, cannot be accessed and known objectively, and it works unconsciously.

So Lacan writes that 'the subject goes far beyond what is experienced "subjectively" by the individual . . . the truth of his history is not at all contained in his script' (Lacan, 2006: 219), i.e. in the lines written down for him for the part he must play. Like actors who have only their own speeches written down, not the rest of the play, the subject does not know the unconscious history that informs his speech: *language is not a means of knowing what I think, it severs me from knowledge, including the knowledge of what I am saying*. The implications of this for literature are crucial; all concepts of 'the author's intention' are almost a waste of time to pursue; we cannot ask 'what did Beckett really mean by Godot?' in *Waiting for Godot*; a text is informed by an unconscious which works through it, which Fredric Jameson, for instance, in his book of that title, calls a 'political unconscious'. In this point lies a principal reason for the significance of psychoanalysis to criticism: we begin with the point that poetic language can never be 'the best words in the best order', as Coleridge said; all poetic language contains something in it which exceeds conscious ordering.

In his following paragraph, Lacan says – in Sheridan's familiar translation – 'the unconscious of the subject is the discourse of the other' (Lacan, 1977a: 55). Here it is possible to see that the unconscious is the symbolic order, which I speak, in a structure of *méconnaissance*; and, since it is structured on the A-B-C-D-E model, every term within the utterance contains the surrounding terms, forming its unconscious desire. Freud had discussed dream images as working by condensation and displacement (*SE* 4.277–309: see below). Lacan relates these to terms derived from classical rhetoric: metaphor and metonymy, which he takes as summing up together a range of rhetorical terms (Lacan, 2006: 221–2), and discusses further in 'The Instance of the Letter in the Unconscious' (Lacan, 2006: 419–24). In condensation, as in metaphor, one term stands in for another, or two terms are compressed together in a high degree of concentration. In metonymy, one term is continually replaced, displaced, by the next, adjacent, term; one term stands for another ('hands' for workers; 'Downing Street said . . .'

means the Prime Minister's office; a flag of a country is a metonym for the country, hence the annoyance the United States feels when its flag is burned; and water and fire are metonyms for each other, because to say one means to think of the other. The subject cannot speak a unique desire, because this is metonymically constructed. Indeed, language is desire, since desire acts metonymically, sliding along the chain of signifiers: not this, but this, but not this, but this. In 'On the Universal Tendency to Debasement in the Sphere of Love' (1912), Freud discusses specifically male sexuality, and an observation that men's sexual object choices are continually degraded. He argues that:

> we must reckon with the possibility that something in the nature of the sexual instinct itself is unfavourable to the realisation of complete satisfaction. If we consider the long and difficult developmental history of the instinct, two factors immediately spring to mind which might be made responsible for this difficulty. Firstly, as a result of the diphasic onset of object choice [the point that sexual desire, and the time when it is possible to satisfy this, do not relate: the child must wait till adulthood] and the interposition of the barrier against incest, the final object of the sexual instinct is no longer the original object but only a *surrogate* for it. Psychoanalysis has shown us that when the original object of a wishful impulse has been lost as a result of repression, it is frequently represented by *an endless series of substitute objects* none of which, however, brings full satisfaction. This may explain the inconstancy in object-choice, the 'craving for stimulation' which is so often a feature of the love of adults. (*SE* 11.188–9, my italics)

The loss of the mother, who, it may be added, is 'only' an embodiment of the 'lost object' – Freud is *not* being strictly literal in saying that the child desires the mother sexually – means that all object-choices run through a pattern whose substitutional nature defines desire as metonymic. Put over-simply, sexuality is unsatisfiable because all object-choices seem empty in relation to those other figures to the left and right of the person chosen. Lacan works with the incompleteness of desire that Freud brings out, adding that desire is caused by this structure of metonymy in language, and with the point that desire, and its symptoms, and the symptoms of repression, therefore, are structured, not arbitrary, according to the formation of the symbolic order. Hence 'a symptom is itself structured like a language' (Lacan, 2006: 223), and, again in Sheridan's familiar translation, 'the unconscious is structured in the most radical way like a language' (Lacan, 1977a: 234). Returning to the image of the play-script, Lacan is fascinated by the gaps on either side of the actor's script; it is, of course, this which constructs the subject as marked by desire.

The Other

So 'man's desire finds its meaning in the other's desire, not so much because the other holds the keys to the desired object, as because his first object(ive) is to be recognised by the other' (Lacan, 2006: 222). Lacan's formulation depends on Kojève's reading of Hegel's *Phenomenology of Spirit*, particularly the section on the master/slave relationship. The master can dominate the slave, but cannot control the slave's desire; possessing the slave's desire would boost the master's narcissism. Seminar XI, *The Four Fundamental Concepts of Psychoanalysis*, expresses this Kojève-inspired point by saying 'when in love, I solicit a look, what is profoundly unsatisfying and always missing is that – *You never look at me from the place from which I see you. Conversely, what I look at is never what I wish to see*' (Lacan, 1979: 103). Love is a desire for the confirmation of what the mirror stage gives. But the loved person does not confirm the narcissism of the lover. There is always something missing in what I see in the other person, always a sense of something else being there. So, in a phrase which runs as a *leitmotif* through Seminar XI, 'desire is the desire of the Other' (Lacan, 1979: 38): I desire the Other, yes, but desire is for what the Other desires, and, if the Other is the unconscious, then *what* is desired remains outside articulation.

It must be added that this is not meant to give a stability to the Other, or to the unconscious. The symbolic order, as a structure, allows some things to be said, and some not, at any one time; it is a structure giving both blindness and insight. When Lacan says that 'God is unconscious', rather than 'God is dead' (Lacan, 1979: 59), that implies that God remains an unstable, deceitful force within language, bringing things out and repressing others, and so unsettling desire, so that it does not have a firm structure at all with which to work. The 'Function and Field' essay distinguishes between full and empty speech, the latter being where 'the subject seems to speak in vain about someone who . . . will never join him in the assumption of his desire' (Lacan, 2006: 211). In empty speech, the patient thinks that his desire is located in himself; as if he was what he sees in the mirror; but the mirror is other and in the sphere of the other. We can say that, though the infant experiences the mirror stage and then enters the symbolic order, that is only the order that experience gives. Actually, the child is inside the symbolic order from the start, for example, from the time the first clothes are bought (e.g. blue for a boy, pink for a girl). The mirror stage is part of the symbolic order. I look because I am in the field of vision; I am looked at already. The difference between the mirror stage and the symbolic order is: the first lures me into thinking I am at the centre; the second decentres, because as subject I must assume a position inside that order, whose alterity can only be guessed at, but which cannot be ignored:

> Freud's discovery was that of the field of the effects, in man's nature, of his relations to the symbolic order, and the fact that their meaning goes all the way back to the most radical instances of symbolisation in being. To ignore the symbolic order [*le méconnaitre*] is to condemn Freud's discovery to forgetting, and analytic experience to ruin. (Lacan, 2006: 227)

Lacan's 'return to Freud' involves, then, the declaration that Freud saw the symbolic order, language, and the symbolic, at the heart of existence. This must be considered through Freud on the dream, where he argues that dreams express themselves in images – symbols – which have their own grammar. Jokes also work by condensation, and so follow the logic of the dream (*SE* 8.88–9, 165–80). Essays by Freud on 'the antithetical meaning of primal words', his discussion of language in *The Uncanny*, and the consideration of the symbolism in the *Fort! Da!* game in *Beyond the Pleasure Principle*, to say nothing of Freud's attention to literary texts, place language at the heart of Freud, but Lacan means more than that. Calling a word 'a presence made of absence', he says that the *Fort! Da!* game makes 'absence itself to be named' (Lacan, 2006: 228). Freud's discovery begins with the primacy of the symbol over the human, because of the primacy of absence, which both necessitates the symbol and is born out of it, but it could not be born out of it if there was no absence. The symbolic order is without 'positive terms', to recall Saussure on language as a system of differences. Here Lacan refers to madness, either as speech which has given up trying to get recognition from the other or as language which, under the power of delusion, 'objectifies the subject in a language void of dialectic' (Lacan, 2006: 231). Either way, such speech lacks the discourse of the other in its language: there is no return from the other upon the subject's speech. John Rajchman says that Foucault makes the absence of dialectic the central term of his definition of modernist writing, which is language with no base in the other (Rajchman, 1985: 20). In that discourse, 'the subject is spoken instead of speaking' (Lacan, 2006: 232). The symbols which have accepted meaning within the symbolic order are not taken up by the subject. What does return in the subject is a symptom, 'the signifier of a signified that has been repressed from the [neurotic] subject's consciousness' (Lacan, 2006: 232). It is always the case, for Freud, and Lacan, that what is repressed, returns. A symptom has no arbitrary form. It relates to the symbolic order, rather, and arises from the subject's specific placement in the symbolic order, however much this may have been repressed.

The mirror stage, enclosing the subject within a 'stadium in which his ego contains his imaginary exploits' (Lacan, 2006: 233), creates a wall which blocks the possibility of the speech from the other, and Lacan quotes T.S. Eliot's *The Hollow Men* (1925) – a poem which draws on Conrad's *Heart of Darkness* (1899) – to enforce the point about absence constituting the subject. The flatness and lack of affect in that poem suggests that 'the mad subject is spoken rather than speaking' (Lacan, 2006: 234). And Eliot is also evoked in the third part of 'Function and Field', which starts with the Roman poet Petronius's epigraph which, evoking the death-drive, opens *The Waste Land* (1922), and it also contains the words of the *Upanishads* which Eliot uses to close that poem (Lacan, 2006: 265), as if Lacan was writing a parallel text to Eliot's. (The notes that Lacan wrote to this and other seminars also compare with Eliot's notes on *The Waste Land*.)

This part of 'Function and Field' is most concerned with what happens in psychoanalysis:

> The function of language in speech is not to inform but to evoke. What I seek in speech is a response from the other. What constitutes me as a subject is my question. In order to be recognised by the other, I proffer what was only in view of what will be. In order to find him I call him by a name that he must assume or refuse in order to answer me. (Lacan, 2006: 247)

Language evokes, calls the other, because it starts from the lack in the ego; it is a recognition of lack, so that we start with a question – as *Hamlet* begins 'Who's there?' – and it asks for recognition from the other. We can add that Lacan's disagreement with Melanie Klein is implicit here, as Lacan argues that 'projection' and 'introjection' are not parallel activities. He argues that projection, which is sending something of myself out into the world, corresponds to the imaginary, while introjection, taking something into myself, corresponds to the evocation of the other, being a need to draw the attention of the other to a lack in the self. He also contends that Klein's psychoanalysis of the child does not allow that call, in that it speaks for the child by naming its desire: 'the child "makes no call"' (Lacana, 1988a: 83; Felman, 1987: 105–28). The call which is made to the other is to receive back from the other not a statement of truth but a 'gift of speech' (Lacan, 2006: 240); and that, he argues, is what Freud was able to give to the Rat Man.

In this last section, emphasising that the analysand has his or her own temporality, that is, an experience of time, and of being in time, and that this includes a movement towards death, Lacan puns on the word 'Da' from the *Upanishads*, which means 'Da' as 'Give', which is how Eliot uses it; and also means 'da' as 'here', from the *Fort! Da!* game, and 'Da' as part of Heidegger's term 'Dasein', 'being here', which is how Heidegger resists speaking of 'the human', or 'man', when thinking of temporality, that being here is in relation to time, and to death, which imposes finitude upon it.

Language and the Dream

That the subject is constituted by language reappears in the 'Seminar on *The Purloined Letter*' (1955), the essay which opens the *Écrits*, and 'The Instance of the Letter in the Unconscious [*l'instance de la lettre dans l'inconscient*], or Reason since Freud' (1957). The first of these was translated in *Yale French Studies* first in 1972, and will be discussed in Chapter 8. The second was translated in 1966. 'Lettre' puns on Heidegger's word for Being (*Sein*), *l'être*. For Heidegger, the unconscious – not that he spoke of it – would mean Being, indeed, it would not be a wrong way to consider what Heidegger means by Being if we consider it as akin to the *langue*; besides this, Heidegger virtually equates Being with language. For Lacan, nothing 'spiritual' subtends being, only the material, literal nature of language, and his essay stresses its literality, just as he also says that the psychoanalyst should have a literary background and training (Lacan, 2006: 413). 'Instance' includes the meanings 'insistence', 'entreaty'; it is what stands inside the subject with the power of insisting, or commanding (compare the legal name 'the court of first instance' to get the sense of its legal power, its decision-making authority). Laplanche and Pontalis (1973: 15–16) indicate that *l'instance* is the word the Standard Edition translates as 'agency', as when Freud thinks of an agency which permits thoughts to enter consciousness (*SE* 4.144); here, the agency certainly has the force of law.

Lacan begins by inverting Saussure's S/*s* distinction, which is the signified (S) placed over the signifier (*s*). Saussure, though stressing the signifier, gives priority to the signified, to meaning, as though this was immediately apparent. The *s* below the bar is unnoticed (repressed, for Lacan); hence Derrida, otherwise no friend to Lacan, calls Saussure logocentric, as believing in immanent, present meaning. For Lacan, the order should be *s*/S; the signifier placed over the signified, and he says 'no signification can be sustained except by reference to another signification' (Lacan, 2006: 415). The signifier does not represent the signified, it does not have to 'justify its existence in terms of any signification whatsoever' (Lacan, 2006: 416). Lacan's argument accords with the fundamental arguments of modernism, that literary language is that which draws attention to language, not meaning, which makes each poem, for instance, self-reflexive.

Lacan's inversion of Saussure which leads to the witty distinguishing of identical doors with two signifiers – Ladies and Gentlemen – makes the point that the signifier, *not* biology, determines sexual difference; that the letter is real and literal because it has material effects (try going into the wrong lavatory in a public building), that it divides places and institutes them, and institutionalises a law around them, and that meaning is derived from the letter, not the other way round. The signifiers Ladies and Gentlemen are two within a chain, as we have seen earlier: Lacan says that 'it is in the chain of the signifier that meaning *insists*, but that none of the chain's elements *consists* in the signification it can provide at that very moment' (Lacan, 2006: 419). Meaning is not the effect of something outside language; nonetheless it 'insists' – with all the implications that word contains – inside the chain of signifiers, which comprise the symbolic order, and the unconscious. At the same time, the signified slides under the signifying chain, never held in place. Lacan is describing a process of destabilisation as well as one of an uncanny persistence, in the way language means something, brings the subject back to itself, particularly, as his example suggests, within sexual difference. Lacan concedes, however, that there are also *points de capiton* within language (Lacan, 2006: 419), like the buttons on a sofa which connect the covering to the insides, stopping the covering moving around. Lacan discusses the bar (i.e. the slash) between the signifier and the signified by punning on 'arbre' (tree), the example he takes from Saussure, and so the point emerges: the bar indicates a primary repression: we are in the world not of objects but of symbols.

The essay then turns towards topics already alluded to: those Freudian concepts of condensation (*Verdichtung*) and displacement (*Verschiebung*), which Lacan compares with Jakobson on metaphor and metonymy; and the dream as a rebus (*SE* 4.277–8), a picture-puzzle, whose separate parts do make sense not when read individually, but only in their symbolic relationship to other signs. When so read, 'the words which are put together . . . are no longer nonsensical, but may form a poetical phrase of the greatest beauty and significance' (*SE* 4.278). And that is what a dream is.

A metaphor puts one term forward instead of another, metonymy shows how a term of language can always be replaced by the next one it has an association with. A metonymic association might run: knife – fork – spoon. One term immediately associates with another, and sets up one axis of language. 'Knife', however, sets up other associations: dagger – sword – blade – spear, all of which relate as metaphors of each other. This metaphorical axis is clearly different from the metonymic, and it is no coincidence that, as an order, the metaphorical examples, arbitrarily chosen by me, all suggest phallic power.

Here we should investigate Freud's terms more completely, starting with 'the interpretation of dreams is the royal road to a knowledge of the unconscious activities of the mind' (*SE* 5.608). The 'royal' road has two tributaries: what Freud calls 'the psychopathology of everyday life', meaning the unintentional mistakes that people make: forgetting things, making slips of the tongue, misreading, making slips of the pen, and bungling actions (*SE* 6.239), all forms of 'parapraxis'; and jokes. One parapraxis from a rich field which Freud gives here and in the joke-book shows how metonymy brings out a secret wish: the President of the Lower House of the Austrian Parliament opening the sitting of the House with the words 'Gentlemen, I take notice that a full quorum of members is present and herewith declare the sitting closed!' (*SE* 6.59). No doubt he wished it closed, and the metonymic interchange of words is revelatory. This example approaches a joke; Freud discusses similarities between jokes and dreams (*SE* 8.88–9). The joke works by condensation, that is, it puts two words together, to make a pun, or it may form a substitute word for one that cannot be said in the particular company (*SE* 8.19–33). One instance is drawn from Heine saying that the millionaire Rothschild 'treated me as his equal – quite famillionairely' (8.16). 'Millionaire' and 'familiar' have been abbreviated into one word; the point that a millionaire cannot treat a poor man as if he was a member of the family has been repressed, but the joke recalls it, meaning that the patronage remains as a symptom in the joke – and the substitute word not only quietly acts as a reminder of the millionaire's thrift – joining two things into one, a principle of accumulation which works throughout his life. But also brings out the point that this patronising treatment is a form of using the other. He is not treating him as a familiar; rather, as a millionaire treats someone he wants to be seen to be good towards.

If a dream is the '(disguised) fulfilment of a (suppressed or repressed) wish' (*SE* 4.160), that relates to recent experience – 'in interpreting dreams we find . . . one component of the content of the dream is a repetition of a recent impression of the previous day' (*SE* 4.180). In a dream, I have my desire in the censored form which means that it appears in disguise. In 1909, Freud added that 'the kernel of my theory of dreams lies in my derivation of dream-distortion from the censorship' (*SE* 4.308n.) How this censorship which disguises operates, Freud summarises at the end of chapter 6, 'The Dream-Work'. Two processes are at work in the production of a dream:

1. the production of the dream-thoughts – these are 'thought-processes that have not become conscious' (*SE* 5.506). Elsewhere, Freud calls the dream-thoughts the dream's 'latent content' (*SE* 4.277).
2. their transformation into the content of the dream. This is 'the dream-work' (*Traumarbeit*), and produces the 'manifest content'.

The dream-work gives another form to the contents of the dream-thoughts, in the primary process. It must evade the censorship, as Freud says, otherwise the dreamer would wake up in alarm, for Freud emphasises that 'dreams are the GUARDIANS of sleep and not its disturbers' (*SE* 4.233). So it displaces the material given, according to 'considerations of representability'. For example, in Wilkie Collins's detective novel *The Moonstone* (1869), the hero, Franklin Blake, unconsciously, drugged by opium, stumbles into the room of Rachel Verinder, at night. He takes her precious 'moonstone'. The jewel displaces the idea of the woman's virginity: how conscious Collins was of all this other sexual reading cannot be answered about him as an individual; it relates to the ideology of the Victorians, to the symbolic order, as it obtained, with its 'considerations of representability' (*Rücksicht auf Darstellbarkeit*). The question is what can be staged, what can be shown. Intensities of feeling in the dream-thoughts are combined: this is 'condensation', giving each figure in the dream an added vividness, like that of characters in melodrama. Freud calls this process of combining several figures into one, 'overdetermination' (*SE* 4.283–4). The dream-work transforms the latent content into 'a single unity in the dream itself' (*SE* 4.179), but Freud does not think that all parts of this can be necessarily interpreted (*SE* 5.525).

The dream-work is further 'distorted' through a 'secondary revision' 'which is to be identified with the activity of our waking thoughts' (*SE* 5.499), in other words, through the secondary processes which now work on the primary processes. Freud sees such distortion (*Entstellung*) as continuous: 'no more than a part of the revision to which the dream-thoughts are regularly subjected as a result of the dream-censorship' (*SE* 5.515). Lacan links this 'distortion', or 'transposition' with 'the sliding of the signifier' (Lacan, 2006: 425), and it is inseparable from processes of repression, and from the point that the subject in language speaks in a situation of *méconnaissance* (Lacan: 1977: 163), always barred from his utterance.

Lacan now passes to his famous 'algorithms', as if using mathematics, to establish a structure which stands, as valid, outside the sliding of the signifier (Payne, 1993: 82–3). The third of these algorithms gives the structure of metaphor, in a formulation deriving from Jakobson, where the poetic use of language is called the intrusion of the metaphoric axis of language on to the metonymic. When the metaphoric drops into the metonymic, the term it replaces becomes 'the occulted signifier' (Lacan, 2006: 422). It dips below the line, it becomes the signified. Lacan's example is a line of Victor Hugo (1869), 'Sa gerbe n'était pas avare ni haineuse', from 'Booz endormi' (Hugo, 2004: 307–13): 'his sheaf was neither miserly nor hateful' – referring to Boaz's generosity to strangers harvesting in his field (see the Old Testament Book of Ruth) (Lacan, 2006: 422). The line substitutes the sheaf for the proper name, Boaz. The old man, perhaps miserly and hateful, as is allowed by the line's negation (*L'avare* is the title of Molière's famous play about the miserly father), disappears, replaced by the generosity of nature's 'sheaf'. Boaz becomes a father; the name of the father, which guarantees a phallic order, implied in the 'sheaf', is meaningful (becomes the signified) after it has disappeared, been repressed (Lacan, 2006: 422–3). Then the power of 'Boaz' dominates the metonymic chain, with the power of a symptom, with which Lacan compares a metaphor, just as he sees metonymy as the expression of desire (Lacan, 2006: 431).

This double determination of the subject by metonymy and metaphor is what Lacan discusses when he replaces the Cartesian 'I think, therefore I am' (*cogito ergo sum*) with a reference to Freud's Copernican revolution, in decentring the subject.

> Is the place that I occupy as subject of the signifier concentric or eccentric in relation to the place that I occupy as subject of the signified? That is the question.
>
> The point is not to know whether I speak of myself in a way that conforms to what I am, but rather to know whether, when I speak of myself, I am the same as the self of whom I speak. (Lacan, 2006: 430)

'Subject of the signifier' means being held in the metonymic shiftings of the signifier, in a situation of desire. That circle is 'excentric' (Lacan, 1977a: 165) to the place of the 'subject of the signified', which Lacan speaks of as 'thought', in exactly the same way that Freud has spoken of 'dream-thoughts' which have been repressed below the 'manifest content' of the dream (which has, then, on this basis, a metonymic structure). The subject is not simply decentred, but it no longer makes sense to speak of one circle at all. Lacan's question is not whether my speech is true, or honest, or authentic – propositions based on saying 'I am' – but whether it relates to my position in the signifying order. For 'I am thinking [i.e. unconsciously] where I am not, therefore I am where I am not thinking'

(Lacan, 2006: 430); Lacan strengthens that with 'I am not, where I am the plaything of my thought: I think about what I am where I do not think I am thinking' (Lacan, 2006: 430). There is a self-division here of the subject as constructed by metaphor and metonymy. Lacan says that Freud has demonstrated why the Saussurian algorithm, signified over signifier, cannot be seen 'in the same plane' (Lacan, 2006: 431). Rather, the signifier must go above, with the signified as its repressed, and the signified is itself a signifier (Boaz's 'sheaf' replaces 'Boaz'), so that what subtends the signifier is itself language. To relate to the signifier, Lacan says, must change 'the course of [man's] history, by modifying the moorings of his being' (Lacan, 2006: 438).

The last section, 'La lettre, l'être et l'autre' (note the aural punning/metonymy here), begins by saying that what thinks in my place is not an 'other' ego, another I. The question is, what is the 'other'? Lacan quotes Freud's statement, *Wo Es war, soll Ich werden*: a statement from the *New Introductory Lectures on Psychoanalysis* (1933). Freud says that psychoanalysis intends to 'strengthen the ego, to make it more independent of the super-ego . . . so that it can appropriate fresh portions of the id. *Where id was there ego shall be.* It is a work of culture – not unlike the draining of the Zuider Zee' (*SE* 22.80, my emphasis). Another translation runs: 'there where it was, I must come to pass' (Muller and Richardson, 1982: 173). What is this 'I'? Lacan translates 'Là où fut ça, il me faut advenir' (Lacan, 1996: 521): 'where it was I must come into being' (Lacan, 2006: 435). Or: it suits that I should come. To come to 'the place where that was' means seeing that the 'I' is rooted in otherness, it means to know 'the self's radical excentricity to itself' (both Lacan, 1977a: 171).

Macbeth *again*

The word 'ça' in the phrase 'there where it was' is the Other, it implies the 'beyond' (Lacan, 2006: 436), which precedes even questions of subjectivity, and intersubjectivity, which is why Lacan recalls Freud's joke about two Jews meeting in a railway carriage at a station in Galicia:

> 'Where are you going?' asked one. 'To Cracow' was the answer.' 'What a liar you are!' broke out the other. 'If you say you're going to Cracow, you want me to believe you're going to Lemberg. But I know that in fact you're going to Cracow. So why are you lying to me?' (*SE* 8.115)

Lacan's sense of the difficulty of anticipating how the other is positioned in language arises from Freud's commentary: 'is it the truth if we describe things as they are without troubling to consider how our hearer will understand what we say? Or is this only jesuitical truth, and does not genuine truth consist in taking the hearer into account [. . .]?' Freud says that jokes of the kind which I have quoted attack 'not a person or an institution but the certainty of our knowledge itself, one of our speculative possessions' (*SE* 8.115).

Historically, the Jesuits could equivocate when accused in a Protestant court: i.e. to answer a straight, but dangerous question, 'Are you a Jesuit?' with something that could be interpreted in two different ways. Yet a 'straight' lie – which would be a sin – had not been told. A 'jesuitical truth' is identical to 'equivocation', which *OED* defines as 'the use of words or expressions that are susceptible of a double signification, with a view to mislead; *esp.* the expression of a virtual falsehood in the form of a proposition which (in order to satisfy the speaker's conscience) is verbally true'. 'Equivocation' is basic to *Macbeth* (it is referred to, in the context of the Jesuits, by the drunken Porter in *Macbeth* 2.3.7–11, and also by Macbeth in 5.5.43–5, with which 5.8.19–22 should be compared).

The Porter's words are worth examining. Pretending to be the Porter of Hell, admitting various classes into Hell as they knock on the door, he begins with a farmer who hanged himself on the expectation of a plentiful harvest, which obviously did not come – so that he must have read the signs of the times, the signs of the weather, wrong. He follows this up with a second person imagined entering: 'Faith, here's an equivocator, that could swear in both the scales against either scale; who committed treason enough for God's sake, yet could not equivocate to heaven: O come in, equivocator' (Shakespeare, 1984: 59). The equivocator does not get away with it, even though he may have said his treason was for God's sake; and the Porter is smug about him being so caught. But in that the equivocator does not resemble the witches, who trade in ambiguities – 'Fair is foul and foul is fair' and 'when the battle's lost and won', both from the first scene. They equivocate with Macbeth and Banquo in their prophecies, and when Macbeth revisits them to find out what will happen to him in the future, in just the way that the first Jew thinks the second Jew is doing, they tell him literal truths which they know will be interpreted another way. Macbeth knows that they are telling him something which cannot be taken in one way only, but he chooses to interpret according to his unconscious desire. The certainty of our knowledge can never be guaranteed because knowledge exists in language, and Lacan's summary of all the terms of rhetoric (Lacan, 2006: 421, 433) are ways of showing how language goes astray in its very being, and its very utterance.

What fascinates in Freud's example is that this 'jesuitical truth' creates a joke. Yet *Macbeth* is a tragedy. And the witches are joking with Macbeth and Banquo. The joke appeals to the primary process, where meanings have not been sorted out rationally. So does the dream, which the *Introductory Lectures on Psychoanalysis* (1916) argues 'does not simply give expression to a thought, but represents the wish fulfilled as an hallucinatory experience. *I should like to go on the lake* is the wish that instigates the dream. The content of the dream itself is: *I am going on the lake*. Thus even in these simple children's dreams a difference remains between the latent and the manifest dream, there is a distortion of the latent dream-thought: *the transformation of a thought into an experience*' (*SE* 15.129). The dream does not distinguish between wish and act. The joke draws attention to that process, whereby one statement includes its opposite: Cracow/Lemberg, as these exist in a metonymic sequence. *Macbeth* makes the doubleness of language itself the tragedy.

This doubleness, relating to condensation, and to thrift, compares with something else. Freud tells the joke of B who borrows a kettle from A. A sues him because the kettle is returned with a hole. B's defence, called 'sophistry' – a word connected to the Jesuits – is first that he never borrowed a kettle from A, second, that the kettle already had a hole in it, third, that he gave it back undamaged (*SE* 8.62, 205). It is not just that jokes are full of holes, but that each excuse is inadequate (has a hole in it) and must be supplemented by another, in a metomymic progression. This allows Lacan to say that metonymy is marked by 'lack' (Lacan, 2006: 439). So jokes point to something missing. Freud continues with the Hungarian village joke, where 'the blacksmith had been guilty of a capital offence. The burgomaster, however, decided that . . . a tailor should be hanged, and not the blacksmith, because there were two tailors in the village but no second blacksmith' (*SE* 8.206). Freud calls this act a 'displacement', and perhaps it relates to the point that tailors are plentiful because things are always needing to be patched, because of 'lack'. So you can become king, or you can become the father of kings, but you cannot do both; you cannot be Macbeth and Banquo.

This illuminates *Macbeth*'s Porter's joke about the tailor, told immediately after admitting the equivocator into Hell: 'Faith, here's an English tailor come hither for stealing out of a French hose: come in, tailor; here you may roast your goose' (*Macbeth* 2.3.12–15). The tailor, who makes and patches, has stolen clothes (as, metaphorically, Macbeth has) out of a basic deficiency, or lack: the French hose would be a gentleman's, and tight-fitting, so there would not be enough to go round, and the tailor has therefore been caught for doing something once too often. The 'goose' is the tailor's smoothing-iron, and also meant syphilis, so that the tailor comes to Hell already deficient by having a disease too many. And 'goose' implies 'penis' and 'prostitute'. If 'stealing' puns on 'staling' (= urinating), several actions seem condensed into one expression; ruining someone else's clothes, wearing stolen clothes, and acquiring venereal disease (the French pox, as the English called it) with trousers down. If it is argued that the tailor could not have done all these things at once, then we have an instance of the primary process at work: all these suggestions, which combine to suggest the pathological nature of what goes into Hell, are non-rationalised, but they co-exist in dream-logic, which is also that of the joke: the tailor (the figure of lack) finds that in Hell he has got his 'goose' in all and more senses than he wanted. His battle is lost, and won.

Equivocation implies an awareness of the doubleness of language, but that doubleness, which does not attempt to prescribe a single meaning, is also basic to the poetry of *Macbeth*. When Macduff – who will kill Macbeth, as Macbeth killed Duncan – hears that his wife and children have been killed by Macbeth's agents, he weeps and swears revenge. Malcolm, Duncan's son, tells him to be comforted, and Macduff replies 'He has no children' (Macbeth 4.3.216). What does Macduff mean? Malcolm has no children, so it is easy for him to say 'be comforted'? Macbeth has no children, so a complete revenge cannot happen, or, if he *had* children, he could not have ordered the execution of Macduff's? He could order murder only because he has no children? In which case, Macduff is, unconsciously, on to the significance of Macbeth being childless, and the line may be a verdict on Macbeth: he is already sentenced. How does that relate to the point that Macduff has no children, and, because he came from his mother's womb 'untimely ripped' (Macbeth 5.8.16), seems to be outside the economy which gives children? 'He has no children' cannot be assigned one meaning only, and its meaning is not one that Macduff knows: meaning belongs in the other, not in the self.

The real

The letter is everywhere present, insisting, but its invisibility is part of what Lacan means by 'the Real', which is the third term introduced in 'Function and Field', along with the Imaginary and the Symbolic. In his first Seminar (1953–54), 'the real . . . is what resists symbolisation absolutely' (Lacan, 1988a: 66). If the Imaginary is the identification made in the mirror stage, which gives the illusion of a complete ego, the Symbolic order is the system of language in which the subject is placed, and which is the Law-of-the-Father. The Real is what cannot be brought into the Symbolic order. Lacan says that 'the Real is the impossible' in Seminar XI: *The Four Fundamental*

Concepts of Psychoanalysis (Lacan, 1979: 167): the concepts are 'the unconscious, repetition, the transference and the drive' (Lacan, 1979: 12). I will discuss 'the Real' via the Seminar, and its use of *Beyond the Pleasure Principle.*

Beyond the Pleasure Principle begins with the pleasure principle as the conservative desire for homeostasis, for non-excitation, overriden by the 'reality principle', which at times impels on the ego the necessity to postpone such satisfaction. Its chapter 2 discusses trauma, which was experienced in a wholly modern and new way in the First World War, and, as meaning a psychic 'wound', rather than a physical one, is perhaps the most critical condition for modernity (see Caruth, 1996). Chapter 2 produces a remark on 'the mysterious masochistic trends of the ego' (*SE* 18.14) before discussing the *Fort! Da!* game, discussed in relation to Klein. Here repetition tries to bind a painful or unpleasant stimulus; it is an attempt to cope with the traumatic.

The text invokes a 'compulsion to repeat' (*SE* 18.19), which works actively, in ways where observers can see that a person's acts of repetition are in character; not the products of a 'daemonic power', they are, in unconscious ways, 'arranged by themselves' (*SE* 18.21). Even more interesting than these instances of a 'perpetual recurrence of the same thing' are passive repetitions, illustrated from the woman whose three successive husbands all die and need nurturing on their death-beds, or from the episode from Tasso's epic *Gerusalemme Liberata* (1580), where Tancred involuntarily twice wounds and destroys Clorinda, the woman he loves (*SE* 18.22). This 'compulsion to repeat', as something inside the system, like the ego, as discussed in relation to the *Project*, overrides the pleasure principle.

Consciousness must protect against stimuli which would disturb the pleasure principle, preventing memory – its impact potentially traumatic (*SE* 18.29) – arising in the place where consciousness of something is enforced. Trauma is aligned with shock (*SE* 18.31), which was discussed before in relation to Freud and Walter Benjamin. When Benjamin links shock to everyday urban existence, he follows the surrealist writer André Breton (1896–1966), who met Freud in 1921, and dubbed psychoanalysis 'the expulsion of man from himself' (Breton, 1960: 24, Cohen, 1993: 57–75, 173–215). And here we can consider Lacan, whose Seminar XI speaks of an 'impediment' which is discovered in the dream, in parapraxes, and in the flash of wit:

> Impediment, failure, split. In a spoken or written sentence something stumbles. Freud is attracted by these phenomena, and it is there that he seeks the unconscious. There, something other demands to be realised – which appears as intentional, of course, but of a strange temporality. What occurs,

> what is *produced*, in this gap, is presented as *the discovery* [*la trouvaille*]. It is in this way that the Freudian exploration first encounters what occurs in the unconscious. (Lacan, 1979: 25)

The lucky find, the discovery, the encounter is basic to Breton, and to Benjamin's discussions of Baudelaire's city poems. The 'discovery' is inseparable from the 'impediment', i.e. the intrusion of the real, which makes the encounter 'the missed encounter' (Lacan, 1979: 55), a phrase which recalls the 'lost object'.

Freud's chapter 5 reverts to the primary processes, which are 'bound' in the secondary processes, and to repetition as an element of the primary process. He defines an instinct (a drive) as 'an urge inherent in organic life to restore an earlier state of things' (*SE* 18.36): i.e., as related to a death-drive. In this, he follows the spirit of 'Instincts and Their Vicissitudes', where instincts have a passive aim (*SE* 14.122). Repetition undoes all organising (binding), all control, but it is a form of control, maintaining self-preservation, and self-mastery which are 'component instincts, whose function it is to assure that the organism shall follow its own path to death' since 'the organism wishes to die only in its own fashion' (18.39). The sexual drives are included here. They contain 'life instincts' which preserve the species (*SE* 18.40), and they are 'ego instincts', but they are also death-drives, as sexual orgasm (*jouissance*) shows, with the joke on orgasm as the 'petit mort', the 'little death'. Freud's chapter 6 discusses death, invoking Plato's *Symposium* for a sense that individual lives are a fragmenting of non-individuated life, and that death is a restoration of what has been broken off; then admits his scepticism about what he has speculatively written (*SE* 18.24). We have seen the scepticism it has received, though not from Klein, or Lacan.

Lacan identifies repetition and the unconscious with each other (Lacan, 1979: 48). Repetition does not just ensure the rule of the pleasure principle (we like things comfortably repeating each other) but *overrides* it; in other words, it has an erotic, or death-driven impulse within it. In what follows, Lacan evokes Aristotle's words for chance, *tuché* and *automaton*. The first is 'the encounter with the real' (Lacan, 1979: 53). It is 'beyond' the *automaton*, which refers to mechanical chance, which relates to the steadiness of the pleasure principle. *Tuché* breaks with the pleasure principle, in the form of a traumatic 'missed encounter'. Lacan evokes the last dream of *The Interpretation of Dreams* (*SE* 5.509), of the bereaved father, who lies down in the next room from his dead son to sleep, leaving an old man – who falls asleep – to keep vigil. He is awakened by the child standing by the bed, holding his arm and saying, *Father, don't you see I'm burning?* And the dead son is burning, because a candle has fallen on to the bed. The candle's sound in falling over (this candle is like the 'impediment') which wakens the father, and the child's words, are from 'the real'. Their force suggests that the father must recognise something, or has missed something he should have seen: the words invite a relooking (repetition) which is traumatic.

The next part, 'The Gaze as *Objet Petit a*', considers Maurice Merleau-Ponty's posthumously published book *The Visible and the Invisible* (1964). Lacan is not interested in the visible/invisible as forming a binary opposition, but rather by the limits encountered in the field of the visible, in the 'strange contingency' – the traumatic is implicit here – which he calls 'the lack that constitutes castration anxiety'. Looking, the scopic drive, is met by something else. There is a split between the eye, and 'the gaze':

> in our relation to things, in so far as this relation is constituted by the way of vision, and ordered in the figures of representation, something slips, passes, is transmitted, from stage to stage, and is always to some degree eluded in it – that is what we call the gaze. (Lacan, 1979: 73)

'The figures of representation' are within the symbolic order. What is missing is the gaze, or the *objet petit a*, or the real, three almost interchangable terms (compare Lacan, 1979: 65 and 83). The 'gaze' is where an object, or something apparently within, or attached to an object, appears as a gaze staring at the subject, or as an hallucinatory voice. The unrepresentable, in symbolic terms, looks, for Lacan speaks of 'the pre-existence of a gaze – I see only from one point, but in my existence, I am looked at from all sides' (Lacan, 1979: 72, compare 75). So, '*Father, don't you see . . .*' draws attention to what the father has not seen: the real, the gaze, which, not reducible to a person, but inherent in vision, looks, as the *objet petit a*. That last phrase combines the sense of the 'lost object' (so connecting with object-relations theory), and the sense of something missing. The letter '*a*' suggests '*autre*', the other, but not the Other with a capital, which is the whole field of the unconscious, but something more elusive within that. Lacan's interest in *das Ding*, the thing, is included.

The ego, the *cogito*, starts by looking. Consciousness starts up through being looked at, by that which is unconscious, and in the field of desire, and which, as the *objet petit a*, gives an imaginary completeness to what is looked at, as the mirror-image seems complete. The strangeness of the gaze makes for a discussion of anamorphosis, where Lacan evokes the soft watches in Dalí's painting *The Persistence of Memory* (1931), or Holbein's painting *The Ambassadors* (1533). Interrupting the perspectival vision in which the ambassadors are seen – and perspective, in the sixteenth-century, establishes the reality of the subject looking at the painting – is the skull. This is an anamorphosis, a shape indiscernible by the usual perspectival mode, visible only when looked at awry (Žižek, 2006: 68–71). For Lacan, the skull shows 'the subject as annihilated – annihilated in the form that is, strictly speaking, the imaged embodiment of the *minus-phi* of castration'. While the soft watches suggest sexual failure, the raised-up skull suggests erection, like the two ambassadors, 'frozen, stiffened', but both states equally suggest sexual failure, castration: the sign of death, of limitations, of the failure of the Imaginary, and the dominance of the law of the father. Correspondingly, Freud, thinking of the snakes forming the hair of the Medusa, who turns men into stone (= a castration image), says that dreams represent castration 'by a doubling or multiplication of a genital symbol' (*SE* 17.235). Lacan calls the skull the gaze (Lacan, 1979: 88–9). It suggests death, imaged in the negating (minus power) of castration. Perspective seems to establish the subject looking, but the anamorphosis, only possible with perspective, destroys the subject. The 'hypnotic value of painting' (Lacan, 1979: 115) is that the picture is a trap for the gaze (Lacan, 1979: 89), it holds it, containing that impossible thing which as the real has such disturbing force.

Continuing with 'What Is a Picture?', which begins 'the *objet a* in the field of the visible is the gaze' (Lacan, 1979: 105), Lacan argues: 'the gaze is outside, I am looked at, that is to say, I am a picture' (Lacan, 1979: 106). The subject is 'photo-graphed', that is, written in light. The mirror stage comes about because I have been looked at since birth: I look because I am inside the field of vision. Discussing mimicry amongst animals, Lacan says that this is not for the sake of adaptation to a hostile environment; he rather uses the surrealist writer Roger Caillois (1913–78) for an argument about the development of *ocelli*, imitation eyes in animals' mimicry. They exist as 'the stain'. Eyes intimidate because they are like *ocelli*, and have the power of fascination. Eyes and stains bring out 'the pre-existence to the seen of a given-to-be-seen'. 'The function of the stain and of the gaze is both that which governs the gaze most secretly and that which always escapes from the grasp of that form of vision that is satisfied with imagining itself as consciousness' (Lacan, 1979: 74). The stain then covers the gaze, as it were, and lets it work, as the real.

To be in the picture is as the stain, the spot (Lacan, 1979: 97). This is a pun: a spot(light) illuminates, but to look at a spotlight is to be dazzled; the spot is darkness and light simultaneously. I cannot see where I am. Wordsworth's *The Prelude* (12.208) says 'there are in our existence spots of time' (Wordsworth, 1979: 577). Punning, it can be said that a 'spot' is a place, possibly accessible to memory, and also, perhaps, a blank, a moment whose content cannot be assessed.

Shoshana Felman emphasises that Lacan returns to Freud as to a master who knows that there is a blank in knowledge, which is the unconscious, and which Lacan images in the purloined letter. That dominates, and dictates repetition, but its content is unknown. 'For the first time in the history of learning, Freud has scientific recourse to a knowledge that is not authoritative, not that of a master, a knowledge that does not know what it knows, and is thus *not in possession of itself*' (Felman, 1987: 92). In the same way, the letter is not possessed by anyone, but possesses them. Lacan's distinction is to have brought out Freud's point, so suggesting that the letter – literature – is not to be deciphered, studied, or taught, for its meaning, but because it undoes certain knowledge. A text is marked by an absence which means that it lacks that which would authorise an interpretation. An attempt at interpretation cannot position itself, so is marked by the stain, the spot. Shoshana Felman's reading of Henry James's *The Turn of the Screw* is significant, in removing interpretations which say either that the governess, who narrates, is hysterical when she thinks that the children, Miles and Flora, are haunted by Peter Quint and Miss Gross, as ghosts, or that the ghosts are real and the governess's fears justified. For Felman, an interpretation which claims that it can know, as the governess interprets, is dependent on reading a signifier whose sense cannot be known. So psychoanalysis is a means not of saying what the text is about but of showing that the text points to an absence at its centre (Felman, 1987: 94–207). The analysand comes to the psychoanalyst thinking he or she is 'the subject supposed to know' (Felman, 1987: 232). Believing that involves 'transference' (Lacan's third concept), the patient transferring unconscious ideas on to the analyst, as though he or she possessed the secret, and could be identified with the parental figure. Freud saw this happen with the 'Rat Man' identifying him with the Father.

The stain resists knowledge, while suggesting that it offers a satisfying illusion. A picture constitutes the stain: Lacan later evokes Cézanne on 'those little blues, those little browns, those little whites', which are called 'touches that fall like rain from the painter's brush' (Lacan, 1977c: 110), and he sees them as stains; Lacan also suggests that there is in the painting something which has the value of eyes (Lacan, 1977c: 101), so that the viewer 'lays down his gaze there as one lays down one's weapons'. Art decentres the gaze of the viewer. The idea of 'laying down weapons' recalls the paranoia of the 'armour of an alienating identity' established in the mirror stage; but while art holds the spectator, it has the force of otherness, preventing the spectator thinking of himself as a single, intending consciousness. Art is marked by the *trompe l'oeil*, that which tricks the eye, in so far as that is an organ demanding 'truth'; it has the *dompte-regard*, the ability to subdue the gaze (Lacan, 1979: 109). Realism is an instance of deception, being the veil which tricks the eye which demands verisimilitude, a representation of reality; what Lacan says critiques realism as a demand for truth. The contrast to the eye which lays down its demand is the eye of envy, the evil eye. Lacan's analysis of *invidia* recalls Klein's, as he thinks of Augustine's envy of his infant brother sucking at the breast. The evil eye has the power of fascination, but so does the picture (Lacan, 1979: 116, 118), and that power makes quiet the power of the subjective consciousness. If 'what one looks at is what cannot be seen' (Lacan, 1979: 182), we have here, something of the power of the real.

The drive

The later parts of *The Four Fundamental Concepts of Psychoanalysis* discuss not desire but the drive, the fourth 'concept'. Drives are the subject of Freud's 'Instincts and Their Vicissitudes' (1915), an essay discusssing *ambivalence*, a word first used in a technical sense by Bleuler, and so virtually a neologism in Freud. Ambivalence is more radical than ambiguity, where one word or phrase can have several meanings, perhaps contradictory. Ambivalence appears in the 'Wolf Man' case (see the next chapter), to imply both sadism and masochism (*SE* 17.26), contradictions in the same subject. Freud says that an 'instinct' – a drive (*Trieb*) – undergoes the following 'vicissitudes': 'reversal into its opposite', 'turning round upon the subject's own self' (a phrase developed by Lacan) and 'repression' and 'sublimation'. Freud considers the first two of these.

In *reversal*, 'the active aim (to torture, to look at) is replaced by the passive aim (to be tortured, to be looked at)' (*SE* 14.127). A sadistic desire, which is that of a voyeur, and scopophilic in character, turns into a second stage, where the desire is to be a self-torturer; turning from active to passive. Here Freud thinks of obsessional neurosis, as with the 'Rat Man'. In the third stage, an extraneous person is sought for to act as the subject. This stage is masochism, which needs a third person for it to work. An example is the desire to be looked at (exhibitionism). Masochism is sadism directed against the subject's own ego, and exhibitionism the desire to look at one's own body. Sadism, and scopophilia, both related to violence and power practised upon some other person as object; and masochism and exhibitionism, apparent contraries, become linked. Inside the switching over is a change from an *active* – traditionally coded as masculine (see 14.134) – to *passive* (feminine) position.

It is not digressive to note that Lacan says that Freud never assumes an 'essential' masculine or feminine position which engenders active and passive positions. Rather, 'the polar reference activity/passivity is there in order to name, to cover, to metaphorise, that which remains unfathomable in sexual difference . . . the masculine/feminine opposition is never attained' (Lacan, 1979: 192). Sexual desire cannot be mapped on-to pre-given gender positions. An example of an active verb in English is 'I decided'. The passive takes the form 'it was decided'. The reversal from active to passive may include the 'introduction of a new subject [*ein neues Subjekt*] to whom one displays oneself in order to be looked at by him'. In the middle, with the autoerotic, looking at the self may be taken as equivalent to the 'reflexive, middle voice', which exists in Greek, Latin (with deponent verbs), and in Romance languages and German, but not in English. In French, it is the reflexive, 'se' form. 'Je me lève' means 'I get myself up', referring to an action that takes place at the beginning of the day; but this is not an English construction. In French, it means that there is no need to make a single distinction between active and passive; the person is active and passive at the same time; the agency implied in any verb is not single.

This turning around of the drive suggests the dominance in the drive of both repetition (the drive does not work towards a linear goal) and ambivalence. Autoeroticism, which Freud links with narcissism (*SE* 14.134), makes the subject active and passive at the same time; it shows what is inherent in ambivalence, that the subject is split, its actions inherently double. Another reversal into the opposite state is the transformation of love into hate. Loving, it will be noted, Freud calls 'the relation of the ego to its sources of pleasure' (*SE* 14.135). He distinguishes three polarities:

- between the subject, the ego, and the object, the external world
- between pleasure and 'unpleasure'
- between active and passive.

The first governs the other two. Love has to do with a relation towards what from the outside world helps to build up what is called 'the extended ego', and it incorporates, or devours, the other's separate existence (*SE* 14.138) – a point important for mourning. Since it destroys the other in its love, Freud calls it ambivalent. Blake's poem 'The Clod and the Pebble', one of the *Songs of Experience*, expresses such ambivalence – love gives itself says the Clod of Clay, but for the Pebble, 'love seeketh only self to please, / To bind another to its delight' (Blake, 1982: 19). The oral stage of devouring is followed by 'an urge for mastery, to which injury or annihilation of the object is a matter of indifference'. At this stage, love is hardly distinguishable from hatred. It is not distinguished until the 'genital organisation' is 'established'; in other words, until genital sexuality appears. Hate, Freud says, 'derives from the narcissistic ego's primordial repudiation of the external world with its outpouring of stimuli', because of the unpleasure these yield (*SE* 14.139). For these reasons, Freud adds that love 'frequently manifests itself as "ambivalent", i.e. as accompanied by impulses of hatred against the same object' (*SE* 14.139). Such ambivalence indicates the subject's split nature: if the two affects are held together at the same time, and the love-relationship can reverse, transform itself, into hate, there is no continuity of being in the subject who has these affects.

Lacan stresses the non-biological nature of the drive, through its relation to the symbolic order. As such, it is a 'fiction' (Lacan, 1979: 163). What is sought is the *objet petit a*, which is unlocatable in any part of the body, being awakened as a desire by the symbolic order. The drive Lacan calls *la pulsion*; he puns with the phrase '*la pulsion en fait le tour*', which Sheridan annotates as 'the drive moves around the object' and 'the drive tricks the object' (Lacan, 1979: 168). The drive goes round, making a detour (a word evoked in Chapter 3), aiming for those areas of the body possessing a 'rim-like structure', that is, areas which are borders, and which have the potential in fantasy to cut off or to separate in a castrating mode (note how Lacan quotes Homer on 'the enclosure of the teeth', 1979: 169).

Lacan then calls the drive a 'montage', as spoken of in a surrealist montage; it goes for heterogeneous images, quite ununified; it is not united in aim: for example, the oral and the anal are not subordinated to a genital desire; all drives are 'partial', incomplete. He draws a model of how the drive moves through an erogenous rim, and 'returns' to it as its target and through it (Lacan, 1979: 178, compare 94). As he draws it, the drive goes through and back on itself as though it was trying to stop a gap, to fill a hole. It goes through three stages: active, then becoming self-reflexive, then passive; in its progress it has gone 'beyond the pleasure principle'. With the third stage emerges Freud's *ein neues Subjekt*; Lacan means that what is new is 'the appearance of a subject which is properly the other' (Lacan, 1979: 178). 'It is only with its appearance at the level of the other that what there is of the function of the drive may be realised' (Lacan, 1979: 178–9). The scopic drive's function – but Lacan mentions all four partial drives: oral, anal, scopic, and invocatory (see Lacan, 1979: 195–6) – is to make a 'vain detour' which will 'catch the *jouissance* of the other', which only happens when the other intervenes, in a way beyond the pleasure principle (Lacan, 1979: 183–4).

The object on which the drive closes as it turns itself inside out, like a needle threaded through a hole and returning through the same hole, an act which is, of course, pointless, 'is simply the presence of a hollow, a void, which can be occupied . . . by any object, and whose agency we know only in the form of the lost object, the *petit a*'. The object is not the origin of the oral drive, for instance, but introduced because 'no food will ever satisfy the oral drive, except by circumventing the eternally lacking object' (Lacan, 1979: 180). In the scopic drive, looking attempts to find the gaze, the object which 'completes' the subject. Lacan is giving another way of conceptualising the Imaginary, which is where the *objet petit a* is to be located. To speak about looking for the phallus is to work in the category of the Symbolic, but Lacan is interested in something much less definable. But there is no completeness to be found in the Other; rather, there is a blank, an absence which denies the subject completeness. Lacan's term for this is *aphanasis*, a term I will return to in Chapter 7. He says that 'when the subject appears somewhere as meaning [i.e. in the Symbolic order], he is manifested elsewhere as "fading", as disappearance' (Lacan, 1979: 218). He has become 'the subject for another signifier'. Being and having knowledge are irreconcilable.

The relationship between the Imaginary (the sphere of narcissism and of the mother) the Symbolic (linked to the father) and the Real, is crucial for Lacan. In Chapter 7, I will discuss the power of the Real in relationship to psychosis.

7

Freud, Lacan: hysteria, paranoia, psychosis

Dora

This chapter begins with three of Freud's 'case-histories': Dora, diagnosed as hysterical; Schreber, a paranoid schizophrenic, and the Wolf Man (a case of infantile neurosis), in order to approach Lacan on paranoia and psychosis. The 'Dora' case turned out negatively. For the other two, Lacan has been one of the most significant commentators.

The *Fragment of an Analysis of a Case of Hysteria* (*Bruchstück einer Hysterie-Analyse*) appeared in 1905, though much of it was written in January 1901, Freud calling it, initially, 'Dreams and Hysteria'. It can be seen as an appendix to *The Interpretation of Dreams*. No case more than this of Dora proves the feminist critique, that Freud gives a theory of male sexuality only. The problem is that psychoanalysis, as here a male discourse, pronounces on women (Frosh, 1999: 183–205). Both 'Irma', co-opted into Freud's self-analysis, and made to serve his reading of himself, and 'Dora' represent cases of the failure of the psychoanalytic method to reach, or help, these women. Freud would have agreed: there is the famous comment which Ernst Jones quotes him as making to Marie Bonaparte, 'The great question that has never been answered and which I have not yet been able to answer, despite my thirty years of research into the female soul is, "What does a woman want?" [*Was will das Weib*?]' (Jones, 1955b: 421).

Freud began work with Dora, an eighteen-year-old, in October 1900, and the analysis concluded on the last day of December. Ida Bauer, the real 'Dora' – the name suggests Dora Spenlow in *David Copperfield*, but Freud also notes, in *The Psychopathology of Everyday Life*, that it was the name he called Rosa, his servant (*SE* 6.241–2) – was born in Vienna in 1882. She had undergone neurotic symptoms in childhood. Her father, a manufacturer, who had taken his family to live outside Vienna, where they had formed a friendship with Herr K and his wife, first visited Freud, as a syphilis patient, in 1894. Ida Bauer, who was married, apparently unhappily, between 1903 and 1932, died in New York in 1945 (Bernheimer and Kahane, 1985: 33–4, Mitchell, 2000: 82–108).

No analysis Freud wrote reads more like a novel of the late nineteenth century, or as a *roman à clef* (*SE* 7.9), or else as modernist literature, if that is defined as, characteristically, the art of the fragment, rather than as literature which makes a claim, through its realism, towards giving a comprehensive sense of middle-class Viennese life. Calling it a 'fragment' includes Freud's knowledge not only of the incompleteness of the case but of the fragmentary nature of the information given to him by the patient, with its lapses of memory. By a strange parapraxis, Freud dated the analysis to 1899 (*SE* 7.13); it has been suggested that this was part of an anxiety that Dora might have read something of *The Interpretation of Dreams*, which had appeared at the end of 1899. Freud analyses Dora and comments on the father, but says nothing about the mother, save that she suffered from what he calls 'housewife's psychosis'. She spent the day cleaning the house in what Freud calls 'obsessional cleanliness' (*SE* 7.20). Yet Freud fails to connect this with the point that the woman had actually been infected by her husband (*SE* 7.75): it confirms a sense in the text that Freud is over-patriarchal, over-anxious, for example, to see Dora's desire as confirming aspects that would satisfy male phantasies; thinking that he had not noticed till too late the phenomenon of 'the transference'; i.e. that process by which Dora identified Freud with her father, so that unconscious feelings were revived, but not as belonging to the past, but in relation to the analyst in the present (*SE* 7.116–17). Such confidence shows itself in a belief that the 'hidden recesses of the mind' of the patient can be wholly read – 'he that has eyes to see and ears to hear may convince himself that no mortal can keep a secret. If his lips are silent, he chatters with his finger-tips; betrayal oozes out of him at every pore' (*SE* 7.77–8). To such confidence, which deconstruction calls 'phallogocentrism', Dora reacted by walking out, giving Freud a fortnight's notice of this, as if, Freud noted, he was being treated as a maidservant or a governess (*SE* 7.105): the point is made in a context that implied that Dora was acting as Herr K with a governess whom he fired.

Dora, her symptoms an insistent cough and aphonia (voicelessness), was brought, reluctantly, to see Freud on her father's authority. The precipitating issue was Dora's accusation that Herr K had made her a proposal while they were walking round the lake, which her father took to be a phantasy, and which Herr K denied. Dora begged her father to break off relations with Herr K and his wife, of whom she had been fond. It seems clear that there was some intimacy between Frau K and Dora's father, which Dora had known about from her governess, whom Dora could see was in love with her father, and who briefed both Dora and her mother against the father's relationship with Frau K (*SE* 7.36–8). Freud considers that the father's agenda in employing him was that he should talk Dora out of a belief that there was sexual intimacy between him and Frau K (*SE* 7.109). So Freud had the awareness that he was being 'used', which may construct something of the over-certainty of interpretation that exists in his reading of Dora.

Freud thinks, from the fluency of the narrative that Dora gives in reproaching her father, that Dora was in love with Herr K (*SE* 7.39). The passage generalises about a patient bringing forth 'a sound and incontestable train of argument', and saying that 'it soon becomes evident that the patient is using thoughts of this kind, which the analysis cannot attack [such as Dora's anger against her father] for the purpose of cloaking others which are anxious to escape from criticism and from consciousness' (*SE* 7.35). That is typical of Freud: he takes as problems what others regard as solutions. We can call his work ideology-critique, since it looks at the solutions that people use to deal with apparently insuperable problems, and shows that these solutions are the work of ideology, what people think they ought to think. Ideology includes, after all, those things which seem so natural that they 'go without saying': these answers, belonging to the sphere of bourgeois ideology, are the problem which psychoanalysis interrogates.

Dora says that Herr K had kissed her before, when she was fourteen. Her revulsion, hysteria, Freud regards as a 'reversal of affect' and a 'displacement of sensation' from pleasure in the genital area to horror expressed in the mouth, as by a nervous cough (*SE* 7.28). Dora's displeasure with her father is that she feels she has 'been handed over to Herr K as the price of his tolerating the relations between her father and his wife' (*SE* 7.34). Her explanation leads to Freud saying that the patient's narrative, in psychoanalysis, has a fluency which suggests there is a covering over of thoughts anxious to escape from criticism and consciousness. 'Reproaches against other people leads one to suspect the existence of a string of self-reproaches with the same content' (*SE* 7.35). Logical accusations are not accepted at face value; this is the section where he discusses the necessity of speaking frankly about sexual matters, though when he does so, it is via *J'appelle un chat un chat* (I call a cat a cat) (*SE* 7.49), which is both sexually provocative and at the same time going round the subject.

Freud considers Dora's blame of her father obsessive, and her relationship to him to have Oedipal resonances; when he mentions this, Dora's response, denying it for herself, but telling of a cousin's love for her own father, makes him think her unconscious is confirming what had been said, adding that 'there is no such things at all as an unconscious "no"' (*SE* 7.57). The statement is developed in the essay 'Negation' (1925), and we shall discuss it later in this chapter, but, if it is true, it makes clear that to deny an Oedipal attachment is not possible; it reveals a repression. The argument suggests that Dora was actually in love with Herr K, but then proposes a lesbian attachment to Frau K, and Freud here adds that he has never come through a single analysis of a man or a woman without having to take into account a very considerable current of homosexuality (*SE* 7.60). Freud considers that Dora was in love with Frau K and angry with her when she thought that, like the governess, Frau K was interested in her only on account of the father. Freud thus concludes that Dora's anger with the father suppressed her love for Herr K, 'which had once been conscious', but also make her, conceal her love for Frau K 'which was in a deeper sense unconscious'. 'She grudged her father Frau K's love, and had not forgiven the woman she loved for the disillusionment she had been caused by her betrayal' (*SE* 7.63); hence her feelings were jealous; here Freud thinks of the jealousy as being masculine-like on Dora's part, so missing a point: the suggestion that Dora had lesbian feelings towards Frau K makes the phallocentric reading which he gives to her dreams, prioritising the woman's feelings towards the man, irrelevant. It does not relate to her desire, misreads the dreams. The technique which allows Freud to detect feminine desire disables him from reading its importance.

Lacan's comments on Dora, which see her identifying with her father, and so with Herr K's wife, and understanding that she had been handed over to Herr K as the price for tolerating the father and Herr K's wife together, treat her hysteria as asking a question in her dreams, which Lacan sees as reacting to insertion in the symbolic order: 'Am I a man or a woman?' For Dora, the question is, 'What is it like to be a woman?' and 'What is it to be a woman?', and specifically, 'What is a feminine organ?' (Lacan, 1993: 171–2). The fourth question is posed because, unlike the phallus, 'there is no symbolisation of woman's sex as such' (Lacan, 1993: 176). Feminine sexuality is not represented in language, in so far as this is patriarchally constructed. The question 'What is a woman?' attempts to symbolise the female organ. And Lacan says that 'the symbolic provides a form into which the subject is inserted at the level of his being. It's on the basis of the signifier that the subject recognises himself as being this or that' (Lacan, 1993: 178, 179).

Schreber

Chapter 6 examined Lacan on paranoia in relation to the imaginary and paranoid knowledge. Paranoia is the subject of *Psychoanalytic Notes on an Autobiographical Case of Paranoia (Dementia Paranoides)* (1911), Freud's 'attempt at an interpretation' of the *Memoirs* of Daniel Paul Schreber: *Denkwürdigkeiten eines Nervenkranken* (1903; literally, *Great Thoughts of a Nervous Patient*). Schreber (1842–1911), a judge in Dresden, and a man of 'strict morals', was born in Leipzig; his father, on whom Freud comments, was Dr Daniel Gottlob Moritz Schreber, a specialist in child care, and in indoor gymnastics, and machines to train youth, physically and mentally. According to Niederland, he acted as an impediment to Schreber being able to assume what he calls 'an active masculine role' (Niederland, 1974: 41).

Schreber married in 1878, a year after the suicide of his brother, and eight years after that of his father; his marriage 'marred only from time to time by the repeated disappointment of our hope of being blessed with children' (Schreber, 1955: 63: alluding to his wife's miscarriages). Schreber spent time in Sonnenstein Asylum near Dresden, and in 1884–85 in Leipzig Psychiatric Clinic, where the director was Professor Paul Flechsig (1847–1929), who cured him of what he called 'hypochondriacal ideas'. If he felt grateful to Flechsig, he writes, 'my wife felt even more sincere gratitude and worshipped Dr Flechsig as the man who had restored her husband to her; for this reason she kept his picture on her desk for many years' (Schreber, 1955: 63). One noteworthy point about Flechsig is that he was one of the first who rejected the view that mental illness had anything to do with the soul; for him, there was an organic basis to mental illness (Lothane, 1992: 212–13).

From a lower judicial appointment, Schreber was promoted to Senatspräsident (i.e. as a district judge) in Dresden in June 1893, but before taking up office in October, and as if as a response to his ennobling, he dreamed that his previous nervous disorder had returned, and had ideas between sleep and waking 'that after all it really must be very nice to be a woman submitting to the act of copulation'. He adds: 'the idea was so foreign to my whole nature that I may say I would have rejected it with indignation if fully awake; from what I have experienced since I cannot exclude the possibility that some external influences were at work to implant this idea in me' (Schreber, 1955: 63). This suggests paranoia, and we perhaps should consider the implicit attitude to male and female sexuality in the word 'submit'. After a second illness that October, he was rehospitalised, transferred to Lindenhof Asylum, and back to Sonnenstein. His *Memoirs* were written to take action for his discharge, in 1902, but he returned, after 1907, dying in the Leipzig-Dösen Asylum.

Freud makes Schreber an instance of paranoia, using for evidence, virtually, only the *Memoirs*, which he reads as a text. He examines his hypochondria, and feelings of being persecuted by certain people including Flechsig, the 'soul-murderer', and his delusional ideas, including believing that he had direct contact with God. The summary that the Court Judgement of 1902 gave of his case was: 'he believed that he had a mission to redeem the world and restore it to its lost state of bliss. This, however, he could only bring about if he were first transformed from a man into a woman' (*SE* 12.16). Freud regards the becoming woman – which he equates with emasculation – as Schreber's primary delusion, and the basis for persecution emanating from the 'rays of God', which Schreber equated with voices which he heard, which talked the 'basic language'. Freud considers Schreber's attitude to God, who was to make him a woman, making him undergo 'voluptuous excesses', as a mixture of reverence and rebelliousness (*SE* 12.29). He spoke of 'miracled' or 'talking birds', threatening him in meaningless phrases, which Freud speculates must be phantasies of young women (*SE* 12.36). Freud analyses the relationship with Flechsig – who had acted as Schreber's doctor in a first period of nervous disorder, spoken of as hypochondria – as one where Schreber phantasised homosexual rape. Indeed Freud speculates that the basis of Schreber's illness was homosexual desire, which he could not endorse in himself; this, directed to Flechsig, meant that God had to replace the latter: making the emasculation 'consonant with the Order of Things'. So 'his ego found compensation in megalomania, while his feminine wishful phantasy made its way through and became acceptable' (*SE* 12.48).

The imaginary persecutor divides into Flechsig and God; while Flechsig divides up into forty to sixty divisions, God divides into the 'lower' and 'upper' God. 'A process of decomposition of this kind is very characteristic of paranoia. Paranoia decomposes just as hysteria condenses. Or rather, paranoia resolves once more into their elements the products of the condensations and identifications which are effected in the unconscious' (*SE* 12.49). Freud intuits from this a dual sexual desire in Schreber in relation to his elder brother and his father, and thinks of desire as directed towards the father, who is also symbolised in the sun.

Freud's third section in his analysis, 'On the Mechanism of Paranoia', considers the part played by a homosexual wish in the development of paranoia. Freud runs through material from his *Three Essays on the Theory of Sexuality* (1905) to discuss the movement from autoeroticism and narcissism to an 'anaclitic' (i.e. heterosexual) object-choice. Evidently, he considers these stages to include homosexual feelings, which, with heterosexual object-choice, are deflected from their sexual aim, and give 'an erotic factor to friendship and comradeship'. Freud discusses the possibility of 'fixation' at any of these stages, thinking it entirely possible that some crisis in life, which he calls 'frustration' – he amplifies this in 'Types of an Onset of Neurosis' (*SE* 12.231–8) – may lead to a reversal, to an earlier object-choice. And such a crisis Schreber faced. At this stage, Freud mentions schizophrenia, (*SE* 12.62), a term which was then new, and coined by the Zürich-based Eugen Bleuler (1857–1939), revising the term used by Emil Kraepelin (1856–1928), who had studied with Paul Flechsig at Liepzig. Kraepelin, in 1892, had called psychosis *dementia praecox*.

The writer Louis Sass considers Schreber's state to be marked by delusions, accompanied by a mood where 'the perceptual world seems to have undergone some subtle but all-encompassing change: unfamiliar events and objects may seem like copies or repetitions of themselves; perceptual phenomena may seem tremendously specific and deeply meaningful, but without the patient being able to explain why' (Sass, 1994: 5). He compares the paintings of Giorgio de Chirico (1888–1978), 'shadowless cityscapes of infinite precision and uncanny meaningfulness with names like "The Enigma of the Day" and "The Mystery and Melancholy of a Street"'. De Chirico paints alienation and melancholia and indifference, what Maurice Blanchot calls 'the madness of the day': the title of one of his *récits* (Blanchot, 1999: 189–99). Schizophrenia is a term applicable to the twentieth century and to modernism, rather than to the nineteenth century, though in the last chapter I argued that it may be even more relevant to think of the twentieth century in relation to trauma.

Paranoia takes the form of contradicting the culturally inadmissible statement '*I* (a man) *love him* (a man)', through such statements, which include those of erotomania, as:

I do not *love* him, I *hate* him
I do not *love* him – I *hate* him because HE PERSECUTES ME
I do not love *him*, I love *her*
I do not love *him* – I love *her* because SHE LOVES ME
It is not *I* who love the man – *she* loves him
I do not love at all – I do not love any one – the equivalent of 'I love only myself'

Freud shows a process of denial taking paranoid form, involving changes of the verb and of the object of the sentence, and even change of the subject (not I – *she* loves). Undeclared love becomes a delusion of being persecuted. An erotomania – Lacan's subject – takes over, which involves exaggerating the sense of one's own desirability as a heterosexual love-object. Delusional jealousy enters in with the 'she loves him' phase. Finally there is megalomania, the strongest form of paranoia, which produces the solipsism of 'I am myself alone', which Richard of Gloucester, on his way to becoming Richard III, announces at the end of *3 Henry VI* (5.6.83). Equally sinister is Iago's 'I am not what I am' (*Othello* 1.1.65). The second of Freud's imagined statements, whereby the other is hated because 'he hates me', is an instance of *projection*, where 'an internal perception is suppressed, and, instead, its content, after undergoing a certain kind of distortion, enters consciousness in the form of an external perception' (*SE* 12.63). So projection is 'when we refer the causes of certain sensations to the external world, instead of looking for them (as we do in the case of others) inside ourselves' (*SE* 12.66). Freud also discusses repression in paranoia, which operates differently from projection, since it involves, first, fixation, where one instinct has been left behind others, and exists at a more infantile stage (*SE* 12.67). The instinct lagging behind is repressed by the ego, but this produces only 'the failure of repression', 'irruption', 'the return of the repressed'. What returns, of a fixated instinct, comes back as a symptom (*SE* 12.68).

Freud also notes Schreber's belief in the imminence of world catastrophe. If for Schreber, other people were 'cursorily improvised men' (*SE* 12.68), because his paranoia or megalomania had withdrawn from all investment in other people, then Freud concludes that 'the delusional formation . . . is in reality an attempt at recovery, a process of reconstruction' of the outer world (*SE* 12.71). Repression detaches the libido (desire) from people, but the process of 'recovery', which is the return of the repressed, brings the outside world back again in hostile form. So 'what was abolished internally returns [as the repressed returns] from without' (*SE* 12.71). The paranoid person has projected so much on to the other, and this makes its return.

Madness and literature

Schreber's *Memoirs* have been examined repeatedly, both corroborating what Freud said about Schreber's father (Niederland, Schatzman) and questioning Schreber's psychosis in relation to his contemporary Germany, whether arguing, like Elias Canetti, that Schreber exemplifies a tendency towards fascism, Canetti paralleling his desire for sole survivorship with the attitudes of Hitler, or whether he was a 'paranoid, molar' type, centralising all power to himself (Canetti, 1973: 505–37, Deleuze and Guattari, 1988: 279, 364). Or was his madness, emerging *before* he could take up the offices he was given, as Eric Santner (1996) contends, a way of resisting the totalitarian temptation? Santner makes comparisons with Kafka, as another figure oppressed by fascist culture, and equally a figure in flight. Michel de Certeau, relating Schreber's text to mysticism, draws attention to the way that he was degraded in the language which addressed him (De Certeau, 1986: 35–46). Deleuze, too, allows for the thought that Schreber's movement is towards 'becoming woman', which cannot be seen negatively (Flieger, 2000: 38–63).

Also interesting is Louis Sass, arguing that madness (schizophrenia) is a condition which increases during the time of modernism. Sass sees Schreber internalising, from his father's control, a sense of being under surveillance, comparable to Foucault's account of the Panopticon, where 'the individual feels constantly exposed to an external, normalising gaze, thus subjecting him or her to the dictates of an authority that must ultimately be internalised'. The internalised surveillance 'eradicates spontaneity, increases the sense of isolation and inwardness, and instills a relentlessly self-monitoring mode of consciousness' (Sass, 1992; 1994: 157–8, Foucault, 1977a: 170–228). Sass opens up Freud's sense of the superego as an internal structure to show it as having a social existence, and source: we have already commented on this through Derrida (see Chapter 3). Derrida situates the causes and effects of neurosis and psychosis not in the subject as source, but as an effect of disciplinary procedures, which construct madness, and a carceral mode of existence, and in this he follows Foucault. This argument may be compared with the psychoanalyst Victor Tausk (1879–1919), writing on the 'influencing machine' (1919), where schizophrenics feel they are under the power of an apparatus which makes them see pictures, projects their feelings on to the wall, and produces motor phenomena in the body. Tausk reads that as the ego splitting off its sexual being, and projecting it as a machine, which then influences the subject. The 'apparatus' is thus phallic, and controlling, and film theory has linked it to the creation of the cinematic apparatus, which is thus narcissistic, projecting sexuality on to the subject (Tausk, 1950, Copjec, 1982).

The difference between Freud and Foucault becomes key to reading modern literature. It seems that madness becomes not a danger for the writer but a condition that attends writing, as though writing had become madness, a marker of alienation. Foucault defines madness as '*the absence of an oeuvre*' (a work); in other words, as the indication that the person has no share in the productive economy, but is functionless; Maurice Blanchot sees that as the effect of writing itself (Foucault, 2006: xxxi, Blanchot, 1982: 13, 23); it takes away the subject's autonomy, or sense of having the power to create a text; it creates *désoeuvrement*, 'worklessness'. The danger of psychoanalysis, as of any interpretative tool, is that it claims to give the truth about the subject, as has been shown in the analysis of James's *The Turn of the Screw* already mentioned, where the governess may be hysterical, as Edmund Wilson thought, or may be seeing ghosts, where the ghosts may be destructive or not (Felman, 1982: 94–207). Claiming the ability to interpret risks paranoia. But a distinction of psychoanalysis is that it does not demonise those it writes of, and becomes a condition in which madness, as a perhaps new phenomenon, can be thought about, not reductively, or in a mode which thinks it knows more than the patient, but giving possible ways of thinking in order to give to the patient different ways of interpreting. This appears in the next case-history: the 'Wolf Man'.

The 'Wolf Man'

'From the History of an Infantile Neurosis' (1918) as a title suggests that the text shows a literary, which is also an interpretative, arrangement, of a case-study. Certainly, there is a history here, which goes beyond Freud's writing, spanning much of the twentieth century (Brooks, 1984: 264–85). The 'Wolf Man', Sergei Pankeev (1887–1979) was born on Christmas Day on his father's estate on the Dnieper river in Russia. He went to Odessa University in 1905; at that time, his sister Anna committed suicide, and he describes how, in the aftermath of that, he made a journey to the Caucasus, in an apparent identification with Lermontov, the author of *A Hero of Our Time* (1840). At the same time his health broke down, apparently after a gonorrhoeal infection. Freud writes that he had attempted an 'intimate physical approach' towards his sister in puberty, and she had rejected him, and he had turned to servant girls as substitutes for the sister, and as subtle forms of, in fantasy, debasing his sister (*SE* 17.22).

Pankeev travelled to St Petersburg, and to Bavaria, meeting psychiatrists such as Emil Kraepelin (Munich, 1908) who diagnosed him as manic-depressive, as he had, apparently, also diagnosed the Wolf Man's father, who died, apparently by suicide, in 1908. At the same time, the Wolf Man met Therese, who was divorced, and had a four-year-old daughter, who was to die from tuberculosis (1919); he married Therese in 1914: being Jewish, she had everything to fear from the *Anschluss* of 1938, when Germany occupied Austria, and she killed herself that year.

Incapacitated, unable even to dress himself, the Wolf Man came for treatment by Freud in January 1910. The case was concluded in 1914; Freud published it in 1918. Pankeev returned for treatment in September 1919, and again in 1926, when Freud assigned him to his pupil, the American-born German-Jewish Ruth Brunswick (1897–1946); this lasted five months, and she wrote up the case, as one of paranoia (Gardiner, 1973: 286–331). He then became acquainted with the American psychoanalyst Muriel Gardiner (1901–95), who was living in Vienna; she remained in contact after she returned to America in 1938, hearing of the privations and hunger in which he and his mother, who died in 1953, had endured in and after the Second World War. He remained in Vienna; Gardiner adds that he was convinced 'that without psychoanalysis he would have been condemned to lifelong misery' (Gardiner, 1973: 9).

Freud sets out a chronology of the events of the Wolf Man's childhood, including an interpretation of events which the Wolf Man never verified: that at the age of one and a half, he either witnessed his parents copulating or had a phantasy of this. At the age of two and a half, there was a scene with Grusha, a nursery-maid, of whom he was fond, whose name ('pear') gave him an association of a big pear with yellow stripes on its skin; Freud thinks that in watching her scrub the floor, 'he had micturated in the room, and she had rejoined, no doubt jokingly, with a threat of castration' (*SE* 17.92). Freud associates her with a fear of a butterfly with yellow stripes, which terrified him when it lighted on a flower: 'it had given him an uncanny feeling. It had looked, so he said, like a woman opening her legs' (*SE* 17.90). Freud thinks of the butterfly as a 'screen memory' behind which was the other fear, of the woman. At the same time, there was another screen memory: 'he saw himself with his nurse looking after the carriage which was driving off with his father, mother and sister, and then going peaceably back into the house' (*SE* 17.14). Freud writes that 'this showed him alone with his Nanya [the older peasant woman who came to look after him] and so disowned Grusha and his sister' (*SE* 17.121). Before the age of three and a half, he heard his mother complaining to the doctor, saying 'I cannot go on living like this' (*SE* 17.77). At the same time as this, Freud notes that the Wolf Man was initiated into sexual matters by his sister, in a quasi-seduction, and Freud also dated to this time his sexual flirtations with his Nanya, which produced from her the threat of castration (*SE* 17.20–1, 24). At this time, an English governess was engaged for the children (*SE* 17.14–15).

Freud dates to the Christmas marking his fourth birthday the dream which gives the clue to his analysis. This was of the bedroom window opening of its own accord and revealing six or seven white wolves sitting on the walnut tree in front of the window. (The drawing the Wolf Man produced, and which Freud reproduced (*SE* 17.30), shows five wolves.) Freud argues that the dream's 'manifest content', where the Wolf Man stressed the attentive looking of the wolves, and their motionlessness, implies that behind the dream was another 'unknown scene', now distorted, 'even distorted into its opposite' (*SE* 17.34). This, and the prominent tails of the wolves, which produced from Pankeev the story of the tailor pulling off a wolf's tail, and then, in a further development, climbing into a tree to escape the wolves who could not climb it, suggests to Freud a castration anxiety. And that is supplemented by folk tales: of the wolf which ate up the seven little goats, and the Wolf with Red Riding Hood, both of which are fantasies of the older eating the younger, and which suggest to Freud, in his first paper on the subject, 'The Occurrence in Dreams of Material from Fairy Tales' (1913), the idea of Kronos eating his sons (*SE* 12.287). These wolf fears make him reverse the situation: the attentive looking was the boy's, so that the distortion was 'an interchange of subject and object, of activity and passivity, being looked at instead of looking', and 'rest instead of motion'.

Digression: ambivalence, and the double

These reversals are basic to much in Freud, and to literary interpretation. They apply to his dream interpretation, which works by seeing images in dreams as constantly displacing themselves, in a process of metonymy. Second, they apply to a paper 'The Antithetical Meaning of Primal Words' (1910, *SE* 11.153–61), which extends the arguments of the philologist Karl Abel whose essay of 1884 considered Egyptian hieroglyphics to show that the Egyptians had a large number of words denoting at once a thing and its opposite. Freud begins by quoting from *The Interpretation of Dreams* chapter 6:

> The way in which dreams treat the category of contraries and contradictories is highly remarkable. It is simply disregarded. 'No' seems not to exist as far as dreams are concerned. They show a particular preference for combining contraries into a unity or for representing them as one and the same thing. Dreams feel themselves at liberty, moreover, to represent any element by its wishful contrary; so that there is no way of deciding at a first glance whether any element that admits of a contrary is present in the dream-thoughts as a positive or as a negative. (*SE* 4.318)

The point recalls Saussure's sense that, in language, 'there are only differences *without positive terms*' (Saussure, 1974: 120). Each term is haunted by another term: to say 'I am a woman' means that 'I am a man' unconsciously haunts the statement. If so, the process of saying 'No, I am not a man' becomes a repression of the possibility that haunts the statement. The dream reveals this, as does language. 'To let' means 'to allow', but it also means 'to prevent', as in the old legal phrase 'without let or hindrance'.

But the essay which is the most obvious for the strange effect of something being what it is and the opposite is 'The Uncanny' – *Das Unheimliche* (1919), which shows that the *unheimlich*, the unfamiliar ('the unhomely') is also *heimlich* (*SE* 17.224–6). *Heimlich* means 'familiar', but, as in English, 'familiar' means 'well known', and implies domestic security, but a 'familiar' is also a ghost, and so something strange, secret, daemonic, so *heimlich* also means its opposite; *das Unheimliche*. Freud quotes the definition of the philosopher Friedrich Schelling (1775–1854): 'everything is *unheimlich* that ought to have remained secret and hidden, but has come to light' (*SE* 17.225). This includes, then, whatever has been repressed. The essay gives a reading of E.T.A. Hoffmann (1776–1822), the German novelist whose work turns so much on the literary figure of the double, on 'characters who are to be considered identical because they look alike'. Hoffmann's fictions turn upon strange repetitions, and makes Freud discuss repetition, arguing:

> the 'double' was originally an insurance against the destruction of the ego, an 'energetic denial of the power of death', as [Otto] Rank says . . . this invention of doubling as a preservative against extinction has its counterpart in the language of dreams, which is fond of representing castration by a doubling, or multiplication of a genital symbol . . . from having been an assurance of immortality, it becomes the uncanny harbinger of death. (*SE* 17.235)

In this reversal, the double, which should seem to guarantee the absoluteness and singleness of the ego, does the opposite: it produces, like repetition, an opposite sense; that there is no single ego, no original: it pronounces death. So it relates to the castration anxieties, related to the fear of the loss of the eyes, which run through Hoffmann's *The Sandman*. Repetition, which threatens because it suggests that life is dominated by the machinic, is uncanny; it contains something in it which is different, which pulls out of any experience something other, double, ambivalent, reversing all senses, and a prompting towards death (Royle, 2003, Cixous, 1976: 525–48).

One further instance of reversal comes from the book published as *Group Psychology and the Analysis of the Ego* (1921), when Freud is discussing the 'herd instinct' and noting the demand for justice as equal treatment for all. Freud argues that a competitive and envious desire to want everything has to be replaced by a group spirit:

> Social justice demands that we deny ourselves many things so that others may have to do without them as well, or, what is the same thing, may not be able to ask for them. This demand for equality is the root of social conscience and the sense of duty. It reveals itself unexpectedly in the syphilitic's dread of infecting other people, which psychoanalysis has taught us to understand. The dread exhibited by these poor wretches corresponds to their violent struggles against the unconscious wish to spread their infection on to other people; for why should they alone be infected and cut off from so much? why not other people as well? And the same germ is to be found in the apt story of the judgement of Solomon [see I Kings 3.16–28]. If one woman's child is dead, the other shall not have a live one either. The bereaved woman is recognised by this wish.
>
> Thus social feeling is based upon the reversal of what was first a hostile feeling into a positively-toned tie in the nature of an identification . . . this reversal seems to occur under the influence of a common affectionate tie with a person outside the group [i.e. a leader, with whom all in the group can identify]. (*SE* 18.121)

The argument is that an earlier envy, which is also an anger, has to reverse into its opposite: into a drive towards asserting a will to justice for all. The basis of justice, is, therefore, envy, or what Nietzsche's *The Genealogy of Morals* calls *ressentiment* (Nietzsche, 1996: 22); here, Freud's analysis comes close to Nietzsche's sense of morality and social justice as the lowest common denominator which is produced by 'preachers of equality' whose anger, and desire for revenge is because they feel they have suffered a personal slight (Nietzsche, 2005: 86). The difference in Freud is that a reversal has happened, as it has not, quite, in Nietzsche: the feeling does not recognise its earlier envy, in its apparent drive towards justice (Forrester, 1997: 13–43).

Nachträglichkeit

Freud's interpretation of the Wolf Man's dream makes it, in his 'unconscious memory traces', a version of witnessing copulation between his parents, where the mother was taken from behind (*a tergo*). Freud takes the woman's sexual position as revealing, magnified in fantasy, the castration threat, and he says the episode received a 'deferred revision' in the dream, a point repeated in the footnote (*SE* 17.38). Freud calls the copulation the 'primal scene' (*Urszene*) (*SE* 17.39). Freud gives an analysis of the whole dream, including the point that the high tree is 'a symbol of observing, of scopophilia' (*SE* 17.43), but, to summarise:

> The steps in the transformation of the material, 'primal scene – wolf story – fairy tale of "The Seven Little Goats"' are a reflection of the progress of the dreamer's thoughts during the construction of the dream: 'longing for sexual satisfaction from his father – realization that castration is a necessary condition of it – fear of his father'. (*SE* 17.42)

The ambivalence of response to the father will be noted (compare *SE* 17.65 and 118). For Freud, the effects of the scene were 'deferred' (*SE* 17.44, see also 17.47, 58, 109), so that the case history illuminates '*Nachträglichkeit*', the idea that the effects of an event, possibly a traumatic one, are not felt at the time, but have an afterlife. The actual 'primal scene' may be beyond recall: the Wolf Man never confirmed the memory, which remained, therefore, a 'construction' on Freud's part, never a recollection (*SE* 17.50–1; see 48–60 generally). Freud is aware that what he writes is speculation; not science, but fiction: creating a past for the Wolf Man. The question of the beginning, of what the primal scene is, becomes something unknowable: this has profound implications for fiction, which is always concerned with what it is that opens a narrative, or makes it possible to launch a series of events.

Since Freud speculated that the primal scene might have been a phantasy of the Wolf Man's, it becomes a question whether there was any 'primal scene'. Here the Wolf Man could not help, for, though he never accepted that he had witnessed the primal scene, the nature of repression would make him an unreliable witness to his defence that he had not. But equally, if the 'primal scene' is echoed in later events, it seems that these are not new, part of a series, but part of a repetition of the primal scene, an event not known, but to be constructed from its symptomatic reappearance at later moments in life. And the primal scene in the life of the boy is already a repetition from the parents; behind the primal scene is an earlier one, which would be the substance of an impossible knowledge: the scene of the boy's own conception.

Three points supplement this analysis. The boy's relation to his father is homosexual, but coded less in male/female terms than in the distinction between active and passive, which is also seen as male/female. Hence the desire to take a feminine role in relation to the father was repressed and replaced by fear of the wolf (*SE* 17.46–7). Freud thinks of a feminine attitude towards men being repressed systematically, and producing as a symptom, in the Wolf Man, intestinal pains (*SE* 17.80). This leads to another point, which is the next stage in the narrative of what happened to the child. He turned towards religion, but set his face against the feature of suffering in the figure of Christ, and then turned his critical dissatisfaction on to God the Father (*SE* 17.62). He also tormented small animals. 'In his sadism he maintained his ancient identification with his father; but in his masochism he chose him as a sexual object' (17.63). Freud considers this as the beginning of 'obsessional neurosis'. The ambivalence towards the father must be remembered.

This relates to a second point: he identifies with his mother and fears the abdominal pains which he thinks she suffers and which he also has. This, Freud says, was his 'repudiation of being identified with her in this sexual scene – the same repudiation with which he awoke from the dream' (*SE* 17.78). 'Repudiation' (*Verwerfung*) reappears in the following paragraphs, first saying that he repudiated the idea of what sexual intercourse involved: i.e. the vagina, which, of course, he did not possess. Freud sees an absolute contradiction in the way the Wolf Man could live having both a fear of castration and an identification with women 'by means of the bowel', i.e. through anal intercourse. Freud thinks this contradiction is characteristic of how the unconscious works, and adds, 'A repression [*Eine Verdrängung*] is something very different from a repudiation [*eine Verwerfung*]' (*SE* 17.80, translation modified).

Repression, disavowal, negation, foreclosure

We must continue with *Verwerfung*. Freud speaks of the attitude the patient took to the problem of castration, and said he rejected (*verwarf*) it and held to his theory of intercourse by the anus. Freud adds that, when he speaks of him having *rejected* it, it was as if it did not exist for him. But at the same time, the Wolf Man recognised castration as a fact. So, says Freud, summarising, with a sense of the difficulty of 'feeling his way' into his mental processes, 'first he resisted and then he yielded, but the second reaction did not do away with the first. In the end there were to be found in him two contrary currents side by side, one of which abominated the idea of castration, while the other was prepared to accept it and console itself with femininity.' But Freud says that beyond this was a third 'current', *Verwerfung*, repudiation, which did not as yet even raise the question of the reality of castration' (*SE* 17.84–5: *Verwerfung* is omitted in the English translation, see Laplanche and Pontalis, 1973: 166). Here, Freud reports a hallucination the Wolf Man had, aged five, of cutting with his penknife into the bark of one of the walnut trees. 'Suddenly, to my unspeakable terror, I noticed that

I had cut through the little finger' of the hand. He did not speak to his nurse, but sat down, and then saw the finger was uninjured (*SE* 17.85). Freud identifies this with a castration anxiety, but, significantly, the boy does not think castration has taken place.

Hence the Wolf Man never accepts the reality of castration, which means that he can both be feminine in relation to the father, and, as with his reaction to God, deny his authority. The absence of speech when the Wolf Man hallucinates cutting off his finger is interpreted by Lacan as a psychotic episode. When castration is not symbolised within the Symbolic order, its non-existence there means that it returns within 'the Real', the domain outside symbolisation, and associated with trauma. We shall examine this in more detail below.

Freud, then, considers the Wolf Man as wavering between activity and passivity, and breaking down after an organic infection had shattered his narcissism, and his sense of being favoured by destiny (*SE* 17.118), something Freud relates to the point that the Wolf Man had been born with a caul, a *Glückshaube*, a 'lucky hood', like a magic protection (*SE* 17.99) – like Dickens's David Copperfield, who feels similarly privileged, and thinks that he cannot drown.

Doubtless a crisis of relationship with the father is at the heart of this case-history. Freud insisted on the infantile sources of the neurosis, and attacks Jung and Adler for disputing the primacy of infantile sexuality, and the Oedipal struggle. An approach to the Wolf Man, and Freud's analysis, comes from Nicolas Abraham and Maria Torok, whom we mentioned in Chapter 5. Their form of psychoanalysis, called 'cryptonymy', is discussed by Jacques Derrida in the Preface: '*Fors*: The Anglish Words of Nicolas Abraham and Maria Torok'. ('Fors' from the Latin *foris*, *foras*, means 'outside' (compare 'foreign'), and is the same as the French 'hors'.) Abraham and Torok consider the meaning of a Russian being analysed in German: the possibility of thinking across different languages further complicating the idea of an 'origin' through the point that the German of the Wolf Man is also not his 'origin'. 'Cryptonymy' as a word combines ideas of the crypt (a place for hiding: language as preserving secrets) and metonymy. Derrida, discussing it, puns, and plays with the antithetical meaning of primal words. Thus, he says, '*for*' implies an interior, 'the innermost heart' is '*le for intérieur*', and an exterior. Repression takes place inside language, which acts as a crypt concealing repressed material, but the material which has been incorporated within the body is already subject to endless displacements inside language. It is impossible here to distinguish an inside and outside of what the self knows and what it has repressed: as Derrida puts it, 'a certain foreign body is here working over our household words' (Abraham and Torok, 1986: xxv). In the same way, Lacan refers to 'intimate exteriority', which he calls 'extimacy' (Lacan, 1992: 139), showing how psychoanalysis makes problematic inside/outside distinctions: the unconscious is extimate, within the subject, but constituting the subject without.

Derrida makes the 'crypt' the foreign body which is included through incorporation in the self, and which is a 'foreigner in the Self, and especially of the heterocryptic ghost that *returns* from the Unconscious of the other, according to what might be called the law of *another generation*' (Abraham and Torok, 1986: xxxi). To unpack this sentence: Abraham and Torok consider that inside the wolf dream there is a memory of the father raping the daughter. They interpret this through attention to the displacements of language that go through several languages (Abraham and Torok, 1986: 67–71). The traumatic memory carries through from a sense of the father's open fly, to the importance of the letter V, suggested in, for example, the pricked-up ears of the wolves, the number 5 (V in Latin), the jaws of the wolf, the first letter of 'wolf', the open window in the dream, the stories his sister told him about Nanya holding the gardener upside-down in order to play with him sexually (*SE* 17.20), the wings of the butterfly, and the idea of the woman's legs being open in the shape of a Roman V, and even the point that from the age of ten onwards the Wolf Man would fall into a depressed state at around five in the afternoon (*SE* 17.37). It should be noted that Freud discusses much of this material (*SE* 17.89–91), even referring to the Wolf Man's suspicions of his father's relations with his sister (*SE* 17.83). The interpretation by Abraham and Torok, which implies that the Wolf Man identified with the sister and told what he had seen to the English governess who 'turned his idea of pleasure into sin, his father into a criminal, and himself, the little Sergei into a court of law raised above his father' could only mean one thing. 'From then on, this pleasure, jealously kept in his innermost safe, could only be the subject of total repudiation' (Abraham and Torok, 1986: 76).

Surrealism and literature

What Lacan says on *Verwerfung* is inseparable from his discussion of paranoia, in which Freud was 'initially and essentially interested' (Lacan, 1993: 4). Lacan on paranoia suggests interest in madness. Freud engaged with that in the Schreber case, but not otherwise: his topic is neurosis. Unlike the psychotic, the neurotic knows that he or she is ill, as inside the symbolic order.

Lacan, from the time of his doctorate, was fascinated by paranoid psychosis, being partly influenced by Gaëtan Gatian de Clérambault (1872–1934), working on erotomania. Part of Lacan's thesis studied a woman he called Aimée, who had tried to stab an actress, Huguette Duflos, in 1930 (Roudinesco, 1994: 32–51; Dean, 1992: 42–7): analysis suggested that Aimée had thought that the actress was secretly in love with her (erotomania) and had attacked her when she felt this was not the case: attacking that which threatened her narcissistic sense of herself, that she was completed by the woman who loved her. 'Erotomania' comes from Esquirol (1772–1840), follower of the French psychiatrist Pinel (1745–1824), in his *Traité des maladies mentales* (1837). Also fundamental to Lacan was the case of the Papin sisters, who were later the theme of Genet's play *The Maids* (1947). In 1933, Christine and Léa Papin had, simultaneously, as under the power of a collective desire, risen up and killed their two employers, mother and daughter, morcellating the bodies, like the *sparagmos*, tearing a body to pieces, in Greek tragedy. Again, the case seemed to be that of two people murdering the basis of what gave them identity (Roudinesco, 1994: 61–5). An article by Lacan on the Papin sisters appeared first in the journal *Minotaure*, a Paris-based surrealist journal (1933–39): here Lacan gave an abbreviated account of his thesis.

Lacan's interests articulated with the surrealists' fascination with the female criminal (someone doubly transgressive), and with hysteria (Foster, 1993: 46–54), as with the case of Violette Nozière, a woman who attempted to murder her parents in 1934. It was turned into a film by Claude Chabrol starrring Isabelle Huppert, in 1978. With the Papin sisters, a quotation from the older, Christine, in prison applies: 'I really do think that in a different life I should have been my sister's husband' (quoted by Macey, 1988: 71). Freud's connections between homosexuality (lesbianism) and paranoia reappear (it was also relevant for Aimée); equally, the impulse towards crime obeys what was discussed in Chapter 4: crime is sought out of a desire for punishment: but Lacan supplements this, calling this desire for crime 'self-punishing paranoia' (Lacan, 2006: 138). Paranoid psychosis is seen as awareness of a 'gap' in the essence of the self (Lacan, 2006: 144), which comes from awareness of the distance between the self that identifies with the image in the mirror, and that image. The relationship between the mirror stage and paranoia will be recalled.

Lacan met Salvador Dalí (1904–89) in 1930 (Dalí met Freud in 1938); and knew the surrealists, including, as already seen, Breton (Dean, 1992, Iversen, 2007: 39–71). Surrealism attempted to paint the 'primary process', to render socially repressed desire, using 'automatism', a passive opening up to irrational images. Dalí's 'paranoiac-critical' method, which argues for the multiple interpretation of a visual image, was the reverse of the surrealists' interest in hysteria. In each case, Dalí insisted on pressing the most paranoid reading, as if paranoid himself. Thus in 1963, Dalí published his 'paranoiac-critical' interpretation of the 'Angelus' (1857–59) painting by Jean-François Millet (1814–75), *Le Mythe tragique de l'Angelus de Millet: Interprétation 'paranoique-critique'*. It had been planned since the 1930s. For Dalí, the man and woman praying in the rather kitsch pastoral painting of peasants at sunset were responding not to the church bells but to a buried child in a coffin between them, which had been painted over. The male's hat before his body conceals an erection. The figures symbolise a mother and son about to have sexual intercourse, the son being terrified by the predatory mother.

Dalí's analysis begins by quoting from Isidor Ducasse (1846–70), the Uruguay-born writer who in Paris, as Le Comte de Lautréamont, wrote *Les Chants de Maldoror*. This famously evokes the handsomeness of a boy, speaking of an aggressive and a passive beauty being like 'the chance juxtaposition of a sewing machine and an umbrella on a dissecting table' (Lautréamont, 1978: 217). The statement, praising a chance encounter, or *trouvaille*, and referring to two males meeting, was taken up by André Breton. Dalí makes the umbrella, as a phallic symbol, male, and the sewing machine female, while reading the woman as destructive, comparing her with the female praying mantis, which devours the male, after mating with him. The homosexuality in Lautréamont has been heterosexualised, by making the woman an image of destructiveness. Is Dalí being anti-feminist, or is he, as he claims, pursuing the imaginary desires of the 1930s, that most fascist decade, and seeing fascism as marked by hatred of the feminine (Greeley, 2001, Dalí, 1996: 273–97)? In other words, is his reading not his personal view, but one allowing us to read the symptoms of the age?

That would mean that the reading hallucinates what is to be seen, as the paranoid does (like Schreber); it is a delirious reading, but here its purpose is critical, in lifting the repression which happens in bourgeois viewing of images. What fascinated Dalí, and Lacan, was the idea that paranoid interpretation changes reality, which begins as if objectively to take on its forms. Breton accused Dalí of sympathies towards fascism; and the connection between fascism and paranoia has already been noticed, giving the sense that single identity is a technologised, armoured narcissistic structure, and that possession of knowledge and identity is aggressive, in its emphasis on a 'hard' masculinity.

Paranoia and the real

The key to paranoia, for Lacan, is *Verwerfung* ('foreclusion' in French, 'foreclosure' in English); he contrasts it with those other words which suggest repression. All four words of these psychoanalytic terms, giving the sense of a defence against the reality of the external world, should be noted:

Die Verdrängung – repression, discussed by Freud in 1915 in an essay of that name (*SE* 14.141–58), and most simply, thought of as a defence reaction to demands made by the drives.

Die Verneinung – negation: title of a 1925 paper (*SE* 19.233–9). Meaning 'negation' and 'denial', it appears when a patient reacts to an attempt to uncover the unconscious by saying, 'I didn't think that'. Since there is no 'no' in the unconscious, such a reaction tends to point to a closing down, a denial of the suggestion, a refusal of it. The French translation is 'la dénégation', which implies a double negative: to negate is already a negation of a something which has been accepted (see below).

Verleugnung – disavowal, denial. This concept appears in 'Fetishism' (1927, *SE* 21.153), and it implies that the person denies the existence of something in external reality: male fetishism specifically 'denies' that the female has no penis, out of fears for its own castration. When Freud mentions *Verleugnung* in 'Some Psychical Consequences of the Anatomical Distinction between the Sexes' (1925), he says this 'denial' for an adult – as opposed to a child – 'would mean the beginning of a psychosis' (*SE* 19.253). (See *SE* 19.143, note; Laplanche and Pontalis, 1973: 118–21).

Verwerfung – foreclosure, or repudiation; this word implies that something has not even been noticed, has not 'taken' in the ego; has just not been noticed. What has been repudiated is the 'name of the father', which secures entry into the symbolic order, and which gives it overall meaning.

Lacan takes from Freud the idea that Schreber's denials mean that 'what was abolished internally returns from without' (*SE* 12.71), since he says in *The Psychoses: Seminar III, 1955–56*, part of which was rewritten for *Écrits* as 'On a Question Prior to Any Possible Treatment of Psychosis': 'whatever is refused in the symbolic order, in the sense of *Verwerfung*, reappears in the real' (Lacan, 1993: 13). To expand: 'in the subject's relationship to the symbol there is the possibility of a primitive *Verwerfung*, that is, that something is not symbolised and appears in the real' (Lacan, 1993: 81).

'The Real', which was discussed in Chapter 6, needs more explanation now. At issue, says Lacan:

> is the rejection of a primordial signifier into the outer shadows, a signifier that will henceforth be missing at this level. Here you have the fundamental

> mechanism that I posit as being at the basis of paranoia. It's a matter of a primordial process of exclusion of an original within, which is not a bodily within but that of an initial body of signifiers. (Lacan, 1993: 150)

Paranoid psychosis, which is not an organic condition, relates to the signifier. Commenting on Dora, who was neurotic, and non-psychotic, Lacan says that psychosis requires 'disturbances of language', which makes it exceed paranoia (Lacan, 1993: 92). Paranoia produces logical processes of thought taken to strange conclusions, but psychosis adds hallucinations and delusions, which, in language, mean outbursts of neologisms, meaningless jingles, logorrhea, what Lecercle calls *délire* (= delirium plus language that 'un-reads', that undoes the symbolic order of language), the two functions of *délire* being 'disruption of the signifying system and reconstruction'. Lecercle finds in Schreber 'the lack of the coherence which makes meaning possible' and 'reconstruction of a whole cosmos as much as of syntax' which 'evinces an excess of coherence which again precludes meaning' (Lecercle, 1985: 138).

We must clarify *Verwerfung*. Lacan introduced a paper on Freud's 'Die Verneinung' by the Hegelian Jean Hyppolite (Lacan, 2006: 308–17, 746–54, 318–33). (Negation is, of course, a Hegelian concept.) Hyppolite draws attention to Freud in saying that '"Affirmation" [*Die Bejahung*] as a substitute for uniting, belongs to Eros; negation – the successor to expulsion – belongs to the instinct for destruction' (*SE* 19.239). Affirmation and unification, introjecting elements into the self, go together, while negation expels unfavourable elements from itself, and belongs to a destructive drive. But, Hyppolite comments, Freud says that the negating judgement is made possible only by the creation of the symbol of negation. So what is negated has already been symbolised in the unconscious, where it is marked. Hyppolite continues with Freud, saying that 'we never discover a "no" in the unconscious':

> in analysis there is no 'no' to be found in the unconscious, but recognition of the unconscious by the ego demonstrates that the ego is always misrecognition; even in knowledge [*connaissance*], one always finds in the ego, in a negative formulation, the hallmark of the possibility of having the unconscious at one's disposal even as one refuses it. (Lacan, 2006: 753)

Negation includes a prior marking in the self, showing there has been a reception, of what is then turned down. There is no unconscious 'no'. Hyppolite brings his Hegelianism to bear in agreeing with this. The negated is kept in a state of repression, and appears as a symptom, within the realm of the symbolic. But *Verwerfung* is 'the absence of *Bejahung*': no sign of the father's authority is left.

Lacan speaks of a 'phallocentrism', wherein the child identifies with the mother, but desires her desire, which is the phallus, and so does not remain in the imaginary, in narcissistic self-completeness. Phallocentrism is 'conditioned by the intrusion of the signifier in man's psyche'. The phallus is 'the pivotal point in the symbolic process that completes, in both sexes, the calling into question of one's sex by the castration complex'. (Neither sex has the phallus: both are as though castrated, i.e. both denied access to full truth, or identity.) The phallus is evoked by 'the paternal metaphor' (Lacan, 2006: 463), which is a recognition of the Name-of-the-Father, as guaranteeing meaning. Lacan cites 'Totem and Taboo', that the murder of the literal father by the sons suggests that 'if this murder is the fertile moment of the debt by which the subject binds himself for life to the Law, the symbolic Father, insofar as he signifies the Law, is truly the dead Father' (Lacan, 2006: 464). There is an inseparable connection between accepting the authority of the Law, or the Name, of the Father, and the symbolic order.

With Schreber, Lacan gives an algorithm. The Name-of-the Father is placed over the Desire of the Mother (meaning 'desire *for* the mother', and 'what the mother desires'), in an order which is S/*s*. (As always, the signifier is over the signified: repression has happened; everything happens symbolically, not in reality). The signifier of the Name means the repression of the signified, the phallic, what the mother desires. But another algorithm places the Desire of the Mother over the signified to the subject. What the subject desires is replaced, superseded, by the Mother's desire. Putting these together, and working backwards, the child's Imaginary has been replaced by the Mother's Desire, but that (as a signifier, proclaiming the supremacy of the mother's will) is, within the first algorithm, repressed beneath the Name-of-the-Father: phallic authority. We are out of the desire of the mother, which represents the lack of the phallus, into apparent independence: the Name-of-the-Father, expressed in another algorithm: an A (*autre*, 'other') over the Phallus. The Phallus, as the mark of difference *and* the mark of authority, is known but is repressed, beneath the Other, the symbolic order, as supported by the phallic (Lacan, 2006: 465). The verticality of this suggests metaphor: the paternal metaphor keeps metaphor in place.

Lacan asks what happens when the Name-of-the-Father is missing:

> At the point at which the Name-of-the-Father is summoned . . . a pure and simple hole may thus answer in the Other; due to the lack of the metaphoric effect, this hole will give rise to a corresponding hole in the place of phallic signification. (Lacan, 2006: 465–6)

Where the Name-of-the-Father has been foreclosed, a hole appears in the symbolic order: this no longer has the coherence that the phallic significance of the Name-of-the-Father gives it: it just seems 'words, words, words', as Hamlet says (2.2.192). The symbolic order seems, normally, to be a protection, which Lacan explains by saying that 'the neurotic inhabits language, the psychotic is inhabited, posssessed by language' (Lacan, 1993: 250). Language has the immediacy and the power of the real, so that words, as things, come back with hallucinatory force. The absence of the father in Schreber's sense of the world produces the homosexuality with which he imagines being a woman, and thinks of being a wife to God; here, Lacan differs from Freud who thinks the homosexual fear launches Schreber's paranoia.

One example of a possible 'foreclosure' is given by Jean Laplanche, using Lacan, writing on the German poet Friedrich Hölderlin (1770–1843), mad for his last forty years (Laplanche, 2007: 40–2, 48–9). At the centre of Hölderlin is perception of absence, the sense that it is not now the time of the gods; that 'we have come too late', as one poem, 'Bread and Wine', says (Tambling, 2010a: 2–4). The poet must now fill the missing space, which produces a failure resulting in absolute collapse. Foucault reviewed Laplanche's work, thus, incidentally, giving the lie to those who argue that Foucault was not interested in psychoanalysis, and Derrida in an essay on the schizoid dramatist and poet Antonin Artaud, reviewed the work of both (Foucault, 1977b: 68–86, Derrida, 1978: 169–95). Foucault diverts Laplanche's attention from the personal events of Hölderlin's biography, and his relationship with Schiller, a father-replacement, towards something else, the ungrounded nature of language. It is not the absence of the father which has produced this sense of signification lacking; it is rather a historical conjuncture which focuses attention that 'language comes from elsewhere, from a place of which no-one can speak, but it can be transformed into a work [i.e. poetry, but note Foucault's definition of madness, already cited] only if, in ascending to its proper discourse, it directs its speech towards this absence' (Foucault, 1977b: 86). Introducing Laplanche's book, Rainer Nägele links that with Lacan on *aphanasis*, when defining the signifier as 'that which represents the subject to another signifier'. I, as a subject, look at another signifier, called S2, as that which is full of meaning, which seems to stand in as a full subject. But of course, there is an emptiness about the other signifier. Nägele cites two passages from Lacan's Seminar XVI (1968):

> This other signifier, S2, represents in this radical connection precisely knowledge, in so far as it is the opaque term, where . . . the subject gets lost, or where it vanishes, something I have underlined . . . in the term 'fading' [*aphanasis*].

> In this subjective genesis, knowledge presents itself from the outset as the term where the subject vanishes. (Laplanche, 2007)

What Lacan calls the fading of the subject may be compared with Blanchot's conception of *désoeuvrement*. As the subject moves into the language of the signifier, so that 'fading' which is like a state of 'worklessness' prevails. Madness is the situation of a loss of difference between the subject and the work that is happening in language, and, in calling it *aphanasis*, Lacan sees it as basic to writing. The alternative, where the writing subject thinks he has knowledge, is conducive of paranoia, as we have seen. Nägele draws attention to Freud's sense of *Urverdrängung* (primal repression), something Freud seems to predate before the ego or superego get to work (*SE* 20.94). Nägele calls it 'a repression before all repression', and quotes Lacan:

> This is what Freud designates as *Urverdrängung*. This so-called originary repression is only seemingly a repression, because it is expressly formulated not so much as repression, but as a kind of kernel already out of the reach of the subject and yet being a knowledge. This is what the notion of *Urverdrängung* means in so far as it makes possible that a whole signifying chain will attach itself to it, thus implying that enigma, the contradiction *in adjecto* [contradiction in terms] which is the subject as the unconscious. (quoted in Laplanche, 2007: xiv)

Before all repression is a repression, which keeps the subject in a state of fixation (*SE* 12.67), where the subject is attached to something left far behind, in its own archaic experience. Freud and Lacan both allow that meaning, and the inflection that all signification has, is attached to something unknown, because primarily repressed. So what supports, or activates, the meaning that the subject works with in writing is unknown. Clarity of utterance because of clarity of meaning, such as the Cartesian subject has, is impossible. The basis of knowledge cannot be had. Foucault reads modern literature, starting with Hölderlin, as working from that groundlessness. A subject is represented by a signifier, because there is no full subject to represent.

The Sinthome

One more take on madness, to be approached indirectly.

For Lacan, the necessity is to keep the Imaginary, the Symbolic, and the Real orders together. From Seminar XIX onwards, he speaks of the Borromean knot, which is illustrated in Seminar XX (Lacan, 1998: 107–38). It is three rings so interlinked that, if one is cut, the whole chain falls apart.

The rings correspond to the three orders. The idea of a failure of coherence points to a basic absence in being, which we have already discussed, through Žižek, as the power of the negative, of absence, of a failure in the Other, which is the topic of psychoanalysis, especially articulated in its Lacanian form. A Marxist critique, as with Althusser, suggests that ideology makes it seem that everything is consistent, that there is a way of representing reality which makes sense of the absences. The symbolic order seems consistent. Lacan, and Žižek, see the failures of representation showing themselves up in the form of symptoms. A symptom reveals a failure; its signifying value is that it shows up gaps, aporias. When Žižek writes *Enjoy Your Symptom* (2001), the title suggests as much that the symptom is produced out of a failure within the symbolic order, as that it points to a repression in the subject. 'According to Freud, when I develop a symptom, I produce a coded message about my innermost secrets, my unconscious desires and traumas' (Žižek, 2006: 11). If 'woman is the symptom of man', as Žižek quotes Lacan as saying, that may mean not only that the place of women, and the way that women are read, in culture (e.g. as marked out by lack, as though castrated) may be read as symptomatic of a failure within masculinity, which desperately attempts to hold on to a patriarchal identity. So it may also mean that 'man himself exists only through woman qua his symptom', that the woman, constructed negatively, patriarchally, with, as we saw with Dora, no signifier to speak her identity, nonetheless brings out something lacking inside the man, in so far as her *jouissance* is different from, outside, the symbolic order, which may try to speak for it, but cannot. These are the arguments of Lacan's Seminar XX (1972–73); *Encore: On Feminine Sexuality: The Limits of Love and Knowledge.*

In the case of James Joyce, the fear is of falling into madness; as though the tie formed by the Borromean knot is in danger of falling apart. In Seminar XXIII, *Le Sinthome* (1975), discussing James Joyce (1882–1941), Lacan began speaking of *le sinthome* as a fourth, which knots together these three orders (R, S, I) (Rabaté, 2001: 154–82, Harari, 2002, Thurston, 2004). *Sinthome*, an old spelling of 'symptom', is like one of the portmanteau words from *Finnegans Wake*, and it combines in itself the sense of something which falls by chance (the old meaning of 'symptom'), and something which cannot be 'read', like the 'stain' discussed in Seminar XI. Something opaque, inseparable from chance, outside interpretation, must be allowed in. Perhaps the *sinthome* is a signifier of the Name-of-the-Father (who is also the Father of the Name). It implies 'saint homme', 'saint Thomas' (Aquinas), and includes 'sin' (including the original sin of the father, HCE, in *Finnegans Wake*). 'Joyce' and 'sens' (sense, meaning) become inseparable from *jouissance*.

Lacan sees *Ulysses* and *Finnegans Wake* as huge linguistic attempts to create the Name of the Father in order not to go mad, as Joyce's daughter, Lucia, was schizophrenic, and was analysed by an unsympathetic Jung. A paternity must be affirmed, and it may said that Joyce shows the necessity of mad writing, with its symptoms, in order to prevent a worse psychosis. In other words, the writing of madness has become indistinguishable from mad writing. Hölderlin and Joyce represent two poles which mark out the modern: writing which because it is based on the ungrounded nature of writing risks madness, and writing which assumes madness to avoid it.

8

Between literature and psychoanalysis

'The Purloined Letter'

How do literature and psychoanalysis relate? The first produces the second; the second interprets the first, the first interrogates the second. Psychoanalysis, as an instance of critical theory, associates with Marx and Nietzsche in analysing modernity, while Marxism and Nietzschean philosophy both question psychoanalysis. Chapter 2 analysed a Sherlock Holmes story, so it seems fit to end with Lacan's study of another, earlier detective story, by Edgar Allan Poe (1806–49) whose hero, Dupin, inspired Doyle. Lacan knew 'The Purloined Letter' (1845) through its French translation as 'La Lettre volée', by Baudelaire, and the essay formed part of Seminar II, *The Ego in Freud's Theory and in the Technique of Psychoanalysis: 1954–1955*). As we have seen, it then headed the *Écrits*, as an example of Lacan's literary criticism; as a contribution to thinking about the detective story; and as central to his thinking about the symbolic order, and the signifier (Lacan, 1988b: 179–80, 186–7, 194–205, Lacan, 2006: 6–48).

Poe's story, easily locatable, is analysed first in terms of repetition. Lacan writes that the 'repetition automatism (*Wiederholungszwang*) has its basis in . . . the *insistence* of the signifying chain' (Lacan, 2006: 6), so making associations with 'The Insistence of the Letter in the Unconscious'. He continues that 'the symbolic order . . . is constitutive for the subject' (Lacan, 2006: 7): these statements reappear throughout the essay. The 'compulsion to repeat', (*Wiederholungszwang*) has already been linked with the death-drive, which *is* the repetition-compulsion, expressed in the movement of the signifying chain. Language insists, and the insistence moves towards death.

Lacan shows how 'The Purloined Letter' is structured by repeating two triangle-like scenes, one with the King (A), the Queen (B), and the minister (C), called the 'primal scene', the second with the police (A), the minister

(B), and Dupin (C). In the first scene, set in the Queen's boudoir, the King (A) sees nothing of the damaging letter in the Queen's possession, but the Minister (C) can see her confusion and the King's blindness, and can purloin the letter, perhaps to blackmail her. In the second, when the letter is in the minister's possession, and Dupin retrieves it, the police (A), like the King, see nothing, though the letter is in the most obvious position, hanging from the mantelpiece. In the first situation, the Queen (B), with the compromising letter, could see what was happening but can do nothing. The minister with the letter can also do nothing; he is now in the same subject-position as the Queen, at B. The minister, at C in the first scene, could remove the letter, because he can see what both A and B can see, know, and do. Dupin the detective can do the same in the second scene.

Lacan's reading makes him say that narrative, far from being a sequence forwards from *a* to *z*, going horizontally, as it were, must be seen as repeating its own obsessions, though these may be disguised, and not appear to be repetitions. No story just goes on till it falls off the edge! Its pattern is one of which the writer is unaware: to understand that pattern it is essential to see its unconscious underpinnings, part of the codes which Barthes saw underlying nineteenth-century realist narratives. As a triangular structure, it repeats something of the Oedipal triangle. Because of repetition, the second scene, by its difference, opens up the first for more understanding (the point returns to Freud's analysis of Emma), but the people in the structure of repetition are in no position to read this; the situation contains an inherent unreadability, which means that the subjects in this signifying structure have no autonomy, as the subject in situation B shows.

The minister changes position in the two triangles, from C to B. As B, he becomes like the Queen, feminised. Bearing the letter turns him from active to passive. The letter 'insists' by creating subjectivity: being a subject means being under the power of the letter. It is unimportant to know the contents of the letter, merely what the effect of the signifier is. The letter makes a detour (a familiar word, now), in a prolonged trajectory: Lacan puns on purloined and prolonged (Lacan, 2006: 21) and a purloined letter points to absence at the centre, but the letter has its pathway 'proper to it', as is implied in the repetition-compulsion. So, 'if what Freud discovered . . . has a meaning, it is that the signifier's displacement determines subjects' acts, destiny, refusals, blindnesses, success and fate, regardless of their innate gifts and instruction, and irregardless of their character or sex; and that everything pertaining to the psychological pregiven follows willy-nilly the signifier's train' (Lacan, 2006: 21).

So the letter will find its way back to the King, via the police. Dupin steals the letter from the minister, and puts in its place, in the phallic position of the fireplace – underscoring how the Minister has been 'castrated' – a facsimile, with the words from the play *Atrée* by the eighteenth-century dramatist Crébillon inside it, 'Un dessein si funeste / S'il n'est digne d'Atrée, est digne de Thyeste' ('A design so deadly / If not worthy of Atreus, is worthy of Thyestes') (Poe, 2003: 299, 481).

The police can do nothing, because they cannot read the situation; indeed, the Prefect of Police despises the minister because he is 'a poet, which I take to be only one remove from a fool' (Poe, 2003: 285). Dupin, at that point, says he has also written poetry: poetry, in the light of Lacan's reading, can be seen to be language which displaces a situation, which disorganises the power of repetition, and which shows the place of the signifier, of the letter. The Queen can read, but she cannot act on her reading. The minister, and Dupin, as poets, understand language, which suggests that they can move the letter: they can see that the letter is always displaced, always needing the interpretation that moving it gives. They hint at the role of psychoanalysis. A stands for a reading that cannot read. B is a position that just takes the text at face value. C is the reading that psychoanalysis gives.

At the end, Dupin has ceased being coolly objective; he has become personally involved, taking revenge on the minister for a wrong he did him once, as a rival, like the brothers Atreus and Thyestes in the Greek myths (in *The Oresteia*, and in Crébillon). Dupin, sending this letter to the minister, while taking back the purloined letter, has become the subject of the letter. Though he thinks he is acting autonomously, he is continuing the pattern, and in any new situation will be at position B. The letter has a 'dumbfounding' [*médusante*] effect (29): it is castrating, as is the figure of the Medusa's head (*SE* 18.273–4, 22.24), and it is death-dealing. Neither the minister nor Dupin can, ultimately, use the letter; both are held by it, and by the symbolic order. So 'the sender [of a letter] . . . receives from the receiver his own message in an inverted form. That is why the "purloined letter", nay, the "letter *en souffrance*" [in abeyance] means that a letter always arrives at its destination' (Lacan, 2006: 30). There is no precedence between sender and receiver, and both are frozen by the effect of the signifier. The argument returns to that discussed with 'The Instance of the Letter'; Lacan removes the subject who thinks he knows, and has authority over his utterance, just as psychoanalysis undoes all thought of 'the author's intentions'. We return to writing as madness: moving the subject both away from that unknown kernel of meaning which constructs language, and into language which abolishes the separateness of the subject who thinks he 'knows' outside the text that is being written.

Derrida, Lacan and writing

Derrida discussed Lacan's reading of 'The Purloined Letter' in the essay 'Le Facteur de la Vérité' (Derrida, 1987: 413–96). He accuses Lacan of framing Poe's story to produce his own meaning: by omitting from his triangular structure the fourth voice which narrates, and which has another vision from the ones already discussed. The structure is not triangular: 'by framing in this violent way, by cutting the narrated figure itself from a fourth side in order to see only triangles, one evades perhaps, a certain complication, perhaps, of the Oedipal structure, which is announced in the scene of writing' (Derrida, 1987: 433). The demand for 'truth' means that the 'scene of writing' is curtailed: Derrida argues too that the itinerary of the letter is made to indicate castration as true of the woman: the truth remains (the letter, as the phallus), but the feminised position (B) cannot claim it, because it is marked by lack.

Derrida writes that 'the lack [i.e. castration] does not have its place in dissemination' (Derrida, 1987: 441). 'Dissemination' is one of the terms by which Derrida describes what happens in 'deconstruction': it is not the centring of the text around a single truth, but letting it go, allowing for dispersal, accepting excess. The statement needs to be compared with what Derrida says about Nietzsche's attempt to write as a woman: 'woman knows that castration *does not take place*' (Derrida, 1979: 61). Castration is a male nightmare, finding its outworkings in fetishism; it does not affect the woman, save from the way the woman is regarded from a phallocentric viewpoint, making her a 'symptom', in that the inadequacies of the male position are pushed on to her.

By keeping the letter on a single itinerary, Derrida claims, Lacan is not just saying that the letter always arrives at its destination, he is acting as the 'postman' (*facteur*). There is the sense that psychoanalysis always delivers 'the truth', in other words, that it knows the truth about you, and delivers it (while charging a fee). Derrida, developing points we have already noted in Chapter 3, argues against the potential of psychoanalysis to deliver 'truth': that 'the letter never arrives at its destination, but it belongs to the structure of the letter to be capable, always, of not arriving' (Derrida, 1987: 444). The difference between literature (the letter) and psychoanalysis inheres in this: literature is not committed to delivering the truth, but psychoanalysis is, and, where psychoanalysis uses literature, it does so by imposing a frame around it, indicating that it misreads, simplifies, represses other possibilities. Derrida says that, despite Lacan's stress on the *letter*, he is more interested in the *voice* (as in the psychoanalytic session), so he is not interested in writing, but only in the semblance of 'presence' that is given by the voice; this interest in voices implies a commitment to immediacy, to 'truth'. We may supplement this through Deleuze and Guattari, who note that, for instance, in the case of the Wolf Man's dream, Freud's interpretation has unconsciously, but symptomatically, turned seven wolves into one (Deleuze and Guattari, 1988: 26–38). This, they say, is part of a 'molar' – as opposed to 'molecular' – tendency in psychoanalysis, to unify, and make single what is plural, to limit the cultural and sexual issues that psychoanalysis notes to the problems of a single subject. In the terms of *Thousand Plateaux*, it is an 'arboreal', as opposed to a 'rhizomatic' tendency within Freudian thinking, which is hierarchical, imposing interpretation, not allowing for multiplicity and plural possibilities. The issue holds equally for Lacan who is also their target.

Such truth, identified with the possession of the phallus, and so unitary, Derrida names as 'phallogocentrism', and 'androcentrism' (Derrida, 1987: 481–2). It puts the woman outside, into the place of the Other (here Derrida cites *Écrits*, Lacan, 2006: 616; Mitchell, 2000: 93; see also Derrida, 1998: 39–69). Here, the stakes are high, and the arguments complex. Lacan's sense of feminine sexuality places the woman beyond the symbolic order, which provides only for a *jouissance* which is phallic in character. If 'there is no sexual relation', as Lacan contends, (Lacan, 1998: 9), that is because *jouissance* is defined as phallic: one signifier has to serve for two, and there is no signifier for the woman's enjoyment as different. Lacan argues for a 'jouissance' for the woman which is supplementary to that which is phallic and patriarchal; and then he refers to the Bernini statue of Teresa of Avila, the mystic who had visions of Christ, and of an angel who pierced her with a spear: 'you need but to go to Rome and see the statue by Bernini to immediately understand that she's coming. What is she getting off on? It is clear that the essential testimony of the mystics consists in saying that they experience it but know nothing about it' (Lacan, 1998: 76, compare Mitchell, 2000: 147). Any language which would speak of such *jouissance* is patriarchal, of the symbolic order, and mysticism risks madness, perhaps *is* madness, in being, strictly non-sense, the language of *délire*.

Lacan says that the woman's experience is outside the symbolic; Derrida thinks Lacanian psychoanalysis is committed to just that order, and by making the woman the other, makes the male experience normative. And at the moment of Lacan's presentation of the 'phallus' – which neither sex possesses – as the marker of a completeness which both sexes lack, French feminist thought, in contrast to Lacan, and in nuanced disagreement with Derrida, has insisted on the woman's body as pointing to a 'completeness' in a way which phallocentric discourse cannot speak about. It asks whether there can be an *écriture féminine*, a woman's writing, which escapes such a stress on lack as normative (Jones, 1981). Yet the feminist argument qualifies the psychoanalytic insight by its 'essentialist' appeal to the nature of women, and, however much psychoanalysis may have omitted the woman, it has at least, in Lacan, put into question such essentialist, and ahistorical arguments about the nature of men and women, and, in that way, it may survive Derrida's critique in *Spurs*.

Returning to the 'postman of truth' argument, it may be said that Lacan sees the letter as an example of the text which moves outside the motivations and intentions of people whom it subjects. Derrida takes that conclusion as imposing a reading on the text, and centring it. Lacan shows that the letter has the power to feminise, and Derrida sees this as making the letter phallic, a model of single truth, but it is not clear that Lacan makes the letter a thing at all; perhaps Derrida makes it too absolute, and so centres Lacan's reading of it (see Barbara Johnson's critique, 1981). Derrida makes fun of Lacan misreading *dessein* in the Crébillon quotation, and making it *destin* instead: so that it translates as 'a destiny so fatal' (Derrida, 1987: 495). He argues that Lacan, possessed by the will to truth, has given the letter a definite destination, and so destiny, so the mistake is symptomatic. Lacan shows, however, that reading literature cannot be a matter of exactitude; while we want to read accurately, all readings of texts are also misreadings, and, in this case, Derrida's matter of the right letter may even be *his* will to truth. Psychoanalysis and deconstruction, as already hinted, may *both* be ways of showing that it is impossible to read a text, because literature's detours exceed all forms of imposition of single meaning. In which case, Barthes urging rereading, because it introduces 'that play which is the return of the different' is wonderful advice: rereading reveals 'not the *real* text, but a plural text: the same and new' (Barthes, 1974: 16). The richness of literature – meaning texts which are not consumable, and so finished, by a single reading – is its excess over single meaning. Another way of putting that is to say it brings back difference, otherness within the text, a lesson which comes from both deconstructive and psychoanalytic readings of literature.

But I conclude with noting, again, the Deleuzian critique of psychoanalysis, which compares with Derrida, and with Foucault, in seeing it as putting all the stress on the single subject, rather than in the conditions of discourse which construct that subject. Žižek questions that point of view in Deleuze, on the grounds that it neglects the place of the signifier, and the sense that this, as it works inside the subject, bars him from his own meaning. We have seen this stress repeatedly in Lacan: utterance is not in the control of the individual subject, who is thus internally divided, while the other, which is desired, as guaranteeing truth and meaning, is similarly marked by absence, incomplete, not what Lacan refers to the psychoanalyst as being, like God, 'the subject supposed to know' (Lacan, 1977c: 224–5). The navel of the dream which cannot be interpreted, the sense that psychoanalysis remains always interminable, undoing the customary senses given to situations and to words, brings us to literature and psychoanalysis not as marked by fullness of meaning, but as making such an idea problematic. Both require awareness of the negative; both work with the unknown, with what is like the stain, or what cannot be pulled into meaning save in condensed and displaced forms, as constituting the reality that we think we know, and needing to be added in to render coherence. That is a different way of seeing psychoanalysis, from the way it is usually characterised, as a box full of meanings ready to be applied. It is different, too, from the way we usually see literature, in making it more strange, always speaking more than it knows, and never simply the sum of the patterns and meanings that may be located in it, which, indeed, it also has the power to negate.

References

Abraham, Nicolas, and Torok, Maria, 1986. *The Wolf Man's Magic Word*. Trans. Nicholas Rand. Foreword by Jacques Derrida. Minneapolis: University of Minnesota Press.

Althusser, Louis, 1984. *Essays on Ideology*. London: Verso.

Anzieu, Didier. 1986. *Freud's Self-Analysis*. Trans. Peter Graham. Preface by M. Masud R. Khan. London: Hogarth Press and the Institute of Psychoanalysis.

Bakhtin, Mikhail, 1984. *Rabelais and His World*. Trans. Hélène Iswolsky. Bloomington: Indiana University Press.

Barthes, Roland, 1974. *S/Z*. Trans. Richard Howard. New York: Hill and Wang.

Benjamin, Walter, 1973. *Charles Baudelaire: A Lyric Poet in the Era of High Capitalism*. Trans. Harry Zohn. London: Verso.

——, 1999. *The Arcades Project*. Trans. Howard Eiland and Kevin McLaughlin. Cambridge, Mass.: Harvard University Press.

Bernheimer, Charles, and Kahane, Claire, 1985. *In Dora's Case: Freud – Hysteria – Feminism*. New York: Columbia University Press. [Essays by Felix Deutsch, Eric H. Erikson, Steven Marcus, Jacques Lacan, Suzanne Gearheart, Jacqueline Rose, Maria Ramas, Toril Moi, Jane Gallop, Neil Hertz, Jere Collins, J. Ray Green, Mary Lydon, Mark Sachner, Eleanor Honig Skoller, Madelon Sprengnether]

Bersani, Leo, 2002. Introduction to Freud, *Civilisation and Its Discontents*. Harmondsworth: Penguin.

Bion, W.R., 1967. *Second Thoughts: Selected Papers on Psychoanalysis*. London: Maresfield Library.

Blake, William, 1982. *The Complete Prose and Verse of William Blake*. Ed. David V. Erdman. Berkeley: University of California Press.

Blanchot, Maurice, 1982. *The Space of Literature*. Trans. Ann Smock. Lincoln: University of Nebraska Press.

——, 1999. *The Station Hill Blanchot Reader: Fiction and Literary Essays*. Ed. George Quasha. Barrytown, NY: Station Hill Press.

Brennan, Teresa 1993. *History After Lacan*. London: Routledge.

Breton, André, 1960. *Nadja*. Trans. Richard Howard. New York: Grove Press.

Brooks, Peter, 1984. *Reading for the Plot: Design and Intention in Narrative*. Cambridge, MA: Harvard University Press.

Butler, Judith, 1990. *Gender Trouble: Feminism and the Subversion of Identity*. London: Routledge.

Canetti, Elias, 1973. *Crowds and Power*. Trans. Carol Stewart. Harmondsworth: Penguin.

Cargill, Oscar, 1963. '*The Turn of the Screw* and Henry James'. *PMLA*, 78: 238–49.

Caruth, Cathy, 1996. *Unclaimed Experience: Trauma, Narrative, and History*. Baltimore: Johns Hopkins University Press.

Cixous, Hélène, 1976, 'Fiction and Its Phantoms: A Reading of Freud's *Das Unheimliche* (The "Uncanny")', *New Literary History*, 7: 525–48.

Clément, Catherine, 1983. *The Lives and Legends of Jacques Lacan*. Trans. Arthur Goldhammer. New York: Columbia University Press.

Cohen, Margaret, 1993. *Profane Illumination: Walter Benjamin and the Paris of Surrealist Revolution*. Berkeley: University of California Press.

Copjec, Joan, 1982. Review: 'The Anxiety of the Influencing Machine'. *October*, 23: 43–59.

Culler, Jonathan, 1980, 1981. *The Pursuit of Signs: Semiotics, Literature, Deconstruction*. London: Routledge & Kegan Paul.

Dalí, Salvador, 1996. *The Collected Writings of Salvador Dalí*. Ed. and trans. Haim Finkelstein. Cambridge: Cambridge University Press.

Dean, Carolyn J., 1992. *The Self and Its Pleasures: Bataille, Lacan, and the History of the Decentred Subject*. Ithaca: Cornell University Press.

Dean, Tim. 2003. 'Lacan and Queer Theory', in Jean-Michel Rabaté (ed.), *The Cambridge Companion to Lacan*. Cambridge: Cambridge University Press.

De Certeau, Michel, 1986. *Heterologies: Discourse on the Other*. Trans. Brian Massumi. Minneapolis: University of Minnesota Press.

Deleuze, Gilles, and Guattari, Félix, 1983. *Anti-Oedipus: Capitalism and Schizophrenia*. Trans. Robert Hurley, Mark Seem, and Helen R. Lane. Minneapolis: University of Minnesota Press.

——, 1988. *A Thousand Plateaux*. Trans. Brian Massumi. London: Athlone Press.

De Man, Paul. 1984. *The Rhetoric of Romanticism*. New York: Columbia University Press.

Derrida, Jacques, 1978. *Writing and Difference*. Trans. Alan Bass. London: Routledge & Kegan Paul.

——, 1979. *Spurs: Nietzsche's Styles*. Trans. Barbara Harlow. Chicago: University of Chicago Press.

——, 1986a. *Memoires: For Paul de Man*. Trans. Cecile Lindsay, Jonathan Culler, and Eduardo Cadava. New York: Columbia University Press.

——, 1986b. 'Foreword: *Fors*: The Anglish Words of Nicolas Abraham and Maria Torok'. Trans. Barbara Johnson. In Nicolas Abraham and Maria Torok, *The Wolf Man's Magic Word: A Cryptonomy*. Trans. Nicholas Rand. Minneapolis: University of Minnesota Press.

——, 1987. *The Post Card: From Socrates to Freud and Beyond*. Trans. Alan Bass. Chicago: University of Chicago Press.
——, 1996. *Archive Fever: A Freudian Impression*. Trans. Eric Prenowitz. Chicago: University of Chicago Press.
——, 1998. *Resistances of Psychoanalysis*. Trans. Peggy Kamuf, Pascale-Anne Brault, and Michael Nass. Chicago: University of Chicago Press.
Dickens, Charles, 2000. *A Tale of Two Cities*. Ed. Richard Maxwell. London: Penguin.
Doyle, Arthur Conan, 1981. *The Penguin Complete Sherlock Holmes*. Harmondsworth: Penguin.
Eliot, T.S., 1974. *Collected Poems, 1909–1962*. London: Faber and Faber.
Ellmann, Maud, 2010. *The Nets of Modernism: Henry James. Virginia Woolf, James Joyce and Sigmund Freud*. Cambridge: Cambridge University Press.
Evans, Dylan, 1996. *An Introductory Dictionary of Lacanian Psychoanalysis*. London: Routledge.
Fairbairn, W. Ronald D., 1952. *Psychoanalytic Studies of the Personality*. London: Tavistock Publications.
Felman, Shoshana, 1982. 'Turning the Screw of Interpretation', in Shoshana Felman (ed.), *Literature and Psychoanalysis: The Question of Reading: Otherwise*, (*Yale French Studies*, 55–6, 1977). Baltimore: Johns Hopkins University Press.
——, 1987. *Jacques Lacan and the Adventure of Insight*. Cambridge, MA: Harvard University Press.
Flieger, Jerry Aline, 2000. 'Becoming Woman: Deleuze, Schreber and Molecular Identification', in Ian Buchanan and Claire Colebrook (eds), *Deleuze and Feminist Theory*. Edinburgh: Edinburgh University Press.
Forrester, John, 1997. *Dispatches from the Freud Wars: Psychoanalysis and Its Passions*. Cambridge, MA: Harvard University Press.
Foster, Hal. 1991. 'Armor Fou', *October* 56: 64–97.
——, 1993. *Compulsive Beauty*. Cambridge, MA: MIT Press.
Foucault, Michel, 1977a. *Discipline and Punish: The Birth of the Prison*. Trans. Alan Sheridan. Harmondsworth: Penguin.
——, 1977b. *Language, Counter-Memory, Practice: Selected Essays and Interviews*. Ed Donald F. Bouchard. Trans. Donald F. Bouchard and Sherry Simon. Ithaca: Cornell University Press.
——, 1981. *The History of Sexuality*. Trans. Robert Hurley. Harmondsworth: Penguin.
——, 2006. *History of Madness*. Trans. Donald F. Bouchard and Sherry Simon. Ithaca: Cornell University Press.
Freud, Sigmund, 1953–74. *The Standard Edition of the Complete Psychological Works*. Edited and translated by James Strachey et al. 24 vols (abbreviated to *SE*). London: Hogarth Press.
Friedman, John, and Alexander, James, 1983. 'Psychonalysis and Natural Science: Freud's 1985 *Project* Revisited', *International Review of Psychoanalysis*, 10: 303–18.

Frosh, Stephen, 1999. 'Freud's Dreams: Dora's Dreams', in Laura Marcus (ed.), *Sigmund Freud's The Interpretation of Dreams: New Interdisciplinary Essays*. Manchester: Manchester University Press.

Gardiner, Muriel, 1973. *The Wolf-Man and Sigmund Freud*. Harmondsworth: Penguin.

George, Diana Hume, 1980. *Blake and Freud*. Ithaca: Cornell University Press.

Greeley, Robin Adèle, 2001. 'Dalí's Fascism; Lacan's Paranoia', *Art History*, 24: 465–92.

Green, André, 1979. *The Tragic Effect: The Oedipus Complex in Tragedy*. Trans. Alan Sheridan. Cambridge: Cambridge University Press.

Greenberg, Valerie D., 1997. *Freud and His Aphasia Book: Language and the Sources of Psychoanalysis*. Ithaca: Cornell University Press.

Groddeck, Georg, 1977. *The Meaning of Illness; Selected Psychoanalytic Writings*. Ed. Lore Schacht. Trans. Gertrud Mander. London: Maresfield Library.

Grosskurth, Phyllis, 1986. *Melanie Klein: Her World and Her Work*. London: Hodder and Stoughton.

Grosz, Elizabeth, 1988. *Jacques Lacan: A Feminist Introduction*. London: Routledge.

Halpern, Richard, 2002. *Shakespeare's Perfume: Sodomy and Sublimity in the Sonnets, Wilde, Freud, and Lacan*. Philadelphia: University of Pennsylvania Press.

Harari, Roberto, 2002. *How James Joyce Made His Name: A Reading of the Final Lacan*. Trans. Luke Thurston. New York: Other Press.

Hegel, G.W.F., 1977. *The Phenomenology of Spirit*. Trans. A.V. Miller. Oxford: Oxford University Press.

Hinshelwood, R.D., 1989. *A Dictionary of Kleinian Thought*. London: Free Association Books.

Holbrook, David, 1964. *The Quest for Love*. London: Methuen.

Hugo, Victor, 2004. *The Essential Victor Hugo*. Trans. E.H. and A.M. Blackmore. Oxford: Oxford University Press.

Ibsen, Henrik, 1958. *The Master Builder and Other Plays*. Trans. Una Ellis Fermor. Harmondsworth: Penguin.

Irigaray, Luce. 1992. *The Irigaray Reader*. Ed. Margaret Whitford. Oxford: Blackwell.

——, 1993. 'Belief Itself', in *Sexes and Genealogies*. Trans. Gillian C. Gill. New York: Columbia University Press.

Irwin, John T., 1994. *The Mystery to a Solution: Poe, Borges and the Analytic Detective Story*. Baltimore: Johns Hopkins University Press.

Iversen, Margaret, 2007. *Beyond Pleasure: Freud, Lacan, Barthes*. University Park, PA: University of Pennsylvania Press.

Jacobus, Mary, 2005. *The Poetics of Psychoanalysis: In the Wake of Klein*. Oxford: Oxford University Press.

Jekels, Ludwig, 1943. 'The Riddle of Shakespeare's *Macbeth*', *The Psychoanalytic Review*, 30: 361–85.

Johnson, Barbara, 1981. 'The Frame of Reference: Poe, Lacan, Derrida', in Robert Young (ed.), *Untying the Text*. London: Routledge and Kegan Paul.

Johnson, Christopher, 1993. *System and Writing in the Philosophy of Jacques Derrida*. Cambridge: Cambridge University Press.

Jones, Ann Rosalind, 1981. 'Writing the Body: Towards an Understanding of *Écriture Féminine*'. *Feminist Studies*, 7: 247–63.

Jones, Ernst, 1955a. *The Life and Work of Sigmund Freud: Vol. 1: The Formative Years and the Great Discoveries, 1856–1900*. New York: Basic Books.

——, 1955b. *The Life and Work of Sigmund Freud: Vol. 2: Years of Maturity, 1901–1919*. New York: Basic Books.

——, 1995c. *The Life and Work of Sigmund Freud: Vol. 3: The Last Phase, 1919–1939*. New York: Basic Books.

Kearney, Lottie, 1970. 'Anxiety', in Humberto Nagera (ed.), *Basic Psychoanalytic Concepts on Metapsychology, Conflicts, Anxiety*. London: George Allen and Unwin.

Klein, Melanie, 1975a. *Love, Guilt and Reparation, and Other Works 1921–1945*. Introduction by R.E. Money-Kyrle. London: Hogarth Press and the Institute of Psychoanalysis.

——, 1975b. *The Psychoanalysis of Children*. Trans. Alix Strachey and H.A. Thorner. London: Hogarth Press and the Institute of Psychoanalysis.

——, 1975c. *Envy and Gratitude and Other Works 1946–1963*. London: Hogarth Press and the Institute of Psychoanalysis. Reprinted with introduction by Hanna Segal, London: Vintage, 1997.

——, 1986. *The Selected Melanie Klein*. Ed. Juliet Mitchell. Harmondsworth: Penguin.

Kofman, Sarah, 1985. *The Enigma of Woman: Woman in Freud's Writings*. Trans. Catherine Porter. Ithaca: Cornell University Press.

Kristeva, Julia, 1980. *Desire in Language: A Semiotic Approach to Literature and Art*. Trans. Thomas Gora, Alice Jardine, and Leon S Roudiez. Oxford: Basil Blackwell.

——, 1982. *Powers of Horror: An Essay on Abjection*. Trans. Leon S. Roudiez. New York: Columbia University Press.

——, 1984. *Revolution in Poetic Language*. Trans. Margaret Waller. Introduction by Leon S. Roudiez. New York: Columbia University Press.

——, 1987. *Tales of Love*. Trans. Leon S. Roudiez. New York: Columbia University Press.

——, 1989. *Black Sun: Depression and Melancholia*. Trans. Leon S. Roudiez. New York: Columbia University Press.

——, 2001. *Melanie Klein*. Trans. Ross Guberman. New York: Columbia University Press.

——, 2004. *Colette*. Trans. Jane Marie Todd. New York: Columbia University Press.

Lacan, Jacques, 1977a. *Écrits: A Selection*. Trans. Alan Sheridan. London: Tavistock.

——, 1977b. 'Desire and the Interpretation of Desire in *Hamlet*'. Trans. James Hulbert. *Yale French Studies*, 33–56, 11–52.

——, 1977c. *The Four Fundamental Concepts of Psychoanalysis* (Seminar XI). Ed. Jacques Alain-Miller. Trans. Alan Sheridan. London: Penguin.

——, 1988a. *The Seminar of Jacques Lacan: Book I: Freud's Papers on Technique 1953–1954*. Ed. Jacques Alain-Miller. Trans. John Forrester. Cambridge: Cambridge University Press.

——, 1988b. *The Seminar of Jacques Lacan: Book II: The Ego in Freud's Theory and in the Technique of Psychoanalysis, 1954–1955*. Ed. Jacques Alain-Miller. Trans. Sylvana Tomaselli. Notes by John Forrester. Cambridge: Cambridge University Press.

——, 1992. *The Ethics of Psychoanalysis 1959–1960: The Seminar of Jacques Lacan*. Ed. Jacques-Alain Miller. Trans. Dennis Porter. London: Routledge.

——, 1993. *The Psychoses: The Seminar of Jacques Lacan, Book III: 1955–1956*. Ed. Jacques Alain-Miller. Trans. Russell Grigg. London: Routledge.

——, 1996. *Écrits*. 2 vols. Paris: Éditions du Seuil.

——, 1998. *On Feminine Sexuality: The Limits of Love and Knowledge: Encore: The Seminar of Jacques Lacan Book XX*. Ed. Jacques Alain-Miller Trans. Bruce Fink. New York: W.W. Norton.

——, 2006. *Écrits*. Trans. Bruce Fink in collaboration with Héloïse Fink and Russell Grigg. New York: W.W. Norton.

——, 2007. *The Other Side of Psychoanalysis: The Seminar of Jacques Lacan Book XVII*. Trans. Russell Grigg. New York: W.W. Norton.

Laplanche, Jean, 1976. *Life and Death in Psychoanalysis*. Trans. Jeffrey Mehlmann. Baltimore: Johns Hopkins University Press.

——, 1992. *Seduction, Translation, Drives*. Ed. John Fletcher and Martin Stanton. London. Institute for Contemporary Arts.

——, 2007. *Hölderlin and the Question of the Father*. Trans. Luke Carson. Introduction by Rainer Nägele. Victoria, BC: ELS Editions, Dept of English, University of Victoria.

Laplanche, Jean, and Pontalis, J.-B., 1973. *The Language of Psychoanalysis*. Trans. Donald Nicholson-Smith. New York: W.W. Norton.

Lautréamont, Le Comte de. 1978. *Maldoror and Poems*. Trans. Paul Knight. Harmondsworth: Penguin.

Lawrence, D.H., 2000. *Women in Love*. Ed. David Farmer, Lindeth Vasey, and John Worthen. Introduction by Mark Kinkead-Weekes. London: Penguin.

Lecercle, Jean-Jacques, 1985. *Philosophy Through the Looking-Glass: Language, Nonsense, Desire*. London: Hutchinson.

Lee, Jason Scott, 1990. *Jacques Lacan*. Boston: G.K. Hall.

Likierman, Meira, 2001. *Melanie Klein: Her Work in Context*. London: Continuum.

Livingstone, Angela, 1999. Introduction to Marina Tsvetaeva, *The Ratcatcher*. London: Angel Books.

Lothane, Zvi, 1992. *In Defence of Schreber: Soul Murder and Psychiatry*. Hillsdale, NJ: Analytic Press.

Lukacher, Ned, 1988. *Primal Scenes: Literature, Philosophy, Psychoanalysis*. Ithaca: Cornell University Press.

——, 1994. 'Chiasmatic Reading: Aporetic History: Freud's *Macketh*', in Sander Cilman et al. (eds), *Reading Freud's Reading*. New York: New York University Press.

Macey, David, 1988. *Lacan in Contexts*. London: Verso.

Mannoni, Octave, 1971. *Freud: The Theory of the Unconsious*. London: NLB.
Marcus, Steven, 1984. *Freud and the Culture of Psychoanalysis*. Boston: George Allen and Unwin.
Marx, Karl, 1977. *The German Ideology*. Ed. C.J. Arthur. London: Lawrence and Wishart.
Masson, Jeffrey, trans. and ed., 1985. *The Complete Letters of Sigmund Freud to Wilhelm Fliess, 1877–1904*. London: Beltnap Press.
Miller, George A., 1970. *Psychology: The Science of Mental Life* (1962). Harmondsworth: Penguin.
Mitchell, Juliet, 2000. *Mad Men and Medusas: Reclaiming Hysteria and the Effects of Sibling Relations on the Human Condition*. London: Penguin.
Mitchell, Juliet, and Rose, Jacqueline, 1982. *Feminine Sexuality: Jacques Lacan and the Ecole Freudienne*. Ed. Juliet Mitchell and Jacqueline Rose. Trans. Jacqueline Rose. London: Macmillan.
Muller, John P. and Richardson, William J., 1982. *Lacan and Language: A Reader's Guide to Écrits*. New York: International Universities Press.
Niederland, William G., 1974. *The Schreber Case: A Psychoanalytic Profile of a Paranoid Personality*. New York: Quadrangle, NY Times Book Club. Hillsdale, NJ: Analytic Press.
Nietzsche, Friedrich, 1996. *On the Genealogy of Morals*. Trans. Douglas Smith. Oxford: Oxford University Press.
——, 1998. *Beyond Good and Evil*. Trans. Marion Faber. Oxford: Oxford University Press.
——, 2004. *Twilight of the Idols and The Antichrist*. Trans. Thomas Common (1896). New York: Dover.
——, 2005. *Thus Spoke Zarathustra*. Trans. Graham Parkes. Oxford: Oxford University Press.
Oliver, Kelly, 1993. *Reading Kristeva: Unravelling the Double Bind*. Bloomington: University of Indiana Press.
Olsen, Ole Andjaer, 2004. 'Depression and Reparation as Themes in Melanie Klein's Analysis of the Painter Ruth Weber'. *Scandinavian Psychoanalytic Review*, 27: 34–42.
O'Pray, Michael, 2004. *Film, Form and Phantasy: Adrian Stokes and Film Aesthetics*. London: Palgrave Macmillan. 2004.
Ornston, Darius Gray (ed.), 1992. *Translating Freud*. New Haven: Yale University Press.
Ovid (Publius Ovidus Naso), 1977. *Metamorphoses*. 2 vols. Trans. Frank Justus Miller, revised G.P. Goold. Cambridge, MA: Harvard University Press.
Payne, Michael, 1993. *Reading Theory: An Introduction to Lacan, Derrida, and Kristeva*. Oxford: Blackwell.
Phillips, Adam, 1988. *Winnicott*. London: Fontana Press.
Phillips, Michael, 2000. *William Blake: The Creation of the Songs: From Manuscript to Illuminated Printing*. Princeton: Princeton University Press.

Poe, Edgar Allan, 2003. *The Fall of the House of Usher and Other Writings*. Ed. David Galloway. London: Penguin.

Priestman, Martin (ed.), 2003. *The Cambridge Companion to Crime Fiction*. Cambridge: Cambridge University Press.

Rabaté, Jean-Michel, 2001. *Jacques Lacan: Psychoanalysis and the Subject of Literature*. Basingstoke: Palgrave.

Rajchman, John, 1985. *Michel Foucault: The Freedom of Philosophy*. New York: Columbia University Press.

Read, Richard, 2007: 'Stokes's Analysis', in *The Coral Mind: Adrian Stokes's Engagement with Architecture, Art History, Criticism and Psychoanalysis*. Ed. Stephen Bann. Philadelphia: University of Pennsylvania Press.

Reinhard, Kenneth, and Lupton, Julia Reinhard, 2009. *After Oedipus: Shakespeare in Psychoanalysis*. Aurora, CO: The Davies Group.

Ricoeur, Paul, 1970. *Freud and Philosophy: An Essay on Intepretation*. Trans. Denis Savage. New Haven: Yale University Press.

Rimbaud, Arthur, 1962. *Collected Poems*. Trans. Oliver Bernard. Harmondsworth: Penguin.

Riviere, Joan, 1986. 'Womanliness as a Masquerade', in Victor Burgin, James Donald, and Cora Kaplan (eds), *Formations of Fantasy*. London: Routledge.

Robert, Marthe, 1977. *From Oedipus to Moses: Freud's Jewish Identity*. Trans. Ralph Manheim. London: Routledge.

Rose, Jacqueline, 1986. *Sexuality in the Field of Vision*. London: Verso.

——, 1993. *Why War? Psychoanalysis, Politics and the Return to Melanie Klein*. Oxford: Blackwell.

Roudinesco, Elisabeth, 1994. *Jacques Lacan: An Outline of a Life and History of a System of Thought*. Trans. Barbara Bray (1997). Cambridge: Polity Press.

Royle, Nicholas, 2003. *The Uncanny*. Manchester: Manchester University Press.

Rudnytsky, Peter L. Bókay, Antal, and Giampieri-Deutsch Patrizia. 1996. *Ferenzci's Turn in Psychoanalysis*. New York: New York University Press.

Sandler, Joseph, Person, Ethel Spector, and Fonagy, Peter, 1991. *Freud's 'On Narcissism: An Introduction'*. New Haven: Yale University Press.

Santner, Eric L., 1996. *My Own Private Germany: Daniel Paul Schreber's Secret History of Modernity*. Princeton: Princeton University Press.

Sass, Louis, 1987. 'Schreber's Panopticism: Psychosis and the Modern Soul'. *Social Research*, 54: 101–47.

——, 1992. *Madness and Modernism: Insanity in the Light of Modern Art, Literature and Thought*. New York: Basic Books.

——, 1994. *The Paradoxes of Delusion: Wittgenstein, Schreber and the Schizophrenic Mind*. Ithaca: Cornell University Press.

Saussure, Ferdinand de, 1974. *Course in General Linguistics*. Ed. Charles Bally, Albert Sechehaye, and Albert Reidlinger. Trans. Wade Buskin. London: Fontana.

Schatzman, Morton, 1973. *Soul Murder: Persecution in the Family*. New York: Random House.

Schneiderman, Stuart, 1986. *Rat Man*. New York: New York University Press.
Schreber, Daniel Paul, 1955. *Memoirs of My Nervous Illness*. Trans. Ida MacAlpine and Richard A. Hunter. London: William Dawson and Sons.
Segal, Hanna, 1979. *Klein*. London: Fontana.
Shakespeare, William, 1984. *Macbeth*. Ed. Kenneth Muir. London: Methuen.
Solomon, Robert, 1974. 'Freud's Neurological Theory of Mind', in Richard Wollheim (ed.), *Freud: A Collection of Critical Essays*. New York: Doubleday Anchor.
Sophocles, 1994. *Ajax, Electra, Oedipus Tyrannus*. Trans. Hugh Lloyd Jones. Cambridge, MA: Harvard University Press.
Stokes, Adrian, 1978. *The Critical Writings of Adrian Stokes*. Ed. Lawrence Gowing. London: Thames and Hudson. 3 vols, cited as 1978a, 1978b, 1978c.
Tambling, Jeremy, 2004. 'Levinas, and *Macbeth*'s Strange Images of Death', *Essays in Criticism*, 54, 4: 351–72.
——, 2010a. *On Anachronism*. Manchester: Manchester University Press.
——, 2010b. *Dante in Purgatory: States of Affect*. Turnhout: Brepols.
Tausk, Victor, 1950. 'On the Origin of the "Influencing Machine" in Schizophrenia', in Robert Fliess (ed.), *The Psychoanalytic Reader: An Anthology of Essential Papers*. London: Hogarth Press.
Thurston, Luke, 2004. *James Joyce and the Problem of Psychoanalysis*. Cambridge: Cambridge University Press.
Trilling, Lionel, 1970. *The Liberal Imagination* (1940). Harmondsworth: Penguin.
Weber, Samuel, 1982. *The Legend of Freud*. Minneapolis: University of Minnesota Press.
Wilden, Anthony, 1968. *Speech and Language in Psychoanalysis: Jacques Lacan, Translated with Notes and a Commentary*. Baltimore: Johns Hopkins University Press (originally called *The Language of the self: The Function of Language in Psychoanalysis*).
Winnicott, D.W., 1971. *Playing and Reality*. London: Tavistock Publications.
Wordsworth, William, 1979. *The Prelude 1799, 1805, 1850*. Ed. Jonathan Wordsworth, M.H. Abrams, and Stephen Gill. New York: W.W. Norton.
Žižek, Slavoj, 2004. *Organs Without Bodies: On Deleuze and Consequences*. London: Routledge.
——, 2006. *How to Read Lacan*. London: Granta Books.

Index